FLAUNTING

Style and the Subversive Male Body in Rei..

In the early modern period, the theatre offered one of the most popular forms of entertainment and aesthetic pleasure. It also fulfilled an important cultural function by displaying modes of behaviour and dramatizing social interaction within a community. *Flaunting* argues that the theatre in late sixteenth-century England created the conditions for a subculture of style, whose members identified themselves by their sartorial extravagance and social impudence.

Drawing on evidence from legal documents, economic treatises, domestic manuals, accounts of playhouse practices, and stage plays, Amanda Bailey critiques the standard accounts, which maintain that those who flaunted their apparel were simply aspirants, or gaudy versions of the superiors they sought to emulate. Instead, she suggests that what mattered most was not *what* these young men wore but *how* they wore their clothes. These young men shared a distinctive sartorial sensibility and used that sensibility to undermine authority at all levels of society. *Flaunting* therefore examines male style as a visual means of subverting the norms of Renaissance England with the stage as the primary source of inspiration for collective identification.

A glimpse into both the celebration of and the opposition to social irreverence in the early modern period, *Flaunting* is a fascinating historical account of drama, fashion, and rebellion with surprisingly close parallels to the contemporary world.

AMANDA BAILEY is an assistant professor in the Department of English at the University of Connecticut, Storrs.

AMANDA BAILEY

Flaunting

Style and the Subversive Male Body in Renaissance England

UNIVERSITY OF TORONTO PRESS
Toronto Buffalo London

Toronto Buffalo London
utorontopress.com

Reprinted in paperback 2019

ISBN 978-0-8020-9242-7 (cloth) ISBN 978-1-4875-2422-7 (paper)

Library and Archives Canada Cataloguing in Publication

Title: Flaunting : style and the subversive male body in Renaissance England / Amanda Bailey.
Names: Bailey, Amanda, 1966– author.
Description: Reprint. Originally published: Toronto : University of Toronto Press, 2007. | Includes bibliographical references and index.
Identifiers: Canadiana 20190054611 | ISBN 9781487524227 (softcover)
Subjects: LCSH: Young men – Clothing – England – History – 16th century. | LCSH: Young men – Clothing – England – History – 17th century. | LCSH: Clothing and dress – England – History – 16th century. | LCSH: Clothing and dress – England – History – 17th century. | LCSH: Costume – England – History – 16th century. | LCSH: Costume – England – History – 17th century. | LCSH: Theater and society – England – History – 16th century. | LCSH: Theater and society – England – History – 17th century. | LCSH: European drama – Renaissance, 1450–1600 – History and criticism.
Classification: LCC GT734 .B332019 | DDC 391/.1094209031—dc23

University of Toronto Press acknowledges the financial assistance to its publishing program of the Canada Council for the Arts and the Ontario Arts Council, an agency of the Government of Ontario.

Canada Council for the Arts Conseil des Arts du Canada

Funded by the Government of Canada Financé par le gouvernement du Canada

For Ross

Fashion can be bought. Style one must possess.

—Edna Woolman Chase

Contents

Acknowledgments

This book began as a dissertation in the Department of English at the University of Michigan, where I had the great fortune to work with mentors whose intelligence, friendship, and perspicuity as readers shaped my own sense of what it means to be a responsible scholar and a caring teacher. I owe much to Leonard Barkan, Steven Mullaney, and Valerie Traub for their direction and encouragement at various phases. A Mellon Foundation Dissertation Fellowship, a travel grant from the University of Michigan's Rackham School of Graduate Studies, a summer research fellowship from the Department of English at the University of Michigan, and a short-term Resident Fellowship at the Newberry Library assisted me in conducting the research necessary for completing the dissertation.

Since graduate school, I have been warmly included in several research groups and have benefited immensely from the camaraderie and suggestions offered by Mary Bly, Judith Ferster, Natasha Korda, Mary Floyd Wilson, and Adam Zucker. Pam Brown and Megan Matchinske deserve special mention for generously reading a draft of my prospectus, and their comments guided me in rethinking the architecture of the book. I am thankful for my colleagues at the University of Connecticut who continue to be energetic fans of this project and of me, notably, Liz Hart, Bob Hasenfratz, and Greg Semenza. Bob Tilton and Bette Talvacchia have gone above and beyond the call of duty. I was recently invited to present my work at Columbia University's Early Modern Seminar, and I am grateful to Jean Howard for her enthusiasm and support.

Parts of chapter 2 have been previously published as "'Monstrous

Manner": Style and the Early Modern Theater,' *Criticism* 43.3 (summer 2001), and a version of chapter 3 has appeared as 'Livery and its Discontents: "Braving it" in *The Taming of the Shrew*,' *Renaissance Drama* 33 (summer 2004). I am grateful for the suggestions of the anonymous readers at both of these journals. My readers at the University of Toronto Press provided thoughtful responses and their incisive observations guided me ably in the later, crucial stages of revision. Suzanne Rancourt has been a terrific editor. Miriam Skey has been a no-less-terrific copy editor.

For their wit, wisdom, and unflagging interest in my intellectual endeavours over the years, I am grateful to Shelley Alhanati, Dana Barton, Rachel Gabara, Phyllis Gorfain, Becky and Bill Gibson, Roze Hentschell, Chris Luebbe, Michael McClure, Marjorie Riepma, David Serlin, and Carrie Wood. My parents have provided much needed support along the way, and I am extremely grateful to them.

Thank you is a woefully inadequate phrase with which to acknowledge the efforts of someone who read draft, after draft (after draft) of this manuscript over the years, and who lived day in and day out with the exhilarations and the anxieties of someone writing a book. If there is an emotion that includes and far surpasses gratitude, then that is what I feel for the gift that is Ross.

FLAUNTING: STYLE AND THE SUBVERSIVE MALE BODY IN RENAISSANCE ENGLAND

1 'Style is the man': Defiant Aesthetics and the Culture of Male Youth

Quicksilver, in *Eastward Ho*, is 'a younger brother and a prentice,' but since his mother is 'a gentlewoman and [his] father a justice of peace and of quorum,' he 'swear[s] by [his] pedigree.'[1] Frustrated by the predicament of being born too late, he does not run away but abandons his flat cap, canvas shirt, and broadcloth trunk hose, and in breach of his Oath of Indenture, 'pumps it' (1.1.82) in 'silks and satins gay' (5.5.65–6).[2]

Throughout Chapman, Jonson, and Marston's play, this 'swaggering gallant' (1.1.126) showcases 'rich clothes' (5.3.55-6) and brags of 'changeable trunks of apparel' (4.2.259). In the end, however, he is reprimanded for his 'dissolute and lewd courses' (4.2.297) and told:

> Thou hast made too much and been too proud of that face, with the rest of thy body; for maintenance of which in neat and garish attire ... thou hast prodigally consumed much of thy master's estate; and being by him gently admonished, at several times, hast returned thyself haughty and rebellious in thine answers, thund'ring out uncivil comparisons, requiting all his kindness with a coarse and harsh behavior, never returning thanks for any one benefit but receiving all as if they had been debts to thee and no courtesies. (4.2.300–12)

Despite having narrowly escaped hanging at Tyburn, there is little indication that Quicksilver will cease wearing his clothes in a flamboyant manner. His final histrionic plea to be paraded home 'through the street in these [prisoner's robes]' so that he may appear 'as a spectacle' is unconvincingly amended by his hasty correction – 'or rather, an example' – a clarification that seems contrived at best (5.5.215–17). All told, what we are faced with in the character of Quicksilver is not unlike what, in Dick Hebdige's assessment, we are presented with in the figure of the Mod: neither resistance nor conformity. Instead, we are confronted with 'a declaration of independence, of otherness, of alien intent, a refusal of anonymity, of subordinate status ... an *in*subordination,' and, at the same time, 'a confirmation of the fact of powerlessness, a celebration of impotence ... a play for attention, and a refusal, once attention has been granted, to be read according to the Book.'[3]

A 'commonly discontented' figure who, according to early modern social commentator John Earle, is 'something better then the Serving-men; yet they more saucy with him then hee bold with the master,' the younger brother's 'neat and garish attire' may be interpreted as the sign of a fantasy in which he embodies the gentility wrested from him by a system of primogeniture.[4] Yet Quicksilver does not so much magically resolve the contradiction between his class background and life circumstances as represent his experience of this dilemma in the form of outrageous display. He expresses the tensions between free citizen and unfree denizen, householder and single man, adult and youth, and master and apprentice on the plane of the aesthetic. His self-presentation is over-the-top, but it offers more than mere theatrics. Despite Quicksilver's marginal position, he occupies centre stage. His sartorial exhibitionism violates his monarch's legislative mandates, trespasses his master's authority, disrupts guild productivity, and diverts household resources.

This book examines the power that resides in the ability to transform the materials of dominant culture into the symbols of subversion, and it explores the sources of this power, its effects upon late sixteenth- and early seventeenth-century English culture, and its relation to the early modern theatre. My consideration of those who used sumptuous apparel to make a spectacle of themselves rests on the central claim that certain young men subordinated by virtue of status, age, and professional prospects did not assume the elite signs of privilege but rather appropriated them for their own ends. Working closely with early modern clothing legislation, didactic literature, and accounts of playhouse practices, as well as popular satiric literature and stage plays, I question the received history of non-elite young men whose sartorial attitudes and behaviour confounded state officials, city fathers, company heads, masters, and university principals. In the pages that follow I ask why Elizabethan authorities consistently identified the sartorial practices of gentle born, socially disenfranchised young men as an affront to established order. The answer to this question, I show, leads to a theatre that did more than produce an awareness that clothes 'made' men and provide the materials for such making. A commercial enterprise that exploited sumptuous clothing as a thematic focus and as an in-house commodity, the early modern theatre encouraged sartorial irreverence among those with little discretionary income and no social authority, and in so doing created the conditions for a subculture of style.

Admittedly, the word 'style' did not achieve its modern sense of 'manner of dress' until the early nineteenth century.[5] In the late sixteenth and early seventeenth centuries, style referred more narrowly to rhetorical practice. Nevertheless, style was, even in these earlier periods, associated with distinctive modes of expression that were likened to the discerning use or flagrant misuse of apparel. Ben Jonson in his polemic on effective writing, *Timber: Or, Discoveries*, for instance, links persuasive argumentation with sartorial conformity. Advising his reader to observe the specific techniques authors employ to distinguish themselves, Jonson defines the art of composition as the mastery of 'what ought to be written; and after what manner.'[6] One's prose, he stresses, should be 'comely' (615), and Jonson cautions against the 'vice' of 'wanton' writing, the earmarks of which are 'far-fetcht descriptions' (617). For Jonson, encountering a work characterized by an incongruity of subject and tone is as disorienting an experience as coming upon a man dressed in clothing unbefitting his rank and place. Undisciplined forms of expressions confront the reader with their illogic, Jonson explains, and violate his sense of the proper in the same way as the 'great Counsellor of state' who wears an apprentice's uniform of 'flat cap, with his trunck hose, and a hobby-horse [long] Cloake,' or the 'Haberdasher' who sports a counsellor's 'velvet Gowne, furr'd with sables' (626). In regard to oration, Jonson censures those who pepper their speech with artificial devices:

> Right and naturall language seeme<s> to have least of the wit in it; that which is writh'd and tortur'd, is counted the more exquisite. Cloath of Bodkin, or Tissue, must be imbrodered ... No beauty to be had, but in wresting, and writhing our owne tongue? Nothing is fashionable, till it bee deform'd; and this is to write like a *Gentleman*. All must bee as affected, and preposterous as our Gallants cloathes, sweet bags, and night-dressings: in which you would thinke our men lay in, like *Ladies*: it is so curious. (581; italics in original)

By likening inflated language to the overwrought 'Cloath of Bodkin, or Tissue' that 'must be imbrodered,' Jonson condemns performative modes of articulation, which, as he emphasizes, mimic in their intricacies the 'preposterous' attire of the ornate and effeminate young man.

In keeping with Jonson, who associates the auditory impression of certain forms of spoken language on the listener with the visual effects of particular sartorial trends on the viewer, Thomas Dekker and Thomas Middleton aver that 'the fashion of playmaking' can 'properly compare to nothing so naturally as the alteration in apparel.'[7] According to Dekker and Middleton the style of clothes worn by those young men who people their audience bears a direct relation to the genre of plays preferred by this constituency. The dramatic trend for clever comedies, they observe, complements the 'niceness' or the fussiness of those garments modelled by the 'Termers,' the Inns of Court students who regularly attended their plays:

> For in the time of the great-crop doublet, your huge bombasted plays, quilted with mighty words to lean purpose, was only then in fashion; and as the doublet fell, neater inventions began to set up. Now in the time of spruceness, our plays follow the niceness of our garments: single plots, quaint conceits, lecherous jests, dressed up in hanging sleeves; and those are fit for the times and the Termers. Such a kind of light-color summer stuff, mingled with divers colors, you shall find this published comedy.[8]

As suggested by their epistle, in which Dekker and Middleton compare their comedy to 'light-color summer stuff,' playwrights were well aware that young men attended the theatre not only to watch stage plays but also to take in the clothes that were 'published' at the playhouse.

Perhaps the term that most closely anticipates the word 'style,' as I use it throughout *Flaunting*, is the early modern verb 'to publish,' which referenced more than the specific task of distributing a literary work. Publishing described the general activity of sharing one's accomplishment with a like-minded community. To 'publish [one's] suit,' for example, could not be achieved simply by appearing in public in new clothes.[9] 'Publishing' one's ensemble involved constituting and reconstituting an ongoing sartorial conversation that included specific venues of display, collective standards of judgment, and a receptive audience. Through this 'publishing' process, one entered into, and in some cases forged, a subgroup that recognized and valued a certain aesthetic, often one that brushed against the standards accepted by members of the dominant culture. To publish oneself sartorially thus entailed authorizing a distinctive manner through the exhibition of particular poses, attitudes and behaviours. By debuting one's hallmark mode of comportment to a wide audience by – in the most literal early modern sense of the verb to publish – *astonishing* onlookers, one could set the terms of a shared sensibility. Just as playtexts would come to be advertised by their decorative frontispieces (made of cloth pulp) as they circulated among an audience of readers, the social meaning of the body of the man, like that of the body of the work, resided not in its temporal endurance but in its value as a nodal point of a contemporary cultural network.[10]

Scholars investigating the history of the subject in general, and the histories of gender politics, class formation, and erotic identities in particular, have intermittently turned their attention to fashion, and their work has laid the ground for my analysis of style. As Ann Rosalind Jones and Peter Stallybrass have suggested, the late sixteenth century may be seen as a transitional period during which items of apparel simultaneously functioned as fetish objects imbued with cultural memory and as exchangeable commodities unmoored from traditions of investiture upon which early modern society relied.[11] The globalization of England's textile trade in this period increased the production and distribution of clothes, creating a surplus of available cast-offs. The far-ranging circulation of both new and used apparel destabilized a traditional social order that depended on an established vestimentary order, and individuals from an ever-widening spectrum of the population found new opportunities to refashion themselves beyond the sartorial expectations of their social rank. Studies that explore the crucial role objects played in the process of subject formation have made great strides in showing the extent to which men and women understood themselves and others as constituted by the land they owned, the food they ate, the furniture they collected, the tools they used, and the clothes they wore.[12]

Building on this scholarship, *Flaunting* takes as axiomatic that subjectivity is mediated and realized by material objects, that the meaning of materiality is culturally constructed and contingent, and that objects produce and sustain various forms of social inclusion and exclusion. This study, however, reintegrates the subject back into the history of the object by examining how increased access to a wider range of commodities stimulated new modes of embodiment. By refocusing critical attention on the subjects, I am not, however, arguing for a return to the category of the individual. My primary interest, instead, is in modes of operation rather than the intentions of their authors (an impossible pursuit, even to those who enacted such operations). It is only through an examination of such modes that we can begin to explore how those who were positioned ambiguously within dominant culture pressured structures of power without breaking from or outwardly rebelling against them. By analysing the various ways that certain early modern young men used and misused apparel to gain from, resist, or ignore patriarchal imperatives, I provide a sustained investigation of the material practices of dress rather than a study of the materiality of clothes.

In what follows, I show that the connections among the social composition of playgoing audiences, types of dramatic representations performed on stage, and the particular sartorial attitudes and practices encouraged at the theatre cannot simply be accounted for by the history of *faci* or making, the root of the word 'fashion,' but must include the hidden history of *art* or the ways of making, the sense of the word 'style.'[13] The premise that guides this project is that style is not a subset of fashion, which was associated with centres of cultural authority, but a performative, adaptable, and innovative modality, which was born of subcultural spaces and groups.[14] If fashion signalled assimilation, style suggested resistance. If fashion was temporal, style was spatial. If the momentum of fashion was mimetic, the energy of style was self-reflective. If fashion promoted accumulation, style advocated waste. Style was multiform and fragmentary, improvisational and situational, and while it lacked a coherent ideology, was not associated with any one institution, and did not conform to a particular set of rules, it had a logic. By performatively modelling incongruous or exaggerated ensembles, practitioners of style de-emphasized the significance of what clothes they wore and forced onlookers to attend instead to how they wore their clothes.

1 Style versus Fashion

By engaging the category of style as both an object of inquiry and as an analytic tool, *Flaunting* revises the standard assumptions that sartorial items are either market phenomena or symbolic signs. Historians and literary critics who examine the circulation of clothes but not the embodied activity of dress are unduly, at times implicitly, influenced by studies that understand men and women's sartorial attitudes and behaviours as responses to the vagaries of fashion.[15] While it is important to acknowledge that at the turn of the sixteenth century textiles served as the premiere commodity form of an emergent global industry, this observation left unexamined perpetuates a critical truism that the consumption of clothes was for buyers a disembodied experience.[16] The notion that early modern consumers perceived the market as primarily a mode of exchange that transcended any specific time and place has recently undergone revision. In light of this scholarship, this book questions the concept of the placeless market and its implied corollary, an all-encompassing, impersonal 'fashion-system.'[17] *Flaunting* demonstrates that the purchase and display of apparel in early modern England entailed heterogeneous, locally defined practices determined by particular subjects' relations to the commercial cultures available to them.

Even though scholars often take for granted the separation between economic agents and the markets in which they participate, the early modern state did not distinguish between the habits of the individual consumer and the working order of the economy, an entity that was itself largely understood in what we would consider highly personal terms. Mercantilists posed the rhetorical question, 'Is not the publique involved in the private, and the private in the publique?' and, as Thomas Mun stresses, 'the corruption of men's conditions and manners' was believed to make otherwise 'rich countries ... exceedingly poor' because the individual's and the nation's economic and social well-being were conjoined.[18] As a result, the state's attempts to manage its subjects' purchase and display of clothes focused on those who participated in diverse networks of cultural and economic exchange. Moreover, the fluctuations of expanding apparel markets did not impose themselves as anonymous ebbs and flows. Rather the rhythms of conspicuous expenditure hastened or slackened in response to shifting definitions of luxury and thrift, prodigality and productivity, and, as I argue throughout, local tensions around status and display. Nascent second-hand apparel markets and the growing predominance of pawnbrokers (which led the way for unregulated enterprises like rag-picking, frippery, and botching), as well as the expanded activities of unfree petty chapmen and hawkers, dispersed market trends and introduced particular items to particular sectors of the population unevenly. While there were fads, such as the popularity of lightweight, imported, Indian calicoes, we need to guard against generalizing these trends to the entire population. Similarly, evidence of provincial fashion-consciousness in probate inventories and personal correspondence needs to be weighed against information about the specific consumption practices of subsets of the population for whom the availability of particular items, as well as attitudes about the purchase and display of clothes, rather than market forces, informed their valuation of certain modes of dress.[19]

Flaunting also aims to complicate the assertion that clothes function like language.[20] The belief that the social meaning of a particular item of apparel remains unchanged across various contexts is based on the presumption that sartorial signification is always determined by those in power. Authority was certainly conferred on the wearer by those items that were associated with luxury, such as furs, velvet, and scarlet-dyed cloth. Yet when such items broke with traditional forms of sartorial incorporation, like livery, and established contexts, like the household, they became illegitimate but by no means devoid of signifying potential. Flaunting it out on the streets of London, the young men I examine openly wrested items of apparel from their 'proper' place, namely the household and the court, and flagrantly modelled extravagant outfits in local taverns, public squares, and at the playhouses. By appearing in hybrid ensembles, composed, for example, of 'thin felt, and ... silk stockings,' or 'foul Linen and [a] fair Doublet,' and by combing second-hand markets for cast-off finery, these men reinvented the meanings of certain items that were traditionally reserved for particular groups and challenged conventional ideals of luxury with subcultural notions of glamour.[21]

The cultural studies model has illuminated the ways in which clothing serves as a visual medium to communicate status, but the notion that clothing in the early modern period constituted a coherent signifying system reduces our understanding of the semiotic potential of dress in light of both diachronic and synchronic approaches. A taxonomic logic that regards style as the *parole* to fashion's *langue* does not allow for analyses of the complexities of corporal performance over time. Future practitioners of style do not merely transgress conventional rules but also cite and elaborate an ever-expanding repertoire of subcultural codes. For this reason, the practices of those young men described by the Elizabethan state as having 'exceeded in the excess of apparel' may be interpreted as setting the stage for the dissident modes by which later marginal subjects subsequently distinguished themselves.[22] The stakes of flaunting for late sixteenth-century English culture may be clarified, for instance, when we put the sartorial exhibitionism of young male servants, students, and apprentices in conversation with the ironic sensibility promoted by the Mods or the kitsch aesthetic associated with Glam Queens, to cite two key modes disenfranchised young men continued to evoke well into the twentieth century. Moving beyond a narrow consideration of clothes as language may also illuminate the links between irreverent sartorial strategies and a range of subversive articulations within the early modern period. Scholars have noted that the late sixteenth century witnessed a rise of new genres and discourses that place mockery, satire, and a sardonic perspective at their centre.[23] *Flaunting* connects modes of insolent embodiment like flaunting not only to parodic trends in dramatic entertainment but also to impudent innovations in the visual arts, such as Mannerism, and to impertinent urban spatial practices, like loitering, posing, and promenading.

2 Sumptuary Discourse

One tool officials had at their disposal to aid them in controlling the flamboyance of sumptuously attired young men was a series of laws designed to restrict the dress of all English subjects in regard to the wearer's rank and income. Over the three-hundred-year period dating from the fourteenth to the seventeenth centuries, the state, in concert with local authorities, attempted to regulate the pomp and circumstance of funerals and weddings, the cost and amount of imported food items at banquets, and the purchase and display of costly apparel. Provisions that addressed protectionist economic concerns were a frequent but by no means consistent feature of English sumptuary law. The persistence of a form of legislation based on the Crown's paternalistic attitude towards what its subjects ate, purchased, and wore marks what appears to be one of the more unusual features of late sixteenth-century English society. Yet on closer inspection, the extended life of sumptuary law is not surprising. In an atmosphere in which a rising merchant class and expanding group of urban professionals competed with a declining aristocracy, it is far from 'peculiar' that elites would attempt to preserve exclusivity by monopolizing the trappings of luxury.[24] When we expand our field of inquiry beyond the actual legal mandates of Elizabethan clothing legislation and consider these laws in the broader context of a range of cultural forces that alternately condemned and condoned sartorial exhibitionism, what comes into sharp focus is, remarkably, a society preoccupied with sumptuousness.

In late sixteenth-century England this preoccupation was expressed by various interconnected discourses, such as the theological moralization of luxury, the secular call for moderation, the elite desire for a legible rank hierarchy, the local need for the observance of deference, and the state's investment in a nationalist discourse that placed proper comportment at the centre of the project of English civility. Thus sumptuary discourse, as opposed to sumptuary law per se, consisted of intersecting, overlapping, and competing ancillary concerns, all of which coalesced around the potentially unruly male body and its various disruptive modes of display. The mutable nature of the concerns that informed sumptuary discourse and the largely unsuccessful application of the various precepts introduced by its constituents suggest that sumptuousness in early modern England entailed much more than a clearly defined legal transgression. For this reason, I read Elizabethan clothing law as a part of a complex discourse of sumptuousness, which, in turn, I understand to be a discourse of anxiety.

Those who readily accept the premise that consumer behaviour is motivated by invidious comparison may also be inclined to regard early modern clothing law as an anxious response to a society strained by a class hierarchy in transition. Yet, as I demonstrate, sumptuous clothes and the young male subjects who wore them participated in a larger field of meaning than one determined by an unending cycle of social emulation.[25] An analysis of sumptuousness as a discourse of anxiety enables us to explore not simply the concerns of state and local authorities as expressed by those in power but also the deeper level of structural tensions of which this legislation served as a barometer. Elizabethan clothing legislation indexes to some degree an elite prejudice against actual or imagined interlopers who diligently worked to approximate the comportment of their betters.[26] Elite fears of encroachment, however, do not speak to why such a wide range of authorities, including guild masters, city alderman, university principals, and householders, targeted young men who lived and worked far from the inner sanctums of power. Nor do the assumptions that members of the lower ranks envied their superiors, sought recognition in the same terms as their betters, and desired inclusion among them address why those young men who were targeted by Elizabethan clothing law were identified not simply by their presumption of costly attire but predominantly by their outlandish or 'monstrous *manner*' of dress.[27]

Using Elizabethan clothing legislation as a jumping-off point and as a touchstone throughout, I show that these laws and the discourse in which they intervened acknowledge the existence of a nascent subculture of youth that began to take shape in early modern London around certain activities and public spaces, and most importantly, around its participants' particular uses and misuses of clothes. As a group of people who shared common interests, practices, and problems, young male social dependents were perceived by their contemporaries as standing apart from a dominant patriarchal culture defined by aristocratic codes of gentility on the one hand, and the citizen and householder's expectations of moderation on the other. The contradictions generated by a changing social hierarchy and by a system of primogeniture that left an inordinate number of young men to fend for themselves certainly remained unresolved within both the Elizabethan and Jacobean eras. The symbolic solutions enlisted by those affected by these phenomena, however, had real economic and social consequences. Through their distinctive rituals of consumption, the young men I examine confronted the material basis of their subordination and infiltrated their society's means of cultural production.

3 Subculture and Youth Culture

In attempting to understand why specific economic and social pressures in late sixteenth-century England created the conditions for a subculture of style, this study investigates the shared experiences of age-related men in a particular class circumstance. The centralization of England's political life in London, an unprecedented surge in population, and economic crises in provincial areas led to the mass migration of 'superfluous' young men, those second and third sons who, because they were not heirs apparent, flooded into the city seeking places at court, in elite households, within guilds, and at the universities and the Inns of Court.[28] In a period marked by a noticeable rise in the number of young men forced to rely on an indifferent system to maintain themselves, the ubiquitous 'younger brother' became a recognizable figure, depicted typically as 'jet[ting] upon the neatest and sprucest leather' and appearing in 'silly and ridiculous fashions' despite an inability to obtain any 'entertainement in the court or *Money*.'[29] Represented in popular satires as having 'little to looſe but their liues,' these '*Infans perdus* (or the Forlorne hope),' one writer observes, nonetheless, project their own version of sartorial grandeur.[30] After all, those disenfranchised young men who found themselves cast upon 'the mercy of the World' had, according to another satirist, been bequeathed '[their] wit' as '[their] best revenue.'[31]

The particular phenomenon of second sons was encompassed within the larger, ongoing social problem posed by bands of male youths.

Historian Keith Thomas has deemed early modern England a gerontocracy, and we are now only just beginning to understand the ways in which generational difference proved as salient to understandings of status and role in the period as distinctions between the sexes and differentials of rank.[32] Evidence from the period shows that 'early modern observers were well aware of the existence of young offenders and youth related social problems' and that 'particular attention was paid to the problems of youth during the years of rising anxiety about crime and vagrancy between 1560 and 1640.'[33] Introduced to curb 'the unadvised rashness and licentiousness of youth,' the 1563 Statute of Artificers, for example, instituted compulsory service by requiring set terms of indenture for servants and apprentices.[34] By restricting participation in certain trades and by urging rural youth to remain in their parishes, the state attempted to 'banish ydlenes' in young men and to stem the tide of those migrating into London, putatively to take up 'a ryotouse life.'[35] Cultural perceptions of the young man as unable 'to curbe' his appetite and as emboldened by 'the season of his Lust, and the houre wherein hee ought to bee bad' inspired a flurry of regulatory activity aiming to anchor this 'Shippe without [a] Pilot.'[36] Social commentators perceived male youths as in danger of becoming engulfed by a surfeit of vitality that inclined them towards overindulgence in alcohol and sexual promiscuity, and young men are warned repeatedly to scrutinize their deportment while in 'the "dark" and "dangerous age."'[37] State and local authorities, such as the Lord Chancellor, Lord Mayor, members of the Court of Aldermen and the Common Council, heads of city corporations, the principals and ancients of Cambridge, Oxford, and the Inns of Court, as well as individual householders, attempted to manage young men by focusing on their 'unseemly excesses,' the primary example of which was sartorial extravagance.[38]

While historians have not reached consensus about whether or not a discrete 'youth culture' thrived in early modern England, most agree that the careful monitoring of the leisure activities of male youths by authorities indicates that young men had some degree of agency in regard to their leisure time.[39] Paul Griffiths, one of the most persuasive opponents of the 'housebound' theory of early modern English youth culture that argues that youths were prevented from forming separate groups independently of supervising adults because they were enclosed within households, sees no reason to abandon the concept of youth culture altogether.[40] He admits there did not seem to be in England highly structured, formal, politicized associations like the youth groups of early modern France, Italy, or Spain, and yet he does provide ample evidence of the strong presence of young men who met together regularly to 'talk, play, drink, eat, gamble, and whore away their time, engaging in some of the bold posturing and subversive impudence which magistrates attributed to ill-advised and ill-nurtured youth.'[41] Advice literature for householders is dominated by accounts of young men's communal 'rioting' at various urban locales, including taverns, ordinaries, St Paul's Cathedral, the Royal Exchange, and the playhouses, where youths 'acquaint themſelues to much with the licentious cuſtomes of the Cittie: as with quarreling, dycing, dauncing, deceiuing, luſtinge, brauing, & indetting.'[42] The influence of young men on the social atmosphere of early modern London was impressive enough that some scholars have cited 'signs of a special culture' that developed among a population that forged networks of alliance beyond the structured atmosphere of guilds, schools, and households.[43] Youth culture may thus prove to be a valuable explanatory framework for historical investigations of subcategories of people who were brought together by shared recreational pursuits or collective expressions of sartorial taste.

What made the subcommunity of male youth that I examine *subcultural* was its ambivalent position to dominant culture, such that members lived alongside and with the very class they were barred from joining and from which the majority had originated.[44] As sociologists have suggested, youth subcultures are marked by a 'double articulation,' first a response to the generational expectations of the parent culture and second a response to the class constraints of the dominant culture.[45] Layered into this bifurcated response is the contradictory need to express autonomy from established cultural codes and, at the same time, the need to maintain some form of identification with them. Importantly, class remains at the heart of the concept of youth subculture.[46] Relations between classes and within class factions, and how these relations affected local communities, economies, family structures, and occupational opportunities, can only be understood within a narrowly defined framework. As Alan Sinfield has suggested, personal subjectivity is an unlikely source of dissident identity and action. Political awareness and self-consciousness of class, race, nation, gender, and sexuality crystallize when one recognizes oneself as belonging to a particular group. Thus, it is through involvement in 'a milieu, a subculture' that individuals develop 'oppositional preoccupations and forms' that, in turn, create the possibilities for alternative subject positions.[47]

4 Sexuality as Social Practice

Flaunting's examination of a subset of men who were sufficiently alienated from dominant structures necessarily complicates studies that overlook the specificity of manhood in a culture in which 'manhood and patriarchy were not equated,' and which, as a result, implicitly posit maleness as an unchanging entity against which femaleness is variously constructed.[48] By exploring the range of corporal practices engaged by those men who used their bodies and the clothes they wore as vehicles for managing disaffection, this study revises standard assumptions about the solidity of masculinity as a category and the security of a social order underwritten by a gendered ideology of power. While some young men no doubt strove to achieve conventional ideals of patriarchal manhood, variant masculinities existed in tension with one another.[49] As much is suggested by the evidence of the inordinate amount of energy that those in positions of power devoted to authorizing certain expressions of masculinity and denigrating others, as they worked to codify the terms of manhood in accordance with the expectations of householders, guild masters, and civic authorities. As a study that seeks to illuminate the full complexity of the workings of gender in early modern English culture by maintaining an awareness of 'gender differences *within* each sex' as well as 'those *between* them,'[50] *Flaunting* emphasizes that male youth were positioned within early modern culture as 'other' culturally, socially, economically, and erotically.

Elizabethan clothing law, as well as local apparel ordinances and by-laws, presumed that economically and socially dislocated young men spent their days and nights together 'haunting ... inconvenient places,' presumably inns, taverns, neighbourhoods associated with disreputable activities, and playhouses.[51] Those who were enrolled at the universities and the Inns of Court lived together as members of all-male societies closed to women. Similarly, servants and apprentices resided in an all-male subculture within larger male-dominated households or corporations.[52] Historians have commented on the late age of first marriage for men. Social dependents did not typically marry until around age thirty, a high proportion remained single throughout their lives, and the bastardy rate in this period was at a 'historically low level.'[53] The assumption of corporation heads and household masters was that male servants and apprentices would refrain from sexual activity with women during the tenure of their indenture. Moreover, in university and household settings, bed sharing was an unquestioned aspect of living arrangements, encouraging physical intimacy between men as a matter of course. The bonds between those young men targeted by Elizabethan clothing laws were based on shared age and a shared state of social dependency, but also, perhaps, on profound fraternal and/or erotic attachments that were forged through the exigencies of everyday life.

Like those whose scholarship addresses sexuality, the family, and the body in the early modern period, I too am interested in the ways in which male same-sex desire signified in early modern English culture beyond the legal and theological category of 'sodomy' and to what extent those who practiced same-sex eroticism in early modern England recognized an affinity with others like them. In pursuing these issues, I have sought recourse to the concept of 'subculture,' a notion that flies in the face of the critical commonplace that an organized urban, subculture of homosexual men or sodomites did not exist in late sixteenth-century England.[54] While this study does not take issue with the historical accuracy of this claim, it does seek to move beyond the theoretical constraints it may impose. In arguing for both the pervasiveness and the diversity of the homoerotic (rather than the homosexual) in late sixteenth-century England, I understand male same-sex intimacy in the period as a significant social practice. *Flaunting* engages the work of those who have elaborated the distinctions between orderly and disorderly homoeroticism, and this study also investigates how the definitional boundaries of homoeroticism came to be informed by and through local struggles over the meaning of the erotic.[55] An understanding of the various ways in which male same-sex desire became intelligible in and through local discursive formations may also allow us to consider not only individual expressions of such desires but also how erotic networks were formed. For instance, same-sex activities such as collaborative authorship, shared school assignments, common leisure pursuits, and agreed-upon sartorial modes may very well have offered more than proximity for participants.[56] By exploring how a certain group of young men defined themselves collectively, I aim to recover the traces of a community made up of those who expressed their connections to one another through shared practices and representational strategies rather than by engaging in specific erotic acts or by promoting certain erotic types.[57]

In early modern England, how people ate, walked, talked, and dressed were not just ways of doing things but the means by which men and women structured and interpreted their world. In his discussion of antiquity, Michel Foucault observes that sexual activity historically was not always 'directed towards a codification of acts' or 'towards a hermeneutics of the subject,' but has often fallen under the auspices of taste. In ancient Greece, for example, erotic predilection was understood as yet another element of 'a stylization of attitudes and an aesthetics of existence.'[58] Not unlike the classical culture with which it identified, late sixteenth-century English culture also understood taste as a key axis of collective identification. To exhibit aesthetic preference was to uphold stylistic coherence within delimited contexts, such that 'the practices of the same agent, and, more generally, the practices of all agents of the same class' demonstrated a stylistic affinity, which made 'each of them a metaphor for any of the others,' thus allowing members of the same group the ability to transfer 'the same schemes of action from one field to another.'[59] Shared assumptions and modes of discrimination gave unity to the experiences of members of a given cohort and created the conditions for a community of users. Habits and preferences, I show, constituted a new kind of symbolic capital for young male subjects to possess, deploy, and develop as they struggled to distinguish themselves through their affiliation with one another.

5 Overview

Throughout this book, I characterize the early modern theatre as a site of contradiction, one that was simultaneously oriented towards the desires of its audience and against authorities. Like the second sons who were its most loyal attendees, the theatre itself traded in a subversive sensibility marked not by a rejection of dominant codes but by a reworking of them. For this reason, the ad hoc commercial ethos of theatrical companies, the thematic concerns of stage plays, and the material practices of acting did not provide an alternative to the dominant values of late Elizabethan culture (contrary to the claims of those who railed against the theatre), but rather offered visitors strategies by which to negotiate a place partially implicated within and partially separated from hierarchic social and economic orders. For instance, the theatre neither forswore nor promoted sumptuousness. By dramatizing the mechanics of style, however, it did entice young men already inclined to sartorial excess to rent and purchase the second-hand items from which company heads such as Philip Henslowe profited, since 'to run a theater was not only to build playhouses but also to own, lend, and sell costumes or to lend money with which to acquire them.'[60] As the one arena that fell outside the regulatory purview of Elizabethan clothing law, the playhouse provided an alternative site of sumptuous display. Here low-born young men, on and off the stage, paraded in luxurious clothes with impunity, like Francis Lenton's 'butterfly' who 'withal his garish tyre,' his 'silken garments and Latin robe ... hath so often outfitted the Globe.'[61]

While literary critics often cite antitheatricalists who blame the theatre for unleashing 'a contagion' upon the 'manners' of its young male attendees, scholars have yet to explore such concerns in the broader context of a culture-wide awareness of the growing problem of sartorially irreverent youth.[62] Playwrights like Ben Jonson periodically acknowledge in their dedications, prologues, and epilogues the significant segment of young men in the audience who came primarily 'to see and to be seen, to make general muster of themselves in their clothes of credit, and [to] possess the stage against the play.'[63] The theatre was perceived as having a particularly pernicious influence upon social subordinates who were putatively 'easily drawne to libertie, pleasure, and licentiousnes,' and likely to engage in any number of dubious activities that further emboldened them to flout conventional codes of deference.[64] Those who objected to the performances of boy companies emphasized the deleterious effects of plays on 'youthe,' who are brought 'to such an impudente famyliaritie with theire betters that often tymes greite contempte of maisters, parents, and magistrats' follows the experience of attending a play.[65] Adding insult to injury, the commercial success of the playhouses and the popularity of the plays performed there ultimately depended upon the theatre's sensitivity to its audiences' desires and, in this case, its ability to express conventional sartorial attitudes and established generic forms in distinctly revised ways. Through 'abus[ing] apparel' (the phrase coined by Elizabethan clothing legislation), by changing and exchanging sumptuous clothes on stage, by renting and selling them off the stage, and by modelling them within the playhouse, company heads, playwrights, and actors created the conditions not only for new disorderly commercial practices but also new disorderly social practices among a particular population.

In the chapters that follow, the playhouse, the household, the court, and the city provide the settings for my analyses of particular social relations and the power dynamics they implied, such as between actor and city father, servant and master, court aspirant and established elite, and gallant and citizen, each of which created unique opportunities for subordinates to challenge codes of deference and for authorities to institute modes of discipline. Engaging dramatic texts that feature young male characters 'flaunting,' 'jetting,' 'braving,' and 'rioting it out' in sumptuous apparel in one of these four arenas, I elucidate how the plays under consideration dramatize both the opportunities afforded as well as the threats posed by sartorially irreverent young men. I focus on plays by Shakespeare, Marlowe, and Jonson to demonstrate that style was neither associated exclusively with any one particular figure in the period such as the gallant, nor the concern merely of any one specific genre, like citizen comedy.[66] Through sustained readings of *The Taming of the Shrew*, *Edward II*, and *Every Man Out of His Humour*, I aim to show that it is more than coincidental that the performance of these plays coincided with the apex of the theatre as a purveyor of clothing and the state as a promulgator of clothing law. Via the three distinct genres of comedy, tragedy, and satire, Shakespeare, Marlowe, and Jonson, respectively, reveal an intimate understanding of the central role of the theatre in the production and proliferation of sartorial irreverence. By elaborating the mechanics of transgressive comportment and by plotting social relations as contests over corporeal legitimacy, the plays I examine acknowledge the extent to which their own dramatic conventions, thematic preoccupations, and commercial strategies are indebted to and in conversation with those audience members who regularly engaged theatrical practice as the basis of their sartorial expression

The playhouses held special appeal for those who understood viscerally the exhilarating and unsettling experience of membership in a *proximate culture*, and as an innovative, profit-driven institution the theatre worked to capitalize on this very sector of its audience. Chapter 2 explores how the category of 'sumptuousness' was mobilized variously by state and local authorities, critics of playhouse practices, and late sixteenth- and early seventeenth-century dramatic and popular texts to characterize the elements of a male youth culture that formed around the theatre. Analysing primary materials, such as Elizabethan clothing laws and state sermons, I explore how the Crown's reliance on the amorphous social category, 'the meaner sort,' enabled authorities to regulate ambiguously positioned male subjects who exhibited sartorial excess. State and local clothing legislation, I show, was ultimately less concerned with those members of the lower ranks who attempted to pass as or to emulate their betters than it was invested in curtailing those whose extravagant self-presentation flouted established codes of deference. In this chapter, I examine the ways in which the theatre provided the physical locale and symbolic centre for young men to come together beyond the supervision of masters, company heads, and principals and bond over shared irreverent sartorial practices.

Chapter 3 brings Shakespeare's *The Taming of the Shrew* into conversation with an incoherent ideology of service that required gentle born, young male domestics to appear as sumptuously attired as their masters. Attending to the changing cultural perceptions of housework that inform *The Shrew*'s representation of mastery, I argue that gender and sexuality are mediated in this play by the contingencies of status and age. While standard readings implicitly regard patriarchy as men's systematic domination of women, this assumption, I show, is not born out in *The Shrew*'s sensitivity towards the generational dimensions of household authority. By exploring early modern cultural fantasies and fears stimulated by a household that was not an orderly arena of reproductive and productive economies but rather a space composed of ambiguously positioned young men who inhabited shifting pecuniary and erotic allegiances, I demonstrate that this play realizes 'shrewishness' as a mode of insurgency made manifest at those moments at which the links among the familial, the erotic, and the economic become exposed by those who 'brave it' in their livery.

Chapter 4 centres on Marlowe's *Edward II* and examines the connection this play establishes between social irreverence and an impertinent foreign aesthetic plaguing Elizabeth I's court off the stage. While I focus on the character of Gaveston and his propensity for 'jetting' in sumptuous Italian apparel through the fictional court of Edward II, I argue that the disruptive force he embodies extends well beyond the bounds of his character and comes to define the sartorial and social politics of the play as a whole. In this chapter, I challenge critical approaches that interpret *Edward II* as primarily concerned with a sodomitical monarch by demonstrating that this play is actually preoccupied with a corrupt court overrun with young male court hangers-on who reinscribe the techniques informing the corporal strategies of their betters as audacious theatricality. As a play committed, in part, to disparaging the connection between stylistic coherence and Elizabethan political order, *Edward II* assumes an ambivalent attitude towards the disruptive potential of the Italianified Englishman.

Ben Jonson's *Every Man Out of His Humour* offered early modern audiences a new form of urban drama. Chapter 5 examines this unwieldy play to show the ways in which it lays bare the stakes of the changing cultural valuation of male comportment at a time when the ethics of courtesy were being replaced by the aesthetics of urbanity, depicted here as 'the disease of the flux of apparel.'[67] Those young men suffering from this disease exhibit a corporal incontinence that undermines ideals of masculine comportment based on moderation and they flaunt a bodily impropriety that thwarts expectations of civil intercourse founded on the proper use of civic space. Yet even as Jonson caricatures those men who promenade down the middle aisle of St Paul's Cathedral in extravagant apparel, he also authorizes their flamboyant practices. 'Flux of apparel' proves to be a crucial strategy engaged in by certain young men to resist and revise patriarchal imperatives. By highlighting the similarities between urban environs and the playhouse, *Every Man Out of His Humour* shows that the affective extremities stimulated by the theatre could be used as a tool to transform particular popular city sites into one's very own stage.

Style still functions as the implicit heuristic by which we interpret and classify the bodies around us, silently, mysteriously, and profoundly determining how we make sense of each other and ourselves. By theorizing and historicizing the claim that 'the style is the man,' my objective in *Flaunting* is to move beyond thinking about sartorial style as a matter of trends in the construction of clothes. Clothes were a medium of power in early modern England because it was in and through clothes that subjects materialized social relations. This study shows that those men who misused apparel exposed the fine lineaments of such relations and revealed their attitudes towards those in power. An investigation of sartorial style in late sixteenth-century England opens up new ways of exploring not merely how subjects formulated identities but also how they revised the terms of their identities. By enlisting style as a heuristic, *Flaunting* begins to forge links among the histories of mobile class politics, social resistance, gender deviance, and sexual dissidence, all of which engage the vexed relationship between being and seeming, appearance and reality, and image and substance. To study style in early modern England is to investigate the birth of subcultural capital, to tease out the multiplicity of masculine identities, to revisit the significance of youth culture, and to begin to unearth the lost history of those transgressive aesthetics that were inspired, enabled, and exploited by the theatre.

2 Monstrous Manner: Clothing Law and the Early Modern Theatre

Oh beware therefore both what you wear, and how you wear it.

Dekker, *The Guls Horne-booke*.[1]

1 The Subculture of Style

Stephen Gosson, one of the most vocal antitheatricalists of late sixteenth-century England, associates the theatre with an irreverent social logic. Actors, Gosson explains, show themselves as 'otherwise than they are,' and in so doing, confound the fundamental distinctions organizing society, such as those between a 'Prince' and a 'mean person':

> For a boy to put on the attyre, the geſture, the paſſions of a woman; for a meane perſon to take vpon him the title of a Prince with counterfeit porte, and traine, is by outwarde ſignes to ſhewe them ſelues otherwiſe then they are, and ſo with in the compaſſe of a lye.[2]

Gosson's distress about actors donning aristocratic apparel as the characters they played is, however, overshadowed by a deeper concern about actors wearing sumptuous clothes as themselves. He reminds his reader that 'her majesty' and 'her honorable council' have repeatedly 'set down the limits of apparel to every degree,' in the form of laws that regulate dress in accordance with the wearer's rank and income. Yet stage players, to Gosson's indignation, disregard these restrictions:

> Overlashing in apparel is so common a fault that the very hirelings of some of our players, who stand at reversion of vi s. by the week, jet under

> gentlemen's noses in suits of silk, exercising themselves to prating on the stage and common scoffing when they come abroad, where they look askance over the shoulder at every man from whom the Sunday before they begged an alms.[3]

The actor who descended from the stage still dressed in his sumptuous ensemble and moved through the crowd long after his role had ended cast a spotlight on the social stakes of a new commercial space where low-born men modelled costly apparel not with the intention of imitating the 'port and train' of their betters but, to Gosson's chagrin, with the aim of asserting their own sense of distinction.[4] According to Gosson, parading in costly apparel relieved these men from emulating elite codes of civility and liberated them from observing expected forms of deference. Sumptuousness granted them licence to mock or, as Gosson puts it, to 'scoff' and 'look askance' at their superiors. Even the hireling, the player's apprentice who was only a temporary company member, Gosson points out, becomes emboldened when he puts on a suit of silk and is inspired to 'jet' by gentlemen with impunity.

By using the word 'jet,' Gosson drives home his point that young men wear sumptuous clothes not simply to role-play but to play it up. To jet meant to carry oneself in an affected way and to convey an ostentatious manner, for instance by strutting 'like a peacock or turkey.'[5] A late fifteenth-century reference to 'the jetters of the Inns of Court' anticipates the exclusive association of jetting with young men, as the word jet appears frequently in late sixteenth-century satires of city gallants who are described as 'jetters.' Similarly, early seventeenth-century sources identify the jetter as a 'spruce minion, gay fellow, and compt [stylish] youth.'[6] Jetting also indexed gender disturbance, as suggested by Robert Burton who, in his *The Anatomy of Melancholy*, links jetting with sartorial excess, theatricality, and effeminacy: '"Good manners" (as Seneca complains) "are extinct with wantonness, in tricking up themselves men go beyond women, they wear harlots' colours, and do not walk, but jet and dance," *hic mulier, haec vir* ... more like players, butterflies ... than men.'[7] In one of his satirical epigrams, Everard Guilpin regards jetting as endemic to the young man who cannot rein in his appetite for extravagant clothes, playgoing, and boy paramours. The 'piertly iet[ting]' gallant, Guilpin explains, 'spends, and out-spends many a pound a yeare,' 'is at euery play,' and 'euery night sups with his *Ingles*.'[8]

Antitheatricalists and satirists were not the only constituencies of Elizabethan culture alarmed by the prospect of 'the meanest sort of men' jetting in suits of silk.[9] Elizabethan sumptuary legislation, which sought to 'reform the monstrous abuse of apparel in almost all estates' was, by its own admission, 'principally' concerned with the meaner sort, an amorphous group of male apprentices, servants, and students.[10] The clothing proclamation of 1574, for instance, directs its provisions to the curtailment of 'the wasting and undoing of a great number of young gentlemen, otherwise serviceable,'[11] who, in the eyes of the law, continued to maintain the habits of expenditure befitting their background despite a change in status. These gentle born, serviceable young men made up the legions of 'superfluous' youths who flooded the city's universities, households, and corporations.[12]

Gentle born young men who sought positions in households and companies or who enrolled in university were not heirs apparent and were thus compelled to pursue a profession to sustain themselves.[13] Facing the same limited social horizons as those who were not of gentle parentage, second sons (or younger brothers as they came to be known) were treated no differently than other young men, who were all regarded as subordinate youths by a legal system on the lookout for sumptuary offenders.[14] The clothing proclamation of 1588, for example, boldly asserts that youths practise 'excesses of apparel' more than any other group. Drafted after a meeting between the Lord Chancellor and the heads, ancients, and principals of the houses of Court and Chancery, the Inns of Court, and Cambridge and Oxford, this proclamation focuses on the 'disordered excess of apparel' most prevalent in places where it had 'spread amongst the youth.'[15] Even subsequent decrees that remain vague about their designated target conclude by enlisting the authority of all heads of households, city fathers, heads of corporations, chancellors of universities, and ancients of the Inns of Court and Chancery to curb the excesses of their charges.

Scholars have demonstrated that a burgeoning, international cloth industry and the rapid proliferation of local second-hand apparel markets produced the material and social conditions for a theatre that revolved around the buying, renting, and selling of clothes. While evidence shows that the early modern theatre capitalized on the wider distribution and rapid accumulation of sumptuous apparel, what has yet to be explored are the ways that it encouraged a new consumer niche made up of ambiguously positioned young men and exploited this niche to promulgate new ideas about the relationship between masculine identity and dress within the culture at large. At the theatre oppositions such as humbleness and vanity, work and play, and substance and surface that structured dominant culture were dismantled and recombined in accordance with a 'transvestite order of knowledge.'[16] This transvestitism, however, went well beyond gender or class crossing. At the playhouse established norms themselves were redressed, as those categories that ratified authenticity became denaturalized by the unorthodox performances that transpired daily both on and off the stage.

The innovative commercial practices sponsored by the playhouse and the novel representational strategies introduced by stage plays lay the ground for a nascent subculture of young men whose sartorial extravagance ruptured rather than sutured the gaps between the position of the wearer and the significance of his clothes. Actors performed in plays that demonstrated the perils and pleasures of changing and exchanging finery, and the playhouse provided a site of flamboyant display where mean young men, on stage and off, could exhibit luxurious clothes without penalty. At the same time, company heads who rented and sold stage costumes, the majority of which were aristocratic cast-offs, placed sumptuous apparel in wider circulation as they introduced young male social dependents to not only the imaginary but also the real possibilities of wearing prohibited apparel. Unlike those cultural arenas where conspicuous consumption was naturalized by the assertion of manner or taste, which served as the symbolic manifestation of authority, the theatre encouraged an alternative form of distinction. By enabling young men to appropriate the proper use of costly apparel, to reinscribe its traditional value, and to remap its assigned contexts the theatre turned status into style.

2 Regulating Monstrousness

On 24 January 1565, Richard Walweyn was detained for wearing 'a very monsterous and outraygous greate payre of hose.'[17] The surviving records do not describe Walweyn's hose, and we can only guess what the arresting officers found to be 'monsterous and outraygous' about them. It is most likely that Walweyn's hose were extraordinarily large due to the impressive amount of padding they contained. Walweyn, a servant, may have violated any number of the provisions that made up the 1562 clothing proclamation, which, among its other aims, attempted to regulate the fad for over-stuffed and elaborately decorated stockings that had 'crept alate into the realm.'[18] Much of the 1562 edict was devoted to determining which rank of men could wear what kind of hose and, according to the proclamation, servants such as Walweyn were allowed to wear plain hose only. As members of 'the meaner sort,' male servants, apprentices, and students were not permitted to wear hose made of velvet, satin, or 'any other stuff above the estimation of sarcenet or taffeta,' or stockings that were stuffed with more than a yard and three quarters of material.[19]

The description of Walweyn's hose as monstrous provides some information about what Walweyn wore, but it also sheds light on how he wore his great hose. Monstrousness indexed a lack of self-control and, more particularly, an inability to master one's urges that was equated with a devolution from a state of civilized manhood. 'Temperance alone,' an advice writer of the period explains, 'is the sustainer of civil fitness, for it taketh care that the realm be not corrupted with riot and wanton delights.'[20] By contrast, intemperance is the 'overflowing in all pleasures, desperately constraining all reason,' which 'metamorphosizes a man into a beast.'[21] Indulging in excess indicated a lapse in rationality and portended a slide into something not human, since, according to one early modern commentator, 'disguised cloathes makes men women, women beasts, and beasts monsters.'[22] In addition to referencing an ungoverned appetite for sensual pleasures, the monstrous also signified that which was extraordinary or strange. In the early modern period the word was used to describe not only the unnatural aspects of an object but also the 'uncivil' ways that an object was put to use.[23] Thus, there was a strong connotative relationship between the monstrous and what we have come to categorize as the obscene, as suggested by the word's connection to the noun 'warning' and to the verb 'to show.'[24] At once performative and perverted, the monstrous anticipated the logic of a theatre that would routinely elaborate the unnatural pairing of conspicuous display and irreverent social practice.

Other than the theatre, the only mechanism within early modern culture that consistently brought the monstrous to light was Elizabethan clothing legislation. The 1562 provisions regulating hose merely hint at the comprehensive nature of this body of law. The queen issued twelve edicts, all of which were primarily directed against men, in a sustained effort to restrict dress in accordance with the rank and income of the wearer.[25] The expansive detail of these decrees, which included an exhaustive catalogue of prohibited items, appended *abbreviats* or schedules, and precise procedures for enforcement, attests to the energy that Elizabeth's administration devoted to the regulation of apparel.[26] Elizabeth promulgated more laws regulating dress than any other British monarch.[27] The urgency of this project is evidenced by the formation of 'Committees for Excesses of Apparel' in and around London, as well as by the increase in the number of assistants assigned to aid London's Lord Mayor and the city's Court of Aldermen in dispatching an explosion of sumptuary cases.[28]

Proclaiming the Crown's intention to penalize those guilty of wearing 'excessive and ordinate apparel' and of 'daily more exceeding in the excess of apparel,' the law presented a grid of sartorial prescriptions and exemptions, articulating the social order in terms of a clearly defined, hierarchical sartorial order.[29] This legislation stressed that only those of 'superior degrees' would be permitted to wear satin, silk, sable, and cloth made of or mixed with gold, silver, or tinsel. While it was determined that knights and men who earned £20 annually or who owned £200 worth of goods may wear silk, it restricted even members of this group to using silk only in their hats, bonnets, nightcaps, girdles, scabbards, hose, or shoes. The 'inferior' or 'meaner sort' was prohibited from wearing silk altogether, as well as other luxurious materials such as velvet, taffeta, satin, damask, and imported wool. 'Mean men' were also forbidden from sporting embroidered clothing that was pricked or pinked with gold, silver, or silk; from trimming their garments with fur like black genet, lucern, and leopard; and from wearing certain colours, like crimson and scarlet. The list of those colours, materials, and types of ornamentation that the inferior sort was barred from wearing expanded with each successive proclamation, and descriptions of newly prohibited items were regularly appended to the standard recommendation that these men wear apparel made of fustian, canvas, leather, and domestically produced wool only.[30]

While there is some truth to the shibboleth that Elizabethan clothing law sought to maintain the integrity of a traditional rank hierarchy strained by increased instances of upwardly mobility, this explanation does not account entirely for the complex role these laws performed in Elizabethan society. [31] Without doubt, the last quarter of the sixteenth century witnessed radical revision to the criteria for status and position as the once rigid boundaries between the upper-elite and the gentry, as well as those between these groups and the professional classes below them, were eroding. Moreover, legal and political criteria such as electorate rights and tenurial status were becoming less reliable as markers of socio-economic status.[32] In rural contexts, where social standing depended upon access to property, many yeomen and husbandmen generated income by combining various modes of land-ownership (for instance, freehold and other tenancies or subtenancies) with participation in local industry. In cities, a burgeoning class of urban professionals complicated older social formations in which typically guild membership or freemen status would have served as an adequate indicator of income or professional standing. By the turn of the sixteenth century, economic development in London alone facilitated the growth of occupations in domestic and national trading, service industries, manufacturing businesses, and government posts. There can be little dispute that even as aristocratic ancestry continued to be the sufficient condition, it was no longer the necessary one for gentility. The myriad indices of status, such as birth, wealth, occupation, political allegiance, and lifestyle, as well as regional, religious, and professional affiliation, overlapped, cancelled out, and qualified one another to the extent that gentility was at once increasingly easier to achieve and more difficult to define.

Yet despite the fact that the categories buttressing an established social order were in flux, there is little evidence to suggest that the traditional structure suffered irreparable damage. If estimations that the population of the upper ranks tripled in the same period that the entire Elizabethan population doubled are accurate, then it appears that the elite successfully expanded its qualifications for gentility to accommodate professionals and members of the lower-gentry.[33] While mobility was a problem in the eyes of some, upward movement was always an integral feature of the social order. Most significantly, the very people who ostensibly threatened this order most wished to preserve its tenets, since their own ascent would be meaningless outside the context of a traditional framework. The aspirant's desire to move up confirmed that he had dutifully internalized the social stakes defined by those above him, and by attempting to emulate his betters, he participated in what was an integrative and reproductive struggle.[34]

The complex dynamics of social mobility in the period are subtly reflected in Elizabethan clothing legislation, which should be interpreted as a sumptuary discourse rather than a measured response to social change. Indeed, upon closer examination we can see that the law is sensitive to the mutability of social configurations, even as it attempts to simplify competing axes of social categorization. These proclamations reveal this dual perspective through their engagement with the ambiguous language of 'sorts.'[35] At first glance, this legislation seems to offer what we have long come to think of as the traditional Elizabethan social pyramid, which includes noblemen at the top, followed by gentlemen, yeomen, citizens, husbandmen, artisans, and labourers. Yet as much as this legislation may have argued for a traditional, hierarchical order, it ultimately divided the population into two broad, vaguely defined camps of the 'better' and the 'meaner' sorts. By promoting a more flexible descriptive apparatus, Elizabethan clothing proclamations created a more inclusive category for the elite, one that cut across the discrete differences that distinguished members within the upper strata, as well as effectively conjoined older and newer definitions of gentility. At the same time, the law was able to designate an amorphous out-group. Unlike the terminology of degrees, the language of 'sorts' did not have to distinguish between the 'better' and the 'meaner' on the basis of rank alone. A more context-specific matrix discriminated between and among any number of related and overlapping distinctions, which could account for the contingencies of gender, local reputation, professional stature, and, most significantly, age.

Indeed, apart from gender, age was the most widely recognized distinction informing constructions of status and authority in the period. Broadly defined as the period after childhood and puberty, and conceived exclusively in terms of the life cycle of men, youth was the stage during which those who were anywhere from twenty-five to thirty-five years old remained unqualified to join the ranks of those who had achieved normative manhood.[36] This life-stage was understood by writers of advice manuals, sermons, and popular tracts as marked not only by social liminality but also by physiological instability; the sins of youth in general came to be regarded as the sins of young men in particular.[37] Young men had yet to achieve the status conferred on those who married, headed up their own households, and obtained professional freedom as indicated by the outward signs of social and fiscal solidity, which, in turn, confirmed an inward state of temperance. According to religious, medical, and secular tracts, youths suffered from a surfeit of vitality and, as a result, more than any other group, young men were 'carried with more headlong force into vice, lust, and vain pleasures of the flesh.'[38] For the physician Levinus Lemnius, youth was the time of life when the 'blood beareth sway abundantly,' and due to 'the boiling of their blood within them,' young men are 'thrall' to the 'pleasures of the body.'[39] The internal hotness and moistness of young male bodies, Lemnius stresses, makes them 'pliant as wax,' upon which vice leaves its impression.[40] In his treatise on gentle conduct, Richard Brathwait also deems youth the 'dangerous time,' in which men give themselves over to 'all licentious liberty.'[41] There is, he emphasizes, 'no time more perilous than the heat of youth, or more apt to give fuel to the fire of inordinate desires.'[42]

The consensus was that during this 'slippery and dangerous age' young men were prone to 'inordinate affections, absurd actions ... extravagance courses and preposterous progressions and aversions,' as well as 'habitual ill customs and unqualified manners.'[43] The two main vices for which young men were regularly censured in the period's advice literature and satirical tracts were intemperance and pride, primarily signalled by sartorial extravagance. In his *Portraitur of the Prodigal Sonne*, Samuel Gardiner describes the 'exorbitant' young man as known for 'gadding abroad after his owne fancies,' and Francis Lenton, in his tract on youth, similarly depicts the young male student as 'ruffl[ing] now in satin, silk and plush' and wearing 'Embroidered suits such as his father never knew / ... / His coin expended by alluring hooks / His parents him supply to buy books.'[44] Lenton's gallant 'courts it' through the streets of London, with 'ostrich on his head [and] beaver rare / Upon his hands a Spanish scent to wear / Hairs curled, ears pearled,' and his body 'clad in the silkworm's winding sheet,' as he casts a 'haughty look' upon those whom he jets by.[45] Thomas Nashe condemns those young men who by consuming what little patrimony they have on extravagant attire, 'cost their dads' a year's toil' as they 'spend that in their Velvets' what their labouring fathers had 'racked up in a Russet coat.'[46] In attempting to provide a physiological explanation for the predisposition of 'young princocks and lusty gallants' who 'make themselves as ridiculous and jesting stocks to the whole company,' Lemnius explains that because of their natural 'digressing and swerving from modesty, temperance, and moderation' young men will always appear 'undecently,' 'brave,' and be inclined to 'deck' themselves out.[47]

Moralists and magistrates perceived youth who appeared in luxurious apparel as 'wayward,' and they too associated sartorial extravagance with a total disregard for, if not a direct challenge to, the social order.[48] Paul Griffiths emphasizes that state and local authorities approached 'the matter of apparel' as a problem of youth, and he notes that this reflected the prevailing assumption that sartorially extravagant male social dependents were inclined towards immorality and criminality.[49] Elizabethan clothing proclamations include mandates instructing householders to regulate the sartorial activities of their charges. These were routinely supplemented by local initiatives, such as the 1559 Privy Council Act that focused on the 'abuses of apparel' among servants. This law instructs masters to search dependents' boxes, chests, and wardrobes for contraband clothing.[50] In 1572 the Lord Mayor of London warns of 'seruantes and apprenteces within [the] cytty [who] ar by indulgence and lack of convenient severytie growne to grete disorder in excess of Apparrell and fasshions' and who, as a result, appear 'uncomly for ther caulinges.'[51]

As historians have observed, guild records reveal 'a preoccupation with the natural inclinations of youth'; increasingly more complaints and committees grew up in the last quarter of the sixteenth century in response to the perceived and actual 'excessive and inordinate pride used by apprentices ... in their apparell.'[52] In 1574 a Merchant Tailors Company apprentice was apprehended in London for wearing a 'cloak of pepadore' (a kind of silk fabric), as well as 'a pair of hose lined with taffety, and a shirt edged with silver contrary to the ordinances.'[53] In 1575 seven apprentices were 'sett up on a scaffold in Cheapsyde' for showcasing 'certyn apparell not being decent for any apprentys to weare.'[54] A 1582 ordinance issued by the Lord Mayor in conjunction with the City Corporation, the Court of Aldermen, and the Common Council of London prohibited apprentices from wearing any clothing except those items they had received from their masters and forbade the wearing of 'ruffles, cuffs, loose collars,' as well as ruffs of 'more than a yard and a half long.'[55] Only canvas, fustian, sackcloth, English leather, or woolen doublets and breeches, 'without any silver or silk trimming,' were permitted, and all hose and stockings were to be 'white [or] blue, or russet kersey or cloth.'[56] 'Plain cloth' or leather upper coats only were allowed, 'without pinking, stitching, edging or silk trimming,' as were cloth gowns and cloaks lined or faced with cloth, cotton, or baize, with 'fixed, round collars, without stitching, guarding, lace or silk.'[57] No one was to wear 'pumps, slippers or shoes, not made of English leather.' Girdles and garters were to be made of 'untrimmed crewel, wool, thread, or leather,' and they were not to be 'pinked, edged or stitched.'[58] Apprentices were instructed to have their clothes held together by 'plaine stringes' with 'plain white seame[s]' and to wear only the woolen caps provided by their masters.[59] Decorative weapons such as swords and daggers, as well as 'jewels of gold [and] silver,' were also forbidden.[60] In the same year, the London Curriers Company prohibited their apprentices from wearing 'silk ruffles or any cloth enriched with gold, silver or silk,' and forbade 'embroidered pumps and slippers, [or] jewelry.'[61] This law also set out to monitor young men who purportedly spent their days 'haunting ... inconvenient places,' presumably taverns, inns, and play-houses, where they modelled their extravagant ensembles.[62]

After the servant and the apprentice, the third most consistent target of state and local sartorial legislation was the male student. Included in the queen's clothing proclamation of 1562 was a special plea to university chancellors and Inns of Court principals to enforce apparel mandates, and in 1564, 1576, and once again in 1583, Leicester, at the Crown's request, initiated internal decrees at Cambridge in the hopes of reforming the sartorial activities of students.[63] In 1565 principals and ancients of both Cambridge and Oxford concerned with the 'disorderly conduct' among students, 'particularly in the article of apparel,' joined forces in an effort to prohibit decorated neck ruffs and sleeve ruffles exceeding the breadth of one finger, as well as the wearing of anything other than 'plain hose' or hose containing one lining.[64] Undecorated hose only were permitted, without any 'slyppe, cut, pownce, welte, or sylke.'[65] In that same year, a report to the crown complained of great 'disorders' of apparel at St John's College, and despite repeated exhortations, in 1566 Cecil solicited the vice chancellor of Cambridge University and all college heads to suppress 'the irregularities of the students respecting apparel.'[66] In 1570 several Cambridge proctors were charged with wearing 'skabilonians [pantaloons] and knitt nether-stockes to[o] fine for schollers,' and in this same period, Cambridge's chancellor initiated a severe penalty dictating that those students who continued to dress extravagantly would be denied lodging.[67] Both universities continued to regulate students' dress independently of the royal administration and passed clothing ordinances in 1578 and in 1585, and as late as 1620, and issued formal complaints to the Privy Council about students' 'excess in apparel.'[68]

Elizabeth's proclamations died with her, and James I, in his first meeting with Parliament in 1604, effectively voided all Acts of Apparel that had been enacted by his predecessors.[69] While James issued only one proclamation in 1610 that made mention of 'the necessity of taking some politic order against excess of apparel,' local authorities continued, albeit sporadically, to issue by-laws and ordinances throughout the first quarter of the seventeenth century in an effort to 'devise some good advise for reformacon of that great disorder nowe as used by prentises in there excesse and monstrousness in apparell.'[70] In the early seventeenth century it became a common complaint of London authorities that young men in the professions had abandoned their traditional uniform of a flat cap, close-cut hair, narrow falling bands, russet coat, and cloth hose for the 'idol of fashion.'[71] A 1603 ordinance of the Newcastle Merchant Adventurers instructed that no company member 'shall permit or suffer his apprentice to ... use anie undecent apparell but plaine,' or to 'weare their haire longe, nor locks at their eares like ruffians' upon pain of imprisonment.[72] Apprentices were ordered to dress in 'coarse side-coat[s], close hose [and] clothe-stockings,' and to trim their 'great ruffes' of velvet, lace, or silk.[73] In 1608 the Merchant Adventurers again attempted to control London apprentices who wore 'apparaile not fytt for [their] ... Estate or qualitie, but rather becominge some Courtier.'[74] A Common Council Act of 1611, for example, prohibited all apprentices from wearing hats that were broader than three inches or that cost more than five shillings. One provision prohibited ruffs from exceeding three yards and stipulated that collars were to be 'close and comelie.' Only cloth, kersey, fustian, sackcloth, canvas, English leather, woolen, and 'Englishe stuff' not exceeding '2s 6d' in cost were permitted for doublets, stockings, and hose. Gloves could not cost more than twelve pence and shoes of Spanish leather were also outlawed. The penalty for infraction of this law was eighteen hours in Little Ease Prison.[75] In that same year, the Grocers' Company legislated against 'Spanish shoes with Polonia heels' and doublet collars with 'poynt[s], well [whale] bone, or plaits;' instead, apprentices were ordered to wear breeches of 'cloth, kersey, fustian, sackcloth, canvasse, English leather or English stuffe,' and stockings of 'woollen, yarn or kersey.'[76] A number of these ordinances cite examples of apprentices behaving 'in a very prodigall manner' and appearing 'as if [they] had bine ... master[s] [themselves].'[77]

Local clothing regulations targeted servants, apprentices, and students because they were youths, but these ordinances also targeted a group that was entirely made up of men. The presupposition of Elizabethan clothing proclamations, as well as local apparel ordinances issued during James's reign, was that young men spent their days and nights consorting almost exclusively with each other, pursuing a shared culture of leisure activities that necessitated frequenting 'unlawful and suspicious places.'[78] Those who were enrolled at the universities and the Inns of Court lived together as members of all-male societies that were closed to women. Similarly, servants and apprentices resided in an all-male subculture within larger male-dominated households or corporations. As historians have noted, it was expected that male servants and apprentices would not engage in sexual activity with women during the term of their indenture, and often not before setting up a household of their own, a period that could extend up to twelve years. Moreover, it was common practice for young men to share beds with one another, as well as with their superiors, in educational and occupational contexts.[79] Even after their terms of service, historians have recently suggested, the patterns of everyday life for working, adult men were more conducive to same-sex than to cross-sex bonding.[80] While rank continued to be the primary organizing principle that structured a highly stratified social order, the heterogeneous social backgrounds of those young men who shared studies, work-lives, homes, and beds did not divide them. Peter Burke has explored what he describes as a '"subculture" of London apprentices,' and Paul Griffiths writes of a distinctive 'apprentice culture.' Paul Seaver, similarly, emphasizes that 'no great gulf of accent or education seems to have separated the gentle apprentice from his fellows recruited from subordinate classes.'[81] The bonds among those young men targeted by Elizabethan clothing laws were based then not only on their shared age and state of social dependency but also on profound fraternal and/or erotic attachments forged through the exigencies of everyday life.

The role of the group proved crucial to youthful expressions of excess in the period, since membership in a subcommunity 'facilitated young men's disruptive assertions' in ways that 'cut across boundaries of social status and geographical origin.'[82] For this reason, youth culture and subculture are key concepts for historical investigations of those who attempted to alter the terms of their identity through the inappropriate use of sumptuous apparel, since it was in the company of other young men and for a predominantly male audience that such transgressions occurred. Importantly, the culture of youth took shape beyond the bounds of the household in contexts that afforded social dependents some degree of autonomy. Unsupervised leisure activities provided opportunities for young men to augment their ties to one another rather than to the guild, household, or educational institution with which they were affiliated. It was through participation in smaller, more localized gatherings with others like themselves that certain young men became emboldened to test the patriarchal ideals of thrift and self-control and to experiment with modes of collective disorder.

3 The 'idlest time of day'

Located in London's Liberties outside the city proper or in deregulated zones within the city, private and public playhouses provided communal sites beyond the jurisdiction of city fathers that offered visitors a permissive atmosphere where they could engage in just the kind of social and sartorial disorder that authorities attempted to curtail. Up until the revival of the boy companies and the hall playhouses in 1599, young men who worked or studied in London made up the largest group of playgoers to the public theatres.[83] The inordinate number of complaints issued about the playgoing activities of male youths in the period suggests that social dependents attended the theatre on a fairly regular basis and that they were not prohibited from doing so either by lack of opportunity or paucity of funds.[84] As early as 1564 Bishop Edmund Grindal, for instance, exhorted Sir William Cecil to 'inhibitte all playes for one whole yeare ... within the Cittie, or 3. myles compasse,' because the theatres are where 'youthe resorteth excessively.'[85] In 1574 the Lord Mayor and the Court of Aldermen initiated what would be one of five petitions for the suppression of the

> Sondrye greate disorders and inconvenyences ... found to ensewe to this Cittie by the inordynate hauntyinge of greate multitudes of people, speciallye youthe, to playes, enterludes, and shewes ... [causing] ffrayes and quarrelles, eavell practizes of incontinencye ... and manie other Corruptions of youthe and other enormyties.[86]

In 1580 the Lord Mayor approached Lord Chancellor Sir Thomas Bromley about controlling the disruptive atmosphere of the playhouses, noting that 'very superfluous sort of men' frequented them. He also reiterated the increasingly common complaint that plays caused the 'great corruption of youthe.'[87] Those who railed against the theatre argued that apprentices were lured away from their posts to visit the playhouses, and in 1582 the Lord Mayor ordered the heads of guilds to prohibit their apprentices from attending plays.[88] In 1597 the Lord Mayor and Court of Aldermen publicly announced that 'divers apprentices & other seruantes' had confessed to using the playhouses as meeting places, where they converged to foment 'designes & mutinus attemptes' against authorities.[89]

Theatre historians have taken great pains to distinguish the social composition of those who frequented London's public theatres and hall playhouses, as well as to delineate the audience to which each playing company appealed. Yet despite the more specialized offerings made available at the Blackfriars or Paul's after 1599, there is no evidence that young men stopped attending the public theatres altogether. As a case in point, in a 1602 private correspondence to his older brother, Philip Gawdy writes of a raid on the public playhouses organized by the Lord Mayor as part of a city-wide attempt to impress young men into serving in the Low Countries:

> So that uppon the Tuesday following their was a proclamation in London that no gentleman or serving man should any more be impressed, for the weake before they did not only press gentlemen, and sarvingmen, but Lawyers, Clarkes, [and] Country men that had lawe causes ... All the playe howses wer beset in one daye and very many pressed from thence, so that in all ther ar pressed fowre thowsand besydes fyve hundred voluntaryes, and all for flaunders.[90]

Gawdy's account suggests that young male gentry, servants, apprentices, and students continued to patronize the public theatre en masse. Other testimonies from the period also indicate that through the end of the century, the Globe Theatre was a regular haunt of those young men who had been known to frequent the more exclusive hall venues.[91] Moreover, those who associated the practices of playgoing with a disorderly culture of young male servants, apprentices, and students focused on the immediate effects of disorder rather than on the particularities of the venue in which the disruption occurred. In *Kind-Harts Dream*, Henry Chettle notes that while plays are being performed anywhere in the city and its immediate environs, 'halfe the day is by most youthes that haue libertie spent vppon them, or at least the greatest company [are] drawne' to the theatres.[92] He calls for 'the yoong people of the Cittie' either to abstain 'altogether from playes, or at their comming thither to vse themselues after a more quiet order.'[93]

Gathered together in 'the afternoon being the idlest time of the day, wherein men are their own masters,' young men at the playhouse enjoyed freedom from the watchful eyes of employers, corporation heads, and principals.[94] City apprentices, household servants, and students at university and the Inns of Court made up the legions of what John Earle describes as 'After-noone's men.'[95] It is not surprising that authorities responded anxiously to such a permissive arrangement, and there are frequent reports of discord among the students, apprentices, servants, and actors assembled together in unsupervised spaces. The Privy Council minutes for 1580 include an account of a brawl among three of the earl of Oxford's players and Inns of Court students in the audience.[96] The following summer, Lord Berkeley reported to the Lord Mayor on 'some broile' that had 'lately fallen owt betwixt certaine of my men and some of the Innes of the Courte.'[97] While the Inns of Court students seem to have always made themselves conspicuous in a crowd, another run-in between a servingman and group of apprentices at the Theatre in 1584 indicates that no single group could bear the blame for the volatile atmosphere at the playhouses.[98] As Ian Archer has suggested, the conflicts among apprentices, servants, and students reflected the status uncertainty of these young men, and he notes that 'such attitudes had a sharper cutting edge in London because many apprentices were recruited from the younger sons of gentry or from the ranks of the yeomanry, the same groups as provided so many servingmen in gentry households.'[99]

'An Order to Cambridge Students,' written on the occasion of a hall performance, provides some information about the general perceptions of the playgoing habits of young men and reveals that the disorder with which they were associated was not necessarily contained within their own ranks. The order instructs that

> No tobacco be taken in the Hall nor anywhere else publicly, and that neither at their standing in the streets, nor before the comedy begin, nor all the time there, any rude or immodest exclamations be made; nor any humming, hawking, whistling, hissing, or laughing be used, or any stamping or knocking, nor any such other uncivil or unscholarlike or boyish demeanour, upon any occasion; nor any clapping of hands be had until the *Plaudite* at the end of the Comedy ... do apparently begin the same.[100]

A disruptive presence to everyone around them, including those trying to perform the play, servants reportedly 'thunder at [the] playhouse, and fight for bitten apples: that no audience but the tribulation of Tower Hill, or the limbs of Limehouse, their dear brothers, are able to endure,' while apprentices 'break in at playes' and 'fight for Apples,' and scholars 'crack Nuts' in the 'peny Rooms.'[101]

Renowned for theatricalizing the very experience of attending a performance, male youths are often depicted by satirists and playwrights as attempting to lay claim to the playing arena in order to show off before their friends. In his mock courtesy manual, *The Guls Hornebooke*, Thomas Dekker mischievously instructs his young male reader on the finer points of how to misbehave at the theatre.[102] He counsels his gallant-in-training to set himself on 'the throne of the stage,' or to rent a stool at the private playhouse (50). Once centrally situated, Dekker explains, he can then compete for the audience's attention by mocking the players, by 'turn[ing] plain ape,' and by 'tak[ing] up a rush and tickl[ing] the earnest ears of [his] fellow gallants' (55). To effectively up-stage the actors, Dekker recommends to his young man that he 'make other fools fall a laughing; mew at passionate speeches; blare at merry; find fault with the music; whew at the children's action; [and] whistle at the songs' (55). Similarly, one of Ben Jonson's characters guides an aspiring gallant on ways to attend a play with the sole intention of garnering attention. He explains to his charge, 'When you come to plays, be humorous, look with a good starched face, and ruffle your brow like a new boot; laugh at nothing but your own jests, or else as the noblemen laugh ... and sit o'the stage and flout: provided you have a good suit.'[103] Another satirist emphasizes that the sumptuously attired young man could create ample distraction for the audience by sitting on the stage proper in an ostentatious ensemble:

> See you him yonder, who sits o're the stage,
> With the Tobacco-pipe now at his mouth?
> It is *Cornelius* that braue gallant youth,
> Who is new printed to this fangled age:
>
> He wears a Ierkin cudgeld with gold lace,
> A profound slop, a hat scarce pipkin high,
> For boots, a pair of dagge cases; his face,
> Furr'd with *Cads*-beard: his ponyard on his thigh.[104]

Jonson also has his Blackfriars' gallant 'sit i' the view, salute all [his] acquaintance, / Rise vp between the *Acts*, [and] let fall [his] cloake,' in order to 'publish' himself as 'a handsome man [with] a rich suite / (As that's a speciall end, why we goe thither, / All that pretend, to stand for 't o' the *Stage*).'[105] John Marston's young men 'load the stage with stuff' or clothes, while Sir Thomas Overbury's gallant 'withers his clothes on a stage, as a salesman is forced to do his suits in Birchin Lane; and when the play is done, if you mark his rising, 'tis with a kind of walking epilogue between the two candles, to know if his suit may pass for current.'[106]

While they no doubt proved an annoyance to other actors and audience members, these boisterous young men were also perceived as victims themselves, insofar as some regarded them as susceptible to the corrosive atmosphere of the playhouse. Authors of advice manuals in the period sympathetically argue that the theatre posed myriad temptations for those who ordinarily struggled to maintain self-control in even more structured settings. According to William Guild, idleness was a vice particular to young men, and Henry Crosse similarly emphasizes that 'youth are made pliant to wantonness and idleness ... the tender buds of good manners utterly rooted out' of them at the theatre.[107] T.F. in his *Newes from the North* designates the theatres among 'such places, where the time is so shamefully misspent,' resulting in the 'vtter distruction of youth.'[108] Richard Brathwait condemns young gentlemen for making playgoing a habit, such that 'they make it their vocation,' as they rise late in the morning, 'put on their clothes formally, repair to an Ordinary, and see a play daily.'[109]

In his defence of stage plays, Nashe attempts to refute the standard claim of 'some petitioners of the Council' that the theatres 'corrupt the youth of the city and withdraw prentices from their work.'[110] Indeed, the Lord Mayor's Petition of 1592 was one of many civic ordinances attempting to delimit the playgoing of servants, students, and apprentices, because at the theatre, the petition asserts, youth 'is greatly corrupted & their manners infected with many euill & vngodly qualities.'[111] The Lord Mayor's Petition of 1597 reiterates the then familiar set of concerns about the 'corrupcion of youth' and the 'contagion of manners' among young men:[112]

> They [the playhouses] are a speciall cause of corrupting their Youth, conteninge nothing but vnchast matters, lascivious devices, shiftes of Coozenage, & other lewd & vngodly practizes, being so as that they impresse the very qualitie & corruption of manners which they represent ... Whearby such as frequent them, beinge of the base & refuze sort of people or such young gentlemen as haue small regard of credit or conscience, drawe the same into imitacion and to the avoidinge the like vices which they represent ... [they] draw apprentices and other seruants from theire ordinary workes and all sortes of people from the resort vnto

> sermons and other Christian exercises, to the great hinderance of traides & prophanation of religion established by her highnes within this Realm.[113]

Corporation heads issued a series of by-laws to buttress city ordinances. A 1582 Order of the Ironmongers Company forbids 'sarvants, apprentices, journemen, or children, to repare or goe to annye playes ... either within the cittie or suburbs' upon punishment at the discretion of one's master.[114] A 1589 entry in the Bakers Company court minutes notes that 'divers journeymen and other servants in this company have heretofore [been] accustomed on the Thursday and other week days to go abroad to gaming houses, taverns, plays, and other suchlike places.'[115] A 1586 ordinance of the Plasterers Company, which echoes regulations passed by the Cloth Workers in 1587 and Tallow Chandlers Company in 1588, warns on the penalty of a fine and corporal punishment that its apprentices should refrain from the daily 'hauntinge of Alehouses, Taverns, [and] plaies.'[116]

While city officials and corporation heads inveighed against a playhouse that inspired idleness in otherwise industrious young men, often such complaints were encompassed within a broader concern, one that is often overlooked by scholars. Early modern advice writers and moralists acknowledge that by attending the theatre, non-elite, young men become exposed to and invited to participate in an illegitimate, ad hoc economy. As Crosse observes in *Vertue's Commonwealthe*, 'At a play, the whole faculty of the mind is altogether bent on delight, the eye earnestly fixed upon the object, every sense busied for the time ... they [stage plays] do not only (as I say) feed the ear with sweet words, equally balanced is the eye with variable delight' (Q2). Comparing the playhouse to the marketplace, Crosse notes that vice is 'set to sale on open Theaters,' and warns against youth attendance, in particular, because the 'internal powers' of young men are 'moved at such visible and lively objects' (P2v). The theatre offered youths the opportunity of 'idleness mixt with a wandering mind' and due to the 'vanity of objects' they observed at the playhouse, Francis Lenton points out, 'ten-to-one' young men who attend plays will 'break the fence of reason and embrace concupiscence.'[117] Philip Stubbes is explicit in his criticism that at the theatre viewers are trained in not only how to 'ſcoffe, mock, & flowt' authority but also in how to 'conſume treaſurs.'[118] In his catalogue of the vices inspired by the theatre, even the Lord Mayor mentions that stage plays induce 'apprentices and servants' to 'maintein their vain & prodigall expenses occasioned by such evill and riotous companie.'[119]

The theatre was renowned for its 'prophane spectacles,' which included the sight of those who attended 'so trimmed, so adorned, so decked, so perfumed' in their 'their holy-dayes appareil,' clothes that were otherwise reserved for church days, that audience members competed to outshine one another, as well as the lavishly attired actors.[120] In a 1587 private correspondence to Walsingham, one visitor to England's theatres is moved to deplore the 'wofull sight to see two hundred proude players jett in their silkes, wheare five hundred pore people sterve in the streets.'[121] Ministers who censured the playhouses condemned 'the gorgeous Playing place' and the 'sumptuous Theatre houses,' which boasted marble columns, spangled heavens, and the lush silks, velvets, and taffetas used to cover and frame the stage.[122] Stage players are described as modelling 'all the best apparell' such as the costly clothes one would ordinarily showcase on only 'the highest day in the yeare.'[123] As the prologue of one play suggests, the performance was hard pressed to satisfy 'so many Ears, so many Eyes,' some which delighted 'in wit,' 'some in shows,' and 'some in Clothes.'[124]

What made the theatre a novel enterprise was its ability to promote a new method of cultural merchandizing in such a way that sumptuous display was transformed into performative practice. As a result, when young men attended the theatre they encountered a wide range of commodities – clothes, wine, beer, ale, tobacco, gingerbread, pippins, and nuts – in the words of Nashe, 'most lively anatomized.'[125] Thus, the activity of playgoing endorsed social dependents as 'self-reliant consumers' who could participate in a market freed from the restrictions of the traditional schedules of the liturgical calendar, guild rules, or even systems of household patronage.[126] At the playhouse direct purchase was made available to an entirely new constituency, young men with diminished prospects, no clearly defined social identity, and few resources.

Through its involvement with unorthodox business practices, the theatre pursued a 'deliberate strategy of economic diversification' which, in turn, enabled it to exploit the peculiar situation of ambivalently positioned young men.[127] The head of the Rose Theatre, Philip Henslowe, for instance, regularly rented out and sold items of apparel that had been used as costumes. Most of the profits that he received from such arrangements were for less than thirty shillings, indicating that small sums of money could allow one to purchase clothes that, although thread-worn, still conveyed some sense of resplendence.[128] In his daily book, Henslowe details a busy traffic in stage costumes and catalogues those items that he received as pledges. He makes numerous references to pieces of material or remnants, such as the 'remnant of black satin' that is pledged along with a scholar's coat 'without lining, cape, or lace,' which he appraises at '£4 and 10s.'[129] Apparently, 62.2 per cent of the apparel that Henslowe rented was to lenders who provided such 'off-cuts,' or smaller items like lace and hose, as their security.[130] While some pledges were, undoubtedly, more valuable, there are many items listed that seem to have belonged to those who worked as servants and apprentices, like 'a doublet of fustian' and 'a pair of breeches of broadcloth.'[131] Perhaps the growing awareness among members of the non-elite that even the more quotidian scholars' gowns and apprentices' hose were assets that could be changed up for better items or for cash motivated some to attend the theatre not only to watch plays but also to supplement their wages, if not their wardrobe.

First-hand accounts tell of young male servants pilfering objects and cash from their masters, as well as of students exchanging law books and their scholars' robes for cash or other cast-off items. In 1598 the servant Robert Saker of London was charged with 'purloyning' his mistress's goods in order to purchase a pair of 'hose and doblett laid out with satten, a payre of jersey stockings, a payre of Spanish leather shoes, a payre of silke stockings, and change of clothes and other apparrell.'[132] The apprentice William Atkinson admitted to taking £10 worth of cash and goods from his master in order to obtain £5 worth of clothes.[133] Servants were regularly accused of stealing household goods to which they had easy access, such as 'apples, aprons, beakers, beef, beer, bottles, brass, bread, candles, candlesticks, cheeses, cloth, clocks, fish, hats, herbs, napkins, plates, rope, sheets, shoes, spoons, spices, stirrups, stockings, sugar, tools, and yarn,' as well as household linens and apparel which they offered as pledges at the brokers' stalls.[134] According to one young man, 'it was a hard matter if an apprentice could not in the tyme of his yeares get some money,' and many bragged that as a matter of course, they regularly pawned various household items 'to fund a trip to the playhouse, alehouse, or bawdy house, [or] to buy clothes.'[135] Contemporary accounts that chart the connections between used clothing markets and the theatre identify the sartorially extravagant young male attendee as the go-between tying together these two enterprises. Lenton, for instance, describes the young man who 'hath so often outfitted the Globe' as reduced to taking 'all his spangled and rare perfumed attire / Which once glittered in the torches fire / ... to the Brokers to compound his debt / Or else be pawned to procure him meat.'[136] Robert Greene has his *Publius Seruilius* remind the stage player, 'bee not so bragge of thy silken roabes, for I sawe them but yesterday make a great shew in a broakers shop.'[137] Jonson writes of the 'Fine-man' who 'thrice chang'd every day' in order 'to teach each suit he has, the ready way / From *Hide-Parke* to the Stage, where at the last / His deare and borrow'd Bravery he must cast.'[138]

The growth of illicit apparel markets specifically geared towards male youth enabled members of this population to not only appropriate the material use of clothes but also to expropriate their social meaning. Consumers of second-hand items identified the surplus value of discarded apparel, and by picking and choosing among aristocratic cast-offs, disenfranchised young men participated in a maverick economy of conspicuous consumption. If aristocratic privilege was defined by a mode of gratuitous expenditure by which the elite lay claim to their largesse by asserting the expendability of the commodity, then mean men, by recycling those items that their betters had exhausted, flaunted their prerogative to revise the material conditions of taste.[139] Indeed, these men, who had limited funds even for second-hand purchases, cobbled together outlandish ensembles by retrieving those items that had been excluded from primary arenas of display, and by infusing them with their own sense of glamour. Their second-hand style, which juxtaposed disparate items, conveyed fragmentation rather than coherence, and by engaging modes of 'confrontational dressing,' they simultaneously assimilated and parodied those aesthetic categories that underwrote the sartorial codes of the dominant culture.[140]

By creating the conditions for a new consumer niche, the theater validated those who through ingenuity procured pledges, by bonding forged networks of credit, and in cleverness discerned the value of cast-offs, allowing them to enter into an emergent world of commercial exchange. At the theatre, young men were identified neither by pedigree nor by social standing but by 'a mode of perception,' whereby they made clothes 'the object of an arrested or fetishistic scrutiny.'[141] For Dekker's young gallant, for example, the distinctions between street clothes and costume, spectator and performer, real life and theatre are meaningless. Having found the perfect moment to present himself to the public surrounding the stage, he inserts himself into the *mise-en-scene* of the play proper as if he were 'one of the properties' that had 'dropped out of the hangings' or 'from behind the arras.'[142] Completely consumed by the steady stream of objects that pass before him, he stands in the middle of the action of the play moved to anger, not by the dramatic narrative but by the sudden realization that his haberdasher sold the stage player before him the very same 'embroidered felt and feather' for which he paid forty shillings not two hours earlier.[143]

4 The Significance of Flaunting

The sentiment 'the clothes make the man' reflected the sartorial philosophy of a period in which clothing constituted cultural authority and conferred social legitimacy.[144] The claim that clothes made men had profound implications in early modern England. Yet, as I have shown, a certain group of men used clothes to make something out of what had been made of them. While Elizabethan clothing law aimed to restrict what the sumptuous dresser wore, it also revealed a peculiar concern with the way the sumptuous dresser wore his clothes. This concern is epitomized by the Elizabethan clothing proclamation of 1580, which condemns 'the great excess of apparel ... in the inferior sort' and commands mean men to 'leave off such fond disguised and monstrous *manner* of attiring themselves.'[145] State and local authorities were as invested in regulating sumptuary practices as they were committed to controlling sumptuous attire. The dual focus of clothing legislation points to a broader anxiety within late Elizabethan culture about the training of youth in proper habits of work and leisure. Deference was crucial in a society marked, on the one hand, by a move towards a service-oriented economy, and, on the other hand, by an upset in established ideologies of super-and subordination. By demonstrating sartorial irreverence, and its accompanying attitude of impudence, certain young men did not simply reject but they also refashioned the terms of their disenfranchisement. Those who frequented the playhouse, with the hope that 'all men may point at [them]' and their clothes, appropriated a disciplinary gaze that rendered them objects of surveillance by boldly remaking themselves the subject of public attention.[146] Although they were 'in the mercer's books' for money owed on satins and velvets and in hiding from their creditors, these young men, nonetheless, unabashedly paraded down the streets of London in flamboyant ensembles.[147]

According to the Puritan social commentator Philip Stubbes in his *Anatomy of Abuses*, young men who procured sumptuous items of apparel by 'any kind of means,' and who were apparently undeterred by the mandates of the Crown's clothing legislation, were guilty of 'riot[ing] and flaunt[ing] daily' (41). While the specific behaviours associated with 'flaunt[ing]' remain unclear, the general sense of the charge is that practitioners openly wrested luxurious items of apparel from their 'proper' place. They may have, in turn, modified the associations of items traditionally used in certain ways by members of a particular social group, producing unorthodox combinations. Or those who engaged in flaunting may have exaggerated a particular aspect of a given item. Stubbes devotes an entire chapter of his *Anatomy of Abuses* to the sartorial practices of 'the inferiour ſorte' (xii), whom he characterizes as men who are 'neither of the nobylitie, gentilitie, nor yeoma*n*ry' but who, nonetheless, 'go daylie in ſilkes, veluets, ſatens, damaſks, [and] taffeties' (34). Mean men, he claims, 'farre ſurpaſſe either noble, honorable, or worſhipfull' in their 'ruffling in Silks, Veluets, Satens, Damaſks, [and] Taffeties' (xii). While he mentions the general 'confused mingle mangle of apparel in *Ailgna* [England],' his primary concern is 'the preposterous excess thereof,' whereby young mean men 'flaunt it out in what apparell [they] luſt [themselves]' (34).

Stubbes, like other popular early modern writers, represents sartorially extravagant young men as insatiable consumers for whom sumptuous clothing is not a means to an end but an end itself. Unlike the ornate courtier or even the affected social pretender, those who flaunted it out did not dress luxuriously in a delimited cultural context or in an effort to promote a social agenda. By treating clothes as fetish-objects of the highest order, they exhibited, instead, a mode of presentation that allowed them to make a spectacle out of the conditions of their own self-fashioning. The notion of excess as a classifiable set of behaviours is articulated within 'An Homily Against Excess of Apparel,' a sermon that Elizabeth assigned to all church officials in 1588. While the sermon sets out to chastise both men and women, a substantial portion is devoted to those men who repeatedly violate the provisions of Elizabethan clothing laws. Invoking biblical authorities and injunctions, the homily ultimately condemns those who practise the 'foul and chargeable excess ... of apparel' on grounds that by violating such 'necessary laws' these subjects pose a 'great peril' to the realm.[148] By reminding its auditors of the four lessons of the Holy Scripture, the sermon conveniently reiterates the state's ideal of a stratified social order as explicated by other state-issued homilies, such as 'An Homily Concerning Good Order.' The sermon's third lesson, for instance, instructs 'that we take in good part our estate and condition, and content ourselves with that which God sendeth, whether it be much or little' (305). The fourth emphasizes that

> Every man behold and consider his own vocation: in as much as God hath appointed every man his degree and office, within the limits whereof it behoveth him to keep himself.
>
> Therefore all may not look to wear like apparel; but every one according to his degree, as God hath placed him. Which, if it were observed, many one doubtless would be compelled to wear a russet coat, which now ruffleth in silks and velvets, spending more by the year in sumptuous apparel, than their fathers received for the whole revenue of their lands. (308)

Here the sermon explicitly targets sons of landowning men who, despite their gentle origins, are consigned to wear russet (a coarse woollen cloth that was not dyed but left its natural reddish-brown or gray colour), the material typically provided to social dependents such as servants and apprentices. According to the sermon, this particular group of young men 'seeketh to excel' all others in 'costly attire' despite their limited resources (310). Spending what little income they have amassed on sable, fur gowns, corked slippers, and trim buskins (308), these young men 'hang their revenues about their necks, ruffling in their ruffs' (310).

The homily forges the link between practising 'excess of apparel' and exceeding one's prescribed social place, and in this respect appears to be an extended meditation on the dangers of a social atmosphere marked by increased instances of sartorial and social illegibility. As described by Henry Crosse, sartorial confusion heralded the overturning of propriety:

> We shall see Pride ruffle in base Rusticks, for everyone will be in fashion howsoever they come by it; the Servant cannot be known from the Master, the Maid from the Mistress, nor scarce any man's estate distinguished by his apparel, but every slovenly Servingmen and greasy Scrape-Trencher will exceed the bounds of his calling and creep into

> acquaintance with velvet, satin, and such costly stuff too high iwis for their low estate and lay all they can wrap and rend on their backs in swaggering and vain apparel to seem a clout of lousy gentility that proving bankrupts in youth are fain to wear rags in age.[149]

'An Homily Against Excess of Apparel,' however, construes the sumptuous dresser as more than a sinner who 'openly contemns' God and an insurgent subject who 'manifestly disobeys' the state by moving outside of his prescribed place (306). The mean, sumptuous dresser does not wear his silks and sables to misrepresent his status, nor does he dress sumptuously to advance himself. Rather he extravagantly 'decks' himself out for the pure pleasure of doing so (308). Those men who 'prepar[e] [themselves] in fine bravery' (306), the homily emphasizes, demonstrate a passion for sumptuous clothes that indexes other 'wanton, lewd, and unchaste behaviour[s]' (306). 'Taking no care at all, but only how to deck themselves [out],' these young men, the sermon explains, will stop at nothing 'to satisfy their wanton lusts' (308).

State sermons and tracts such as Stubbes's *Anatomy of Abuses* were correct in regarding sartorial excess as a sign of social and economic disorder, yet by reading such condemnations of sartorial extravagance only in terms of class transgression and gender dissonance, modern scholars have overlooked how sensitive contemporaries were to expressions of masculinity that, unlike failed or anxious approximations of patriarchal ideals, demonstrated a bold rejection of these ideals. The word 'masculinity,' which did not enter the English language until the middle of the eighteenth century, referred to the privilege awarded to men in matters of inheritance. 'Manhood' and 'manliness' were the terms used in the sixteenth century to connote those qualities essential to civility, which was identified teleologically as the definitive characteristic of the adult man.[150] Effeminacy signalled the inability to control one's passions, and immoderation in dress was both the cause and the sign of incivility and hence of unmanliness. In *A Discourse of Trade*, Thomas Mun, for example, explains that the consequences of 'following our pleasures' are ruinous to the virility of the nation and the citizen alike:

> The sum of all is this, that the general leprosy of our Piping, Potting, Feasting, Fashions, and mis-spending of our time in Idleness and Pleasure (contrary to the Law of God, and the use of other Nations) hath made us effeminate in our Bodies, weak in our Knowledge, poor in our

> Treasure, declined in our Valour, unfortunate in our Enterprises, and contemned by our Enemies.[151]

The excesses that made young men susceptible to flaunting it out in extravagant ensembles threatened to compromise their claims to self-mastery and their prerogative to become masters over others.[152] Like Marston's gallant, who is 'nothing but his clothes,' young men who 'strut[ed] in vice' also modelled their 'effeminate inuention,' as made evident by a propensity to 'ryot [and] lust,' making them 'sencelesse, sensuall Epicure[s].'[153] Barnaby Rich warns against young men who chronically consider themselves to be 'quite out of *fashion*,' if they are not '*strumpet* like attired.'[154] Manhood was what male youth were expected to strive for, and those who resisted its imperatives by partaking in activities that were not politically necessary, socially useful, or economically beneficial, theatrically flouted its codes.

5 Conclusion

Those young apprentices, servants, and students who peopled the theatre and trafficked in used clothing perceived the city to be 'a Commodie [comedy], both in partes and in apparell,' and themselves as 'the Actors,' daily dramatizing the fact that even men such as themselves who 'could scarce get Veluet for [their] Cape[s], [have] nowe linde [their] Cloake[s] throughout with it.'[155] Changes in cultural technology made it possible for these young men to reorient their position towards and to intensify their participation in a new world of consumption and leisure. In particular, the theatre enabled and elaborated the various ways that the disenfranchised could distinguish themselves beyond simply procuring specific costly items of apparel. Rather, through the selection and reorganization of sartorial items, in tandem with the adoption of specific attitudes, poses, and ways of being in the world, certain young men on stage and off could act out the process whereby they altered the social uses and meanings of crucial cultural commodities.

Did the sartorial practices of this subculture alter the philosophies and processes of the dominant culture against which they were reacting? Certainly the demonstration of sartorial irreverence did not generate more social options for these disenfranchised young men. Arguably, their display of excess set them back even further, since they were inevitably chastised, if not penalized, for such impudence. Moreover, the success of the theatre may suggest that the subculture of style I have been describing became robbed of its oppositional power as its tactics of irreverence became commercialized. Yet when we consider the subversive sartorial strategies these men engaged in specific settings, such as the household and the court, as well as at certain civic sites like St Paul's Cathedral, we can begin to identify the disruptive effects of sartorial excess on both the state's perceptions of its own authority and on very real structures of local power. The early modern emphasis on youth as a transitional moment and on young men as an inherently unstable cohort was symptomatic of a parent culture that was itself becoming fractured by changing criteria of gentility, shifting expectations of work and leisure, and debates over the meaning of conspicuous consumption. As I have suggested in this chapter, the concept of youth in early modern culture was especially complex because youth was understood as at once a stage of life, a physiological condition, a social position, and as an attitude marked by wilful impertinence. Focusing on the period's concerns about male youth may ultimately reveal the ways in which wider socio-economic transformations were starting to unhinge the material and cultural forms that organized systems of deference in early modern English culture. Youth as 'a metaphor for social change,' signalled both the vanguard of the new and the erosion of the old, and thus the attitudes and behaviour of young men indexed a fundamental shift in those traditional relations that had provided hierarchic stability to late sixteenth-century English society.[156] In the chapters that follow, I will show that while young men were perceived as agents of social breakdown in this period of change, excessive young men who flaunted a monstrous manner of dress were seen as an especially subversive minority.

3 Livery and Its Discontents in *The Taming of the Shrew*

And trick't and trim'd, thus bravely he supposes himselfe another man.

Anonymous, *Witt's Recreations*.[1]

1 The Limits of Livery

The contentious dynamic between husband and wife has dominated critical approaches to *The Taming of the Shrew*, while the volatile interactions between masters and servants have remained largely unexplored.[2] Yet the taming of Kate and the disciplining of various servants deserve equal attention, since both are integral to the play's representation of mastery as besieged by a domestic economy increasingly oriented towards sumptuous display. In the late sixteenth century, the household moved away from the production of goods and towards the procurement of them, altering the work of domestics from the labour of creating products to the task of exhibiting commodities. Indeed, Shakespeare's shrew-taming narrative distinguishes itself from other early modern ballads and jest-book tales by its interest in the home as a site of consumption.[3] As a barometer of fluctuating notions about the meaning and purpose of housework, Shakespeare's play measures the variable responses of a culture poised between residual and emergent ideals of domesticity. On the one hand, *The Shrew* recognizes the decorative housewife as the new emblem of the consumer home. On the other hand, it acknowledges that even as the housewife arrived on the domestic scene, the household continued to be populated by extra-familial young men who were not expected to engage in manual toil but were encouraged to participate in conspicuous display.

Traditionally masters in early modern England expressed social prestige through the splendour of their male charges. Servants embodied the largesse of the household and became integrated into its hierarchy through the donning of livery. They were provided costly clothing with which to proclaim not their own, but their master's status.[4] Despite the Crown's attempts to ensure that members of the elite did not dress their men beyond the sumptuary dictates of their own rank, and in spite of the censure of moralists, householders continued to rely on young male domestics to showcase their magnificence.[5] The institution of livery went hand in hand with an ideology of service that encouraged domestics to engage in 'histrionic "self-fashioning,"' producing the conditions for young men to use the sartorial expectations of their position to outshine their masters and to potentially disobey them in other matters.[6] For the majority of England's male youth who spent some part or all of their lives in service, their identity, to the distress of their masters, was not apparently fully formed by, or in some cases even informed by, their household position.

Because as many as 60 per cent of young men between the ages of fifteen and thirty-five were employed in a household, historians have deemed late sixteenth-century England a 'service society.'[7] Although contemporaries claimed that those young men who lived in represented the 'vntryed dregges and droſſe of leſſe eſteeme,' as opposed to the 'pure and refined' gentlemen of yesteryear, evidence shows that among this 60 per cent there was only a slight drop in the number of gentle-born servants.[8] Many domestics hailed from non-gentle backgrounds, but a significant portion continued to come from the ranks of those second sons whose life circumstances compelled them to take up positions in elite households.[9] As A.L. Beier importantly emphasizes, even though the economic realities of over-population recommended a career in service as one of few viable prospects, young men from gentle backgrounds persisted in perceiving their household status as indicative of a temporary phase in their life-cycle.[10]

Critics have observed that Petruchio's tactics for inducting Kate into her new domestic role revolve around the manipulation of 'household stuff.'[11] Yet the exclusive focus on marital dynamics in *The Shrew* has caused readers to overlook the ways in which household stuff occupies an equally prominent place in masters' methods of managing a domestic space peopled by ambiguously positioned young men. Household stuff is a primary prop in the maintenance of domestic order, but throughout the play, such stuff also provides the material for domestic subversion. A system of service that made masters dependent on their subordinates for the promotion of their own status, Shakespeare's play shows, allowed those servants who were aware of their decorative role and willing to abuse it the latitude to construct *and* to deconstruct their masters' claims to social legitimacy. By engaging its audience in an ongoing, pitched battle between masters and servants for supremacy over the material resources and the social significance of the domestic sphere, *The Shrew*, unlike the advice manuals upon which it draws, offers viewers more than a depiction of domestic rebellion and a prescription for household order.

Performed daily before a cohort of young men, the majority of whom served in households, by actors who themselves served wealthy patrons, this play exposes its bias in regard to master-servant relations. In the Induction, serving and playing are conflated when one character likens the play about to be enacted before the others, on the stage and off, to 'household stuff' (Ind. 2.131). When the players who will present this 'pleasant comedy' (Ind. 2.121) arrive, they characterize their performance as an 'offer [of] service to [their] lordship' (Ind. 1.74). *The Shrew*, then, not only frames the action that follows with a depiction of domestic labour as a theatrical endeavour but also comes to represent the household itself as a space not unlike the theatre insofar as it enables more than constrains young men's unruly desires and identifications. Like the masters it portrays, Shakespeare's play was also dependent on the acquiescence of young men for its success. For this reason, it devotes a substantial portion of its comedic energy to elaborating the performative strategies employed by those who skilfully manipulate the props of servitude by transforming the insignia of obeisance into the signs of resistance.

2 The Comely Servant

By the end of the sixteenth century, the ideal of service based on a fraternal and militaristic conception of *comitatus*, exemplified by the retainer system that obligated servants to protect their masters' physical person, had been effectively replaced by a mode of service in which young men were expected to represent their masters' prestige. They did so by dressing sumptuously and by adopting what one popular manual, I.M.'s *Servingmans Comfort*, describes as a 'comely' demeanour (139). Household status in this period became so closely tied to vestimentary display that the appearance of a man's servants was considered tantamount to 'the physical presentation of the attributes of the man.'[12] John Earle describes the servingman as 'one of the makings up of a Gentleman, as well as his clothes ... for hee is cast behind his master as fashionably as his sword and cloake are, and he [the master] is but *in querpo* [half-dressed] without him.'[13] The main qualification of a servant, Earle emphasizes, is that he has a 'good legge,' because 'he is indeed wholly his Master's ... of his pleasures; he is handsome for his credit.'[14] This ideology of personal service inadvertently made those in authority dependent on the social and sartorial conformity of their domestics. The perspective that viewed 'Every Mans proper *Mansion*, House, and *Home* [as] the *Theatre* of his *Hospitality*' recognized male servants as star players in an elaborate costume drama.[15]

The anonymous author of *Civil and Uncivil Life* discusses the decorative function of male servants, stressing that young men working in the home should not be expected to engage in 'labour or drudgery.'[16] Rather, this author avers, servants, rightfully, 'take great ſcorne' when they are requested to perform menial tasks 'being cumly perſonages,' whose primary function is to adorn their master by 'attend[ing] vpon [his] Table ... follow[ing] [him] in the ſtreetes ... and furniſh[ing] [his] Halles at home' (34). Like the gentlemen they served, the author explains, domestics ought to be trained to become 'expert in ſundry ſeemly, and neceſſary knowledges' (38). Among their areas of distinction, servants should be practised in how to 'decently weare their garments' and to entertain with witty 'table talke,' since they will be expected to discourse on either 'pleaſure or profit' (38). A servingman, Sir Thomas Overbury concurs, 'is a creature' whose 'life is for ease and leisure, much about gentleman-like ... His discretion is to be careful for his master's credit, and his sufficiency to marshal dishes at a table and to carve well. His neatness consists much in his hair and his outward linen ... his courting language ... [and] he is always ready furnished with a song.'[17]

On account of the strong correlation between the social position of the master and the number of male domestics he employed, even heads of more modest households were compelled to keep conspicuously idle servants, whom they furnished with clothing as costly as their own. According to *Civil and Uncivil*, 'no man wil put off his cap or do him reuerence' who 'walke[s] in the Cittie without ſeruants attending on him' (43). I.M., in *The Servingmans Comfort*, satirizes the upstart whose 'Fathers chiefe Badge or Cogniſance was the Weauers

Shuttle, or the Taylors Sheares' (126). Iohn Makeſhift, 'whoſe laſt acre lyes morgaged,' nonetheless, struts down the street attended by six to eight elaborately attired fellows (125). Another new man 'treade[s] the ſtreetes ſo ſtately attended, and ſo gallantly garded' that he 'floryſh[es] [his] fayre Cloakes, as though he were the Prince of Peacockes' (126). To augment his portrait of those who compensated for their lack of pedigree by keeping ostentatiously attired men, I.M. describes a Justice of the Peace worth 2000 marks annually whose servant wore apparel 'much better than his Maiſters' (123). One visitor to England confirms I.M.'s sense of the heightened incidence of sartorial imbalance between master and servant; he claims that servants of all ranks of men who once were 'wont to wear blue Coates, and their Masters badge of silver on the left sleeve,' now 'most commonly weare cloakes garded with laces' and are 'apparelled with no less pride and inconstancie of fashions than other degrees.'[18] An ideology of service that linked sumptuousness with obedience represented dressing extravagantly, a practice that according to Elizabethan clothing law violated the tenets of established social hierarchy, as a servant's duty to his master.

In *The Shrew* the servant Grumio showcases his ability to manipulate the circumstances in which his master looks to him to proclaim his magnificence. Instead of promoting his master, Grumio exposes Petruchio's lack of mastery by pushing him to the point where he can no longer maintain his persona as a gentleman. Grumio achieves his goal by choosing to perform his submission in a histrionic fashion. Having arrived at the home of the wealthy Hortensio, Grumio expresses his willingness to protect his master and follow Petruchio's order, 'Sirrah, Grumio, knock, I say' (1.2.5) by knocking or hitting a potential attacker. Yet no one else is present, and it becomes apparent that Petruchio has not been abused, or in the words of Grumio 'rebused' (1.2.6–7). Grumio then decides to interpret Petruchio's command, 'knock me here soundly' (1.2.8) as an order to hit *him*. By insisting on this literal interpretation of his master's words, Grumio implies that it would be more comprehensible if Petruchio were to have Grumio inflict violence upon him, a distortion of the role of the loyal retainer, than to expect Grumio to uphold his sense of entitlement by 'soundly' or loudly knocking to ostentatiously signal his arrival. Petruchio is after all a country rube who has just recently come into a sizable enough but by no means impressive inheritance. The precarious nature of his station is confirmed by his having come to Padua to 'wive it wealthily' (1.2.70), and his willingness to marry 'an old trot with ne'er a tooth in her head' (1.2.74) so long as she comes with 'gold enough' (1.2.73). Nevertheless, Petruchio wishes to broadcast his newly elevated status to his urbane friend by having his servant pretentiously announce him. As Grumio continues to thwart his master's instructions, Petruchio becomes provoked into beating him. Hortensio is thus drawn to his door by Petruchio's disgraceful display, exemplified by the commotion he causes as he fights with his servant on the city street.

Thomas Moisan has examined such moments of 'verbal misprision' in early modern drama by focusing on plays that feature servants purposely 'misunderstanding' their masters' commands while continuing to maintain a subservient posture.[19] He argues that the antagonistic emotions that are provoked by the breakdown in communication between superiors and subordinates are successfully dispelled by comic dramaturgy. Yet if we interpret such exchanges in *The Shrew* as not merely discrete moments of insolence but as connected to other instances in the play when servants appropriate the decorative function of their role to break – rather than to make – their master's status, these interactions point to a subtle but coherent strategy of resistance. For instance, without violating the strictures of his subordination, Grumio continues to push against the parameters of his role as a 'comely' servant to undermine Petruchio's mastery. In the wedding scene, Grumio elaborates further how to dedicate the materials of servitude to the expression of dissidence.

Apparently, Grumio has exceeded the expectations of his 'wedding garments,' described in act 4 as the privilege of household servants on special occasions (4.1.34). He has not simply dressed up for Petruchio's wedding ceremony; he arrives 'caparisoned' or flamboyantly decked out in his apparel (3.2.57). He wears 'a linen stock on one leg and a kersey boot-hose on the other' (3.2.58). In the place of a garter, he sports a flourish of red and blue strips of cloth. His hat, having 'the humor of forty fancies pricked in't for a feather' (3.2.60), boasts a crown of feathers that is so ornate that it defies description. A member of the wedding party characterizes Grumio as not unlike Petruchio's horse insofar as he too is 'infected with the fashions' (3.2.60). Grumio is described as 'a monster, a very monster in apparel,' or, alternatively, as having dressed 'not like a Christian footboy or a gentleman's lackey' (3.2.60–1).[20] Yet another observer, remarking on Grumio's sartorial extravagance, speculates that 'some odd humor pricks him to this fashion,' since 'oftentimes, he goes but mean-appareled' (3.2.62–3).

Petruchio, on the other hand, is dressed in such a way that he constitutes an 'eyesore' (3.2.91) and a 'shame to [his] estate' (3.2.90). His ensemble conveys a general state of destitution: he wears 'an old jerkin' and a pair of 'old breeches thrice turned; a pair of boots that have been candle-cases,' and he carries 'an old rusty sword ... with a broken hilt' (3.2.41–4). The points or strings attaching his clothes are 'broken' (3.2.45). Critics have correctly interpreted Petruchio's unseemly appearance as an early instance of his taming strategy whereby he publicly humiliates Kate with his sartorial misconduct.[21] Yet these readings of Petruchio's sartorial misbehaviour do not account for Grumio. As a result, readers have consistently overlooked the most startling aspect of the visual tableau produced by the under-dressed Petruchio and the over-dressed Grumio. Only by analysing Petruchio's sartorial performance not as a solo act but as in concert with Grumio's can we begin to understand this complex sartorial contrast.

Explaining that he intends his impoverished attire to serve as an object lesson on the relationship between proper household management and thrift, Petruchio tells Kate's father Baptista that 'to me [Kate's] married, not unto my clothes. / Could I repair what she will wear in me / As I can change these poor accoutrements, / 'Twere well for Kate and better for myself' (3.2.108–10). In emphasizing the 'wear' Kate will effect, Petruchio refers to the favour he performs for Baptista, since once Kate and her sister are married off they will no longer wear away or consume their father's resources. Petruchio's comments about wear certainly reference a host of concerns expressed within sixteenth-century household manuals, sermons, and ballads that women drive their fathers and husbands to ruin by their habits of excessive expenditure and particularly by their sartorial extravagance.[22] In the ballad 'The Cruel Shrew,' for instance, the speaker describes a typical day for his wife:

As soon as she is out of bed
  her looking-glass she takes,
(So vainly is she daily led);
  her morning's work she makes
In putting on her brave attire,
  that fine and costly be,
Whilst I work hard in dirt and mire
Alack! What remedy?[23]

Since the primary goal of the household was the maintenance of order, the spendthrift wife challenged the sovereignty of her husband by her refusal to be a productive domestic and by her exhaustion of his estate. A compensatory fantasy disavowing the dependency of those men, such as Petruchio, who sought to avoid work and to elevate their station by marrying wealthy women, this ballad depicts the wife as threatening her husband's gentle status by reducing him to manual toil. Yet advice writer William Vaughan, who bemoaned that 'every servingman in England, nay, every Common Jack, flaunts it in silks and velvets,' understood the threat to household resources and to the status of its head as emanating from another source.[24]

Grumio's outrageous ensemble speaks to the equally urgent and arguably even more pressing concern among householders that their male domestics perceived their chores as the consumption rather than the guarding of their masters' goods. Even though the inordinate dress of servants had been a typical preoccupation of householders throughout the sixteenth century, at the end of the century official complaints about domestics' attire 'assumed a particularity and an intensity unrivalled in previous decades.'[25] These complaints focused on servants consuming householders' goods, such as those admonitions issued by the anonymous author of *Civil and Uncivil Life* who rebukes his servants for wearing out household 'ʃtuffe,' in particular bed linens, wall hangings, and 'Curtaines and Canopies of ʃilke' (64). He is distressed that 'within a litle time' such a 'great deale of good ʃtuffe' is ruined that he, 'the poore Maiʃter of the houʃe,' ends up with 'al his linnen ʃoul[ed], al his prouiʃion eaten & his houʃehold ʃtuffe made vnʃauery, & oft times torne and ʃpoiled' (64). I.M. chastises those servants who are not satisfied with the clothes with which they have been provided but must wear 'Apparrell of the neweʃt faʃhion,' which, as he notes, they will inevitably sell to the second-hand markets at Birchin Lane.[26] The period's court records attest to the inordinate number of complaints lodged against domestics who 'pilfered,' 'cozened,' 'misspent,' and 'wasted' household stuff, and who fenced stolen items in exchange for cast-off clothes.[27]

Masters' anxieties about their servants wearing out household stuff were well founded, since, as Kate Mertes points out, the household's most significant resource was its members' ability to recycle food stuffs, the metals of pots and pans, and linens and cloth.[28] In 1601 the Court of Aldermen in London appointed a special committee to 'consider what course is fitt to be taken touching bankrupt mens servants and apprentices which deceave their masters.'[29] Contemporary sources indicate that servants were regularly accused of raiding household cupboards, chests, and their masters' purses for 'petty things' or 'trifles,' and, as historians note, articles of clothing were stolen more than any other item.[30] A series of laws was issued in the last decade of the sixteenth century by city authorities, the Lord Mayor, the Corporations, the Court of Aldermen, and the Common Council, in conjunction with the royal administration, aiming to regulate the costliness of apparel awarded to servants by making heads of households responsible for the sartorial propriety of their charges and by fining them for their subordinate's sartorial misconduct.

While Petruchio seeks to assert his newly established authority as head of the marital household by illustrating to Kate the importance of reining in one's appetite for household stuff, Grumio's over-the-top outfit suggests that Petruchio's attempts to manage his wife's habits of consumption bear no relation to his ability to control his servants' extravagances. Tranio, Lucentio's servant, who having traded places with his master attends Petruchio's wedding in Lucentio's apparel, amplifies Grumio's visual irreverence by showing off his resplendent attire. Significantly, Tranio is the only onlooker who claims to understand the sartorial tableau before him. He announces to the bewildered crowd that '[Petruchio] hath some meaning in his mad attire' (3.2.114). Yet rather than explicate this meaning, he exploits the attention of the wedding party by diverting focus onto his own ensemble as he urges Petruchio to remove his 'unreverent robes' (3.2.102) and gallantly offers to loan him some of the costly clothes with which he is adorned. Referring to the sumptuous clothes he wears as 'clothes of mine' (3.2.103), Tranio reveals the ease with which servants count their master's finery as their own stuff. While his master stands off to the side in the humble attire of an impoverished tutor, Tranio demonstrates himself to be well versed in the intricacies of the relationship between sartorial display and social authority, as well as ready to seize the opportunity to manipulate the relation between the two. Thus, while Tranio may apprehend Petruchio's desire to use his inauguration into his new role of householder as an occasion to discipline Kate, he understands, like Grumio, how to take advantage of such public occasions to challenge the monopoly that masters tried to maintain over sumptuous display.

Conduct manuals in the period did not focus on servants' sartorial practices in isolation but addressed the sartorial relationship between master and servant, which signalled, as advice writer William Gouge emphasizes, 'the wisdom of the master ... in well-governing [his] servants.'[31] Sartorial disarray in a domestic context broadcast the head's loss of mastery since there was 'nothing more vnſeemely in a ciuile Gentleman, then his apparell out of repayre, torne, or broken.'[32] Stressing the importance of maintaining proper sartorial balance and the appropriate visual proportion between superior and inferior, Gouge avers that when masters 'carry themselves basely and abjectly before their servants, being light in their behavior, foolish in their carriage, given to ... uncleanness ... and other vices,' they have abdicated their authority.[33] Failures to 'order [one's] own person' indexed, according to Cleaver and Dod, one's inability to 'rule [one's] own house' and, by extension, to properly govern the commonwealth.[34] The intimacy between master and servant that was instrumental to the working order of the household also potentially led to the blurring of boundaries and the straining of those hierarchical distinctions around which the household was organized. Subordinates were at once confidants and companions and as such served as potent flash points for the contradictions that inhered in domestic arrangements, since they were, as Frances Dolan notes, 'dependent yet depended upon, familiar yet not wholly known or controlled, a class and yet not one.'[35]

3 The Braving Servant

Rather than resolving the tensions generated by contestatory sartorial and social orders within the household, Shakespeare's play offers its audience a wholly unique perspective on the relationship between sartorial practice and social power. The opportunities afforded by the contradictions that inhered in an ideology of service that conceived of servants as accoutrements to their masters' ensembles inform *The Shrew*'s representation of young male domestics performatively citing and irreverently transforming the institution of livery, even as masters continue to look to clothing as a primary medium by which to articulate their authority. In the first half of the play, servants couch their resistance in exaggerated expressions of subordination. By the middle of the play, however, they enlist a bolder tactic of subversion, one that more often than not shades into insubordination. This more forceful strategy, characterized by 'braving,' enables subordinates to use the clothes assigned to them and the rhetoric of obedience as the basis of *disidentification* rather than as the material reminder of their servitude.[36]

An early form of ritualized insult anticipating later subcultural signifying practices such as the dozens, reading, shading, or dissing, braving in the early modern period entailed a demonstration of verbal bravado that allowed one to simultaneously disguise and convey hostility.[37] When engaged in braving, each participant was pressed to devise a progressively cleverer comment by which to diminish his opponent, since wit carried the day. Just as verbal braving allowed the speaker to show off his rhetorical agility, sartorial braving enabled the wearer to display his stylistic sensibility. Braving was a competitive mode by which the wearer attempted to outshine someone else, for instance, by wearing his apparel in a way that made him to appear 'more gayer' than 'a lord.'[38] The verb 'to brave,' with its connotations of to boast, to vaunt, and to gloat was, according to early modern usage, associated with inappropriate or combative sartorial behaviour exemplified by those men who 'strut it, stout it, [and] brave it in [their] costly apparel.'[39]

Lucentio's servant Tranio calls attention to his skill at braving when he suggests that he and his master trade places, allowing him to assume Lucentio's dress and 'port' (1.1.194–5) and 'bear [his] part' in Padua (1.1.186), while Lucentio dresses as Bianca's impoverished tutor. Adorned in his master's apparel, Tranio's first task is to outbid the competition for Bianca by convincing her father that he is the most lucrative prospect. Basing his negotiating strategy on the promotion of promised rather than actual wealth, Tranio reveals an uncanny ability to manufacture the illusion of largesse. The other suitor, Gremio, dutifully catalogues his holdings, which include a farm of one hundred cattle and one hundred and twenty oxen, and a house in the city 'richly furnished' with plate and gold, basins and ewers, Tyrian tapestries, ivory coffers stuffed with crowns, cypress chests full of costly apparel and expensive linens, Turkish cushions embossed with pearl, gold trimmed draperies, pewter, and brass (2.1.339–51). Stressing that he is his father's immediate 'heir and only son' (2.1.358), Tranio, even in the fictional scenario he creates, credits himself with goods that, perhaps like the borrowed robes he wears, he regards as his intrinsic due. His initial assertion that he will inherit 'houses three or four as good ... Besides two thousand ducats by the year of fruitful land' is reasonable enough under the circumstances (2.1.361–2). When, however, Gremio comes forward with a merchant vessel, Tranio goes overboard. He cannot resist flamboyantly topping this offer with 'three great argosies, besides two galliases, and twelve tight galleys' (2.1.371–2) and, finishing with a flourish, turning to Gremio to boast, 'These I will assure her, / And twice as much, whate'er thou off'rest next' (2.1.372–3). Despite potentially casting doubt on his creditability, Tranio is compelled to vaunt, and he seizes the opportunity of a simple tallying up of goods to show up his opponent with aggressive ostentation.

Through a demonstration of impudent showiness, Tranio continues to bend the normative rules of livery as he mutates the ideal of decorative service from within. Once he doffs his blue cap of service and dons Lucentio's 'colored hat and cloak' (1.1.199), he decides not only to 'keep [his master's] house' but also to 'welcome his friends, visit his countrymen, and banquet them' (1.1.188–9). What the other characters and the audience witness is not simply a servant dressed in his master's clothes, but rather, as the stage directions are careful to indicate, a servant who enters '*brave*' (1.2.209).[40] In other words, onlookers are stunned not simply by what Tranio wears (his master's luxurious apparel) but also by how he wears his sumptuous ensemble, apparently in a manner whereby he brazenly promotes his own sense of glamour. The adverb 'brave' informs us that Tranio, described by one critic as an 'upstart knave,' dresses ostentatiously with a confidence bordering on impertinence.[41] Unleashing the full potential of term, Tranio wears his apparel with the explicit aim of showing off. Indeed, by defying all expectations of sartorial propriety, he transforms himself into a 'brave,' another term for a gallant or a young man renowned for his 'upstart bravery' or the insolent manner with which he wears his finery (*OED*).

On one level, Tranio's over-the-top self-presentation reassuringly affirms the immutable difference between masters and servants by demonstrating that when subordinates dressed in sumptuous apparel, they could only reproduce the sartorial splendour of their superiors as garish exaggeration since they could not convey the necessary *sprezzatura*. On another level, Tranio's flamboyance carries the sting of parody. His sartorial hyperbole suggests that Lucentio's magnificence, which Tranio putatively imitates, has always bordered on gaudy ostentation rather than tastefully connoted entitlement. Yet the extreme reactions that Tranio's appearance stimulates suggest a third reading that points to the truly transgressive nature of his sartorial extravagance.

Those who encounter the transformed Tranio are genuinely disturbed by the sight of his braving it out in silks and velvets. Biondello, a fellow servant, does not perceive Tranio's sumptuousness as safely inscribed within the bonds of service, and he accuses the lavishly attired domestic of having stolen his master's clothes (1.1.215). Nor are Biondello's doubts about Tranio's loyalty to the household in which they serve assuaged by Lucentio's explanation that Tranio has 'changed into Lucentio' and is in effect the new master. Biondello's cynical response, 'The better for him. Would I were so too!' (1.1.229) suggests that he is well aware of the ways that servants exploited such circumstances. Lucentio's father Vincentio, who later arrives unannounced in Padua, interprets Tranio's sartorial splendour neither as gauche exhibitionism nor as pointed mockery. Rather he is alarmed by what he regards as evidence that his son's servant, who is for all intents and purposes his servant, has taken advantage of being beyond his supervision and squandered his allowance on luxurious clothes, which he models throughout Padua with impunity. Assaulted by the sight of Tranio dressed in finery and with a man in tow, Vincentio laments, 'O immortal gods! O fine villain! A silken doublet, a velvet hose, a scarlet cloak, and a copintank [high-crowned] hat! O, I am undone, I am undone! While I play the good husband at home, my son and my servant spend all at the university' (5.1.51–4). When he discovers that Tranio has also assumed his son's name, Vicentio immediately concludes that Tranio has murdered his master in order to steal his apparel (5.1.67). Tranio's obedience to Lucentio justifies maintaining the lie that he is indeed a gentleman and that Biondella is his servant. Moreover, it compels him to speak imperiously to Vicentio, asking (a question that anticipates Jonson's saucy apprentice Quicksilver), 'Why, sir, what 'cerns it you if I wear pearl and gold? I thank my good father, I am able to maintain it' (5.1.58–9). Tranio's impertinent assertion of the prerogative to wear luxurious apparel generates a series of misunderstandings such that Tranio orders the arrest of Vicentio on the grounds that *he* is impersonating a gentleman. The confusion is cleared up only by the last minute arrival of Lucentio. Lucentio's sudden appearance and his revelation that he has authorized Tranio's fabulousness averts, as if with the wave of a magic wand, an otherwise dire situation in which the resplendent servant effectively strips the elite patriarch of his authority and sends him off to prison.

The various points at which onlookers accuse Tranio of abusing his master's generosity, of stealing from him, and even of murdering his master function as commentaries on the hermeneutics of suspicion employed by those who encounter a flamboyantly attired servant who conveys confidence in his appearance. Despite the hasty resolution to the misapprehension inspired by Tranio's sartorial performance, the play cannot entirely disavow the subversive implications of its subplot. Such moments of rupture index how quickly the social fabric is rent when the familiar/familial figure of the dutiful servant becomes strange. Even the use of doubling, by which the harmonious servant and master pair of Tranio and Lucentio are juxtaposed with the suspicious servant and master pair of Tranio and Vincentio, does not keep the subterranean threat of insubordination safely buried. Rather, such doubling offers the audience a dual perspective, allowing Shakespeare to simultaneously secure and remove the veil of loyalty and goodwill between master and servant.

Advice writers like William Gouge were well aware of the hazardous consequences of a system in which servants' apparel credits their master. In *Of Domestical Duties* he warns his readers of the tensions generated within a domestic context in which gentle-born servingmen are provided with expensive clothing, and he cautions householders against dressing servants too extravagantly. He stresses that 'the apparel also which servants wear must be so fashioned and ordered, as it may declare them to be servants and under their masters, and so it will argue a reverend respect of their masters' (337). For Gouge, the end of costly apparel is to show 'a difference betwixt superiors and inferiors, persons in authority and under subjection'(337). Observing that 'through too much familiarity' servants will come to 'carry themselves fellow-like,' he explains:

> Exceeding great is the fault of servants in their excess apparel. No distinction ordinarily betwixt a man's children and servants: nay none betwixt masters and their men, mistresses and their maids. It may be while men and maids are at their masters' and mistresses' finding, difference may be made: though, even then also, if they can any way get wherewithal, they will do what they can to be as brave as they can. But, if once they be at their own finding, all shall be laid out upon apparel, and they will also be as fine as master or mistresses: if not so costly, yet in show as specious and brave. (337)

'Being born of gentlemen' and 'of good degree,' servants, Gouge cautions, are apt to 'forget their present place and condition; or else (which is worse) ... willfully presume above it' (335).

The resentment of young men who took up positions in elite households, despite having come from elite homes themselves, is suggested by satirical portraits such as that of the young man who muses:

> What bred a Scholar; born a Gentleman
> Of five years standing an Oxonian
> Of person Proper: of a comely Feature
> And shall I basely now turn Serving-Creature?'[42]

For these men the acquisition of luxury occupied a central place in their fantasies of service, which for them entailed a life akin to a life of gentility. In *A Diamond Most Precious, Worthy to be Marked*, a manual 'instructing all masters and servants how they ought to live their lives,' one gentle-born young man dreams of serving in the household of a wealthy Londoner so that he can 'have [his] delight as a gentleman hath ... two new coats a year ... suits of hose ... hats with feathers' and to 'be all in bravery.'[43] Richard Climsell also depicts the life of a domestic as an enticing possibility for the young man who boasts,

> Why should I labour, toyle, or care,
> since I am fed with dainty fare?
> My Gelding I have for to ride,
> my cloake my good sword by my side,
> My bootes and spurres shining like gold,
> like those whose names are high inrold:
> What pleasure more can any crave,
> then such content as I now haue?[44]

The Shrew demonstrates that the vexed issue of authority in a household composed of ambiguously positioned men is only aggravated when servants apply the principles of sartorial braving to the practice of rhetorical braving. In the only scene in *The Shrew* in which sartorial style is addressed explicitly, Petruchio's servant Grumio and the tailor engage in an extended verbal battle over who actually commissioned the design of Kate's gown. Petruchio objects to the gown on grounds that it is overly ornate, boasting 'curiously cut' sleeves (4.3.137). Although the literal definition of 'curious' was careful, skilful, or well done, in early modern usage 'curious' also referenced an artistic manner marked by heightened artifice or hyperbole. Petruchio chastises Grumio for presumptuously commissioning an outfit bearing the mark of his curious or flamboyant sensibility.[45] Insult is added to injury when Grumio resorts to a flashy rhetorical mode to deflect blame. Denying that he authorized the 'note of fashion' (4.3.126), Grumio engages the tailor in an exchange marked by boasting and exaggeration that recalls Tranio's vaunting rhetoric. Insisting that he dutifully followed his master's directions in constructing the dress, the tailor points out that his master in turn faithfully adhered to Grumio's 'order how it should be done' (4.3.116). Grumio, abdicating all responsibility for the dress's design, defends himself from *his* master's reproof by denigrating the tailor. He emphasizes that a tailor's job is to 'fac[e] many things' or to artificially dissimulate, and Grumio establishes that tailors are experts at masking blemishes and, by implication, fabricating the truth (4.3.121).

By mobilizing the terms 'face' and 'brave,' words meaning to decorate and to defy, Tranio highlights the elements of baiting and boasting subtending style. He warns the tailor, 'Face not me. Thou hast braved many men; brave not me. I will neither be faced nor braved. I say unto thee, I bid thy master cut out the gown, but I did not bid him cut it to pieces. Ergo thou liest' (4.3.123–5). Grumio's defensive strategy is itself, though, an example of facing, in which he engages the tactic of taking an implied accusation (that he is a liar) and boldly puts it right back in his opponent's face.[46] In addition to mocking the tailor's profession, Grumio plays off of the early modern stereotype of tailors as sexually ambiguous, lascivious peddlers of exotic wares who seduced men and women alike into economic and erotic excesses.[47] Tailors, Grumio points out, are known to indiscriminately shift from facing to braving, and this one, as far as he is concerned, is no less guilty of a suspicious bi-modality whereby he may attempt to unfairly gain rhetorical advantage. By dramatizing how those who engaged in braving were able to confound authority and defer punishment, *The Shrew* connects rhetorical and sartorial irreverence as it identifies both as crucial modes of symbolic aggression that subordinates utilized to manipulate the constraints of their circumstances.

Because braving in its sartorial and verbal forms always illuminated the stakes of insubordination for household order, more often than not it could only be curtailed by the threat or implementation of corporal punishment. In the tailor scene Grumio's braving provokes his master to beat him, which, in turn, exposes the tenuous nature of Petruchio's authority and the extent to which his household revolves around intimate contact between men. While masters relied upon physical discipline to reassert household hierarchy, in certain contexts such close contact between master and servant (whether defined as sport or discipline) endangered domestic order by violating those prescriptions that called for a strict separation between superiors and inferiors.[48] As the debate over style between Grumio and the tailor reaches its pitch, Grumio activates a series of homonymic puns whereby he pushes the word 'cut' along the signifying scale. Through his repetition of the word 'cut' (which appears five times over the course of thirty-five lines), Grumio makes Kate's gown recede as the word's proper referent and uses cut to signify elliptically Kate's cut, a 'conceit' that is, Grumio notes, 'deeper than you think' (4.3.153).[49] Reacting with shock to Petruchio's request that the tailor 'take up' or take away Kate's gown for his master's 'use' (4.3.149), Grumio insists on understanding Petruchio's directive as an order to lift Kate's dress to assist another man's erotic use of her. His wilful misinterpretation serves to highlight the tenuous nature of the distinction between eros and discipline within the male-dominated household. By persisting in sexualizing the word 'cut' and conceiving of service as the duty to obey erotically those in authority, Grumio's astonished exclamation, 'Take up my mistress' gown to his master's use! O, fie, fie, fie!' (4.3.154–5) is a histrionic response that exaggerates his master's perversity and his own unavoidable complicity.

In the spirit of performative obeisance, Grumio lays out the protocol for his own punishment by declaring that if it can be determined that he ordered the curiously cut, 'loose-bodied gown,' then his master should dress him in it and beat him 'with a bottom of brown thread' (4.3.130–1). By assuming this new livery, the 'loose-bodied' gown intended for Petruchio's new bride, Grumio takes the place of Kate as the object of Petruchio's corrective and, by implication, erotic energies. Moreover, by constituting himself as the object of pedagogical violence, Grumio's request invokes the homosocial/homoerotic milieu of the early modern grammar school where schoolmasters disciplined their young male students with corporal punishment that consisted of flogging them with birch rods.[50] By attending to bottoms – of the brown thread with which he is being beaten and his own where the beating is being applied – Grumio invokes his own cut, highlighting the corporal site upon which disciplinary activity and sexual subordination converge. The ass was a potent social symbol in the period since the beast of burden was the primary emblem for the dutiful servant.[51] The ass was also a key erotic symbol, which appeared frequently in not only the public discourse of male dominance but also in the private language of male desire.[52] Indeed, the sexual, sadistic, and scatological are invoked a few lines later when Grumio resolves to continue to rally for his innocence, even if the tailor's 'little finger [is] armed in a thimble' (4.3.141), to which the tailor replies, 'This is true ... An I had thee in a place where, thou shoulds't know it' (4.3.142–3). While the 'it' refers to the correct version of the bill and the 'place' a court of law, the tailor's 'it' may also reference his little finger, which, if the tailor had Grumio in a more private place, Grumio would have the opportunity to 'know' intimately. Grumio's retort, 'I am for thee straight' or I am ready (4.3.144), 'Take thou the bill, give me thy mete-yard [a long measuring stick] and spare me not' (4.3.144–5) continues in the vein of outrageous posturing, as he claims that he will not only withstand being penetrated by the tailor's little finger but also can tolerate the forceful insertion of a bill or a halberd, or even a long measuring stick. Luxuriating in the possibilities of the cut, semantic and otherwise, Grumio unleashes the semiotic surplus of the signifier to illuminate the economic and erotic links that both constituted and endangered master-servant relations in the early modern household.

4 The Rioting Servant

The desires and fears associated with the sartorial, social, and sexual proximity between masters and their domestics are played out in *The Shrew*'s Induction, in which a drunken tinker of pedigreed ancestry (Ind. 1.4) is temporarily elevated to the station of a lord. This framing device highlights the ways in which domestic order depends on the proper use of household stuff, and in the Induction sumptuous clothes and docile attendants assume a crucial role in the confirmation of status. Accordingly, the Induction also dramatizes the tinker Sly's wily ability to appropriate the situation as an occasion to enjoy the luxuries offered him. Sly's skilful manipulation of the circumstances anticipates the play's preoccupation with a system of service that although designed to uphold hierarchic distinctions between households always had the potential to confuse relations within the household.

Sly's profession as one who repairs household objects recommends him as a young man who is able to render the household a productive space of mobile identifications rather than simply a site of discipline. In the eyes of the lord who happens upon the drunken Sly, he is simply a 'beggar' (Ind. 1.37), one who, once he is conveyed to bed and 'wrapped in sweet clothes' (Ind. 1.34), will 'forget himself' (Ind. 37). Unaware that Sly has previously proclaimed that 'the Slys are no rogues' (Ind. 1.3) and that he has laid claim to an elite pedigree dating back to 'Richard [the] Conqueror' (Ind. 1.4), Sly's drunken mistake for William, the lord miscalculates his subject. Moreover, his experiment seems especially ill conceived in light of the tendency of sumptuously attired servants not to forget themselves but rather to become reminded of their origins once outfitted in costly apparel. As William Gouge points out, extravagantly dressed servants are apt to 'forget their *present place* and condition; or else (which is worse) ... willfully presume above it.'[53]

Creating an in-joke between those young male servants peopling the audience off the stage and the lord's attendants on the stage, who ironically reassure their misguided master that Sly 'cannot choose' (Ind. 1.38) but to believe himself to be gentle once he awakens in such lavish attire, Shakespeare highlights the theatrical foundation of compliance. Here the play makes the sly suggestion that all masters are hoodwinked into believing their own authority, which relies on the performative obeisance of servants who regard *themselves* as entitled. The lord's men lay bare the mechanics by which they 'will play [their] part,' as they vow to perform so well that their new master Sly will be convinced of their 'true diligence' (Ind. 1.65–6). Taking a moment to vaunt, they brag of their impressive acting abilities that will aid them in persuading Sly that 'he is no less than what *we* say he is' (Ind. 1.65–7, emphasis mine). The trick, it appears, is now on the lord who believes he will successfully prove the essential nature of class difference. Indeed, all seems in keeping with the lord's plan when Sly upon waking requests ale and not the more genteel sack. Yet despite occasional lapses into lower rank modes of expression, Sly seems to recognize intrinsically the value of the items with which he is surrounded, as well as how to take advantage of the 'sweet clothes,' 'delicious banquet,' and the 'brave attendants' bestowed upon him (Ind. 1.34–6).

Critics who read the Induction as a testament to a rigid notion of class distinction have been hoodwinked, like the lord. Upon closer inspection, these opening scenes reveal a nuanced perspective on status and identity. The character of Sly functions as a reminder to viewers that one's own understanding of one's status, as well as one's likes and dislikes, is not determined by a specific social context or institutional setting, but rather by a complex overlay of life circumstances and family background. Sly has been placed in the lord's 'fairest chamber' (Ind. 1.42), and he luxuriates as his servants:

Balm his foul head in warm distilled waters,
And burn sweet wood to make the lodging sweet
. . . .
. . . [are] ready straight,
And with a low submissive reverence
Say, 'What is it your honor will command?'
. . .
. . . [are] ready with a costly suit,
And ask him what apparel he will wear. (Ind. 1.44–56)

The servants' acquiescent behaviour performs a decorative function as they transform themselves into ornate objects ceremoniously presented to Sly. It is, however, at the point when Sly attempts to disrobe his 'lady,' the cross-dressed page, in hopes of consummating their relationship (Ind. 2.109) that the results of the lord's experiment begin to founder.

As the play takes great pains to show, Sly has not magically transmogrified into an entirely different person. He repeatedly requests 'a pot o' the smallest ale' and periodically calls out for his tavern friends Cicely Hacket, Stephen Sly, old John Naps of Greet, Peter Turf, and Henry Pimpernel (Ind. 2.84-89). Along similar lines, there is little reason to believe that Sly is convinced that the cross-dressed page before him is indeed a 'lady.' Yet his desire for the page complicates the lord's stark assessment of the difference between gentle and mean. Sly's predilection for the effeminate, young male servant, unlike his taste for ale, is in keeping with a sensibility associated with those in positions of mastery. Only those who enjoyed some sense of entitlement could, after all, appreciate the allure that a culture of super- and subordination conferred upon the socially dependent and sexually available young man. In this respect, Sly represents a hybrid figure, part beggar and part gentleman, insofar as he reveals that he has not forgotten himself, but, at least in regard to his erotic taste, remembered a place of common ground with the lord.

The promiscuous intermingling between superiors and inferiors in the household was a concern of those who warned that 'when masters are over-ruled by their servants ... servants soon prove [to be] masters.'[54] Tellingly, many late sixteenth-century advice manuals do not chastise heads of households for deploying overly strict measures in exacting deference but rebuke householders for being too lenient or too familiar with their dependents, thus inspiring them to 'take libert[ies].' Masters who treat their servants 'too delicately,' Gouge avers, cause servants to 'forget [their] place, scorn to be as a servant, [and] aspire to be [their] master's child, which is next to [their] master's mate.'[55] Sexual intimacy between master and servant was not prohibited, as scholars have shown, but when masters were perceived as overindulging domestics, as one manual cautions, subordinates 'are brought vp ... to[o] proudely.'[56] Those servants who are 'wan tonly' supplied with an 'excesse of bothe meat and apparell' are inevitably the young men who indulge in 'ryoting' and participate in various 'lewd [ ]' practices.[57] Perceiving the anarchic city as an apt analogue for the disordered home, Cleaver and Dod observe:

> For as in a city there is nothing more unequal than that every man should be like equal, so it is not convenient that in one house every man should be like and equal together. There is no equality in that city where the private man is equal with the magistrate, the people with the senate, or the servant with the master, but rather a confusion of all offices and authority.[58]

Householders in this period were regularly reminded of the importance of maintaining a proper distance from their domestics and of not mistaking their subordinates for 'fit companions.'[59]

The blurring of distinctions between master and servant is represented in the Induction as akin to an overturning of the natural order. The disruptive effects of unregulated eros between high and low are amply illustrated by the 'wanton pictures' (Ind. 1.43) furnishing Sly's bedchamber that depict the transgressive union of gods and mortals. One portrait represents Cytherea/Venus voyeuristically peering through the hedges at the bathing Adonis, while the thrushes 'move and wanton with her breath,' (Ind. 2.47) as her pants of desire suggest frantic autoerotic activity. There is a portrayal of Jove's 'surprise' (50) of Io 'as lively painted as the deed was done' (51). Apollo's pursuit of Daphne is also represented, in which Daphne's loss of virginity is anticipated by the vivid presentation of her white legs pricked and bloodied by thorns (55). Ovidian representations of seduction and rape, as Leonard Barkan suggests, narrate the forcible joining of those things that should be kept separate, initiating 'an experience that breaks all previously accepted rules.'[60] While the moment of consummation produces ecstasy, these illicit unions also bring about irreversible transformations.

The absent-presence of the 'best known myth of homoerotic desire in early modern England,' that of Jupiter's seduction of his page

Ganymede, is reinserted into the pantheon as Sly assumes the role of Jupiter by commanding his lady/page to lie with him.[61] In this myth unbridled passion between master and servant is linked explicitly to domestic upheaval. Signs of dissolution in the make-believe household of Master Sly become pronounced when Sly's once dutiful lady/page resists his/her master's authority. She/he responds to her master's command that she/he 'undress ... and come now to bed' (Ind. 2.109) not with compliance but with the bold assertion that they observe a 'pardon' for 'a night or two' (Ind. 2.111). Sly's desire does indeed promise to destabilize the precarious tenets of his own authority, since once he removes his sweet clothes, he strips himself of not merely the trappings of his elite status but, in this case, the very materials that constitute it. Once divested, the master Sly reoccupies the space of a dispossessed tinker, despite his claims to an elite pedigree. He will then be revealed as inferior to his gentle-born servant, whose obeisance – like Sly's elevated status – will be exposed as an elaborate fiction.

Yet metamorphosis in *The Shrew* does not simply instigate the annihilation of identity. Transformation also functions throughout the play as a crucial strategy whereby elites such as Lucentio realize their goals and subordinates like Tranio successfully satisfy their own desires for luxury and display. Even in their invocations of danger, the pictures surrounding Sly's bed also advertise the erotic potential of such fraught pairings between higher and lower, exemplified by the dramatic consummation that is associated with the volatile coupling of mortals and gods. These pictures, after all, like Shakespeare's play, do not merely discipline the viewer but also stimulate pleasure within him. Similarly, the visiting players offer Sly, and those in Shakespeare's audience, yet another opportunity to experience the *frisson* that may be generated by an atmosphere in which the operative categories underwriting a traditional patriarchal order become upended. The visiting actors describe the play they intend to perform as a source of both pleasure and educative value, since it is at once a 'pleasant comedy' (Ind. 2.121) and a 'kind of history' (Ind. 1.132), one, significantly, of 'household stuff' (Ind. 1.131).

5 To Serve, Love, and Obey

The Shrew ultimately narrates the history of one kind of domestic regime while at the same time anticipates another. The play begins with an all-male household, which is inaugurated in the Induction by the disappearance of the tavern hostess and the appearance of the decorative young male page, who summarily 'usurps' the 'voice, gait, and action of a gentlewoman' (Ind. 1.127–8). The all-male household is then reconstituted at Petruchio's country home, where he resides over a domestic staff composed of men only. While the play continues to explore the intimacy between master and servant and its potential to derail the productive and reproductive mission of the patriarchal household, in the final instance, *The Shrew* shifts its focus to the relationship between master and mistress. Marriage, the play shows, can function as a regulatory apparatus with which to secure a new, gendered division of household labour.[62] By predicting the instantiation of the private, bourgeois home, which featured the housewife as the manager of household stuff, the play portends the growing irrelevance of the lavishly attired male servant whose primary function was to appear comely.[63]

In designating the household as a sphere in which the mistress performs the task of enjoying the products retrieved by her husband, whose work is significantly represented as merchant adventurism and not as manual labour (5.1.153), *The Shrew* does not simply register the regendering of domestic management but also alludes to its implications. As Kate is progressively interpellated into her new role as domestic consumer, the household becomes increasingly populated by reluctant and seemingly incompetent male servants. Despite Grumio's instructions to Petruchio's steward to dress the staff in 'their new fustian' with 'white stockings' (4.1.33–4) and to ensure that the head servingmen are 'sleekly combed, their blue coats brushed and their garters of an indifferent [plain] knit' (4.1.64–6), such expectations of propriety are painstakingly detailed only to culminate in disappointment. The servants do not greet their master with a 'curtsy with their left legs' and a 'kiss' on his hand (4.1.67). Petruchio arrives home, instead, to 'loggerhead and unpolished grooms' (4.1.94), who show 'no attendance,' 'no regard,' and 'no duty' (4.1.95). His domestics are in an extreme state of sartorial disarray, as Grumio reports:

> Nathaniel's coat, sir, was not fully made,
> And Gabriel's pumps were all unpinked i' the heel.
> There was no link to color Peter's hat,
> And Walter's dagger was not come from sheathing.

> There were none fine but Adam, Ralph, and Gregory.
> The rest were ragged, old, and beggarly (4.1.101–6).

Their sartorial unseemliness is matched only by their impudent behaviour. One servant 'plucks' Petruchio's 'foot awry' in removing his boots (4.1.116), another ignores his request for his slippers (4.1.122), a third spills water on him (4.1.124), and yet a fourth domestic serves him burnt meat (4.1.130). As Kate's rebelliousness subsides, insubordinate behaviour becomes exclusively associated with male servants, who provoke Petruchio to engage in corporal punishment.

Over the course of the play, Kate comes to understand her commensurability with these recalcitrant male domestics. This may be gleaned by the report that she 'waded through the dirt to pluck [Petruchio] off Grumio' when Petruchio began to beat him because her horse stumbled (4.1.55–6). Petruchio has, after all, identified his wife as integral to the public presentation of household status. After they are married, he explains to her that her person is tantamount to '[the] house' itself and that her body is a part of '[his] household stuff' (3.2.219–20). Along similar lines, Petruchio demonstrates that her provision of 'livery,' as with other household subordinates, will be dispensed in accordance with her demonstration of compliance. He promises to provide her 'silken coats and caps and golden rings, / with ruffs, and cuffs, and farthingales, and things, / With scarves, and fans, and double change of bravery, / With amber bracelets, beads, and all this knavery' (4.3.54–8), when she is 'gentle' (4.3.71). Petruchio's directive in the final act, 'Katherine, that cap of yours becomes you not. / Off with that bauble. Throw it underfoot.' (5.2.125–6), broadcasts his prerogative to control her sartorial presentation, which he understands, all too well, reflects upon the integrity of his authority over his new household.

By having Kate invoke the language of service in her final speech, Shakespeare explicitly connects domestic prescriptions for the comely servant with the obligations of the dainty wife. Kate, the play shows, has also come to appreciate the extraordinary power she has over Petruchio's prestige, which is tied to her willingness to perform her decorative function. In the end, Kate willingly positions herself as a domestic who is 'bound to serve, love, and obey' (5.2.168) the head of the household, whom she describes as her lord, keeper, head, king, sovereign, and governor (5.2.143–51). She also, though, pointedly reminds her 'forward' (5.2.173) listener to 'unknit' her 'unkind brow' (5.2.140) because it 'blots thy beauty' (5.2.143). A woman 'moved'

(5.2.146), Kate stresses, is 'bereft of beauty' (5.2.147). Beauty, or the proper observance of decorum, she explains, is what housewives must promote in exchange for the 'tribute' with which they are awarded (5.2.156). The assumption of 'fair looks and true obedience' (5.2.157) seems a reasonable exchange for the 'payment' (5.2.158) of household stuff, which, as Kate has come to realize, housewives may manipulate to satisfy their own desires. By detailing the benefits of lying 'warm at home, secure and safe,' while her 'lord' and 'keeper' 'commits his body to painful labor' (5.2.156,152–3), Kate articulates the tenets of a domestic scenario in which the master's duty is to procure the commodities that the housewife will exhibit.

In accordance with an evolving gendered ideology of domestic management, which was subsequently explicated and promoted in early seventeenth-century economic treatises, conduct manuals, and theatrical representations, men who consume stuff outside of the context of the patriarchal household come to be associated with unruly excess. Ironically, the conspicuous consumerism of the young, unmarried man is cited as causing the demise of traditional forms of service. This is exemplified by descriptions of city gallants stripping their male servants of their liveries and discharging them so that they can have more money to spend on their own sumptuous apparel and on urban pleasures such as playgoing. Henry Crosse asks, 'Is it not a token of a covetous mind that men of good possessions and fair livings should break up house and sojourn only with one or two servants that they may horde up with their rents when they are able to keep a good house themselves?'[64] William Vaughan, likewise, attributes the 'decay' of housekeeping to those young gentlemen who divert their revenue on the purchasing of 'gorgeous attire.' They 'cavalier it abroad,' and, having 'given up housekeeping at home, [...] take a chamber in London,' where they consume their time 'in [the] viewing of stage plays.'[65]

Conclusion: Shrewishness

Throughout this chapter I have focused on the multiple ways in which 'shrewishness' is embodied by several characters at various moments throughout the play. 'Shrew,' like the words 'harlot,' 'punk,' or 'scold,' was a term of denigration that referred to both men and women until it underwent a semantic shift in the late sixteenth century.[66] Even as the gender valence of shrew changed, the word remained haunted by associations with male class revolt. As David Underdown points out, scolding was predominantly a juridical offence ascribed to lower-rank women, but 'the shrew' was a social outcast or newcomer to the community of either gender. Shrews were singled out for causing disturbances within a given community, for instance, by instigating local resistance and even fomenting popular rebellion.[67] Like the 'skimmington,' a violator of community conventions, as well as more generally 'something or someone undesirable,' the shrew in this period was first and foremost someone who challenged authority. Historians have shown that women accused of being shrews were subjected to shaming rituals such as the cucking stool, but male shrews were also 'tamed.'[68] Literary critics that call on this historiography often underplay the role of men as objects of public shame and targets of retributive violence. Reviving the bi-gendered history of the shrew enables us to explore those sites in Shakespeare's play where shrewishness is deployed to signal class antagonism as well as gender conflict.

When we read *The Shrew* as a play that divides its dramatic focus between the fraught relations between men and women and the no less fraught relations between men, we can begin to see how it may offer a window onto a complex domestic arena whose working order relied upon the submissive young man as much as upon the dutiful woman. In *The Shrew*, the household is not a private enclave, but a socially fluid and at times chaotic space. Like the atmosphere of the male-dominated guilds and the universities, settings all too familiar to Shakespeare's audience, the organization of the household is shown to be particularly vulnerable to the disruptive behaviours of young men. By attending to those young male domestics who showcase their ability to use the clothes assigned to them as the raw materials of dissident style, *The Shrew* identifies shrewishness as a viable mode of insurgency for men and women alike.

4 The Italian Vice and Bad Taste in *Edward II*

Taste is the form par excellence of *amor fati*.

Pierre Bourdieu, *Distinction*.[1]

1 The Infection of Foreign Style

The true subject of Christopher Marlowe's tragedy *Edward II* is not a king failing in the duties of his office but a court overtaken by 'the infection of foreign style.'[2] The symptoms of the sickness contaminating Edward's realm are those 'abhominable vices' that members of Marlowe's audience associated with the Italianified Englishman, namely, 'vaineglory, ſelfeloue, [and] ſodomie.'[3] Even in the most vital period of cultural exchange between England and Italy, the cultivation of an Italian sensibility was perceived, both on and off the Elizabethan stage, as a blessing and a curse. Late sixteenth-century Italy was the centre of classical learning, mercantile activity, and artistic innovation. It was also the site of political intrigue, courtly idleness, and erotic temptation. Young men travelled to Italy to perfect the courtly graces of Castiglione, yet, as one contemporary warned, 'few young travellers have brought home [from Italy] sound and safe, and (in a word) English bodies.'[4] In the eyes of some, Italy's Mediterranean climate had a corrosive effect even on young men's minds. As one early modern dramatic character exclaims:

> Brother, I fear me in your travel you have drunk too much of that Italian air, that hath infected the whole mass of your ingenious nature, dried up in you all sap of generous disposition, poison'd the very essence of your

> soul, and so polluted your senses that whatsoever enters there takes from them contagion, and is to your fancy represented as foul and tainted, which in itself perhaps is spotless.[5]

While the contagions of Italy poisoned those who travelled abroad, mysteriously, those who never stepped foot on Italian soil, young men composing 'the great army of younger brothers' overtaking the English court, manifested the most dramatic symptoms of the disease of Italianness.[6] Those 'with little patrimony or none at all, either threatened with the loss of status or desperately anxious to attain it' flaunted ensembles of 'maruellous, curiouſly ouerwhipt,' 'Neapolitane ſtuff.'[7] The established elite regarded these *Ingleses Italianatos*, who 'rvffeled [it] out' in 'the habit of a *malcontent*,' not as masters of the arts of Castiglione, but as practitioners of the so-called Italian vice.[8]

In *Edward II*, no figure is more closely associated with the telltale signs of the Italian vice – 'the art of epicurising, the art of whoring [and] the art of Sodomitrie' – than Piers Gaveston.[9] The king's infatuation with the aspirant Gaveston, and later with the court hangers-on Baldock and Spencer Junior, lead him to dismiss his advisors' warnings about the treachery of flattering favourites. Marlowe's play, critics have argued, shows that a king who disregards the counsel of his barons is setting himself up for a fall. One reader avers:

> Not only is Edward homosexual – not necessarily contemptible in itself, as even his worst enemy agrees – but the private speeches of Gaveston and the Spencers as they gloat over how they intend to use their illegitimate influence are enough to convince a reasonable audience that Edward has demonstrably bad taste.[10]

The characterization of Edward as vulnerable to the dangerous dyad of irresistible temptation and uncontrollable desire is in keeping with the critical consensus that he becomes seduced by Gaveston's alluring aesthetic.[11] Yet despite the attention scholars have devoted to Gaveston's inappropriate exhibitionism, analyses of the source and the effects of the power wielded by someone who promotes outrageous display presuppose that the aesthetically unconventional is 'either grossly unintelligible or grossly immoral.'[12] Such readings ignore the play's awareness of the potency of aesthetic defiance and thus fail to illuminate how sexual and stylistic excess are linked in this play and what is at stake in their overlay.

Edward's barons disapprove of Gaveston's intimacy with the king, whose 'amorous lines' have recalled him from exile to join his 'dearest friend,' and they also resent his assumption of privileges unearned by birth. They are, though, especially offended by Gaveston's sense of style.[13] As the king's chief advisor asserts, it is not Edward's 'wanton humour' per se, meaning his erotic relationship with Gaveston, that disrupts the working order of the court (4.403). Rather the issue is that Gaveston 'should by his sovereign's favour grow so pert' (4.405). In describing Gaveston as 'pert,' Mortimer Junior uses the adjective reserved for 'children, young people, or persons in inferior positions, such as are considered to be too "uppish" or forward in their address.'[14] By characterizing Gaveston as a 'brisk,' 'dapper jack' (4. 413), Mortimer Junior also discounts him as someone who is 'overly attentive to his attire and scornful of others.'[15] While Mortimer Junior inventories Gaveston's wardrobe with obsessive precision, the details of his 'short Italian hooded cloak, larded with pearl' (4.414) and 'Tuscan hat' (4.415) are not nearly as impressive as the way he wears his Italian clothes. Gaveston 'jets it in the court' (4.409).

Scholars have looked to the continent for antecedents for Edward and Gaveston's love affair, notably the relationship between Henri III and his favourite Epernon, yet no one has offered a sustained investigation of Gaveston's Italianness. This critical lacuna is especially surprising since Gaveston's foreign aesthetic serves as the centrepiece of a shifting constellation of offences, all of which involve his cavalier rejection of the codes of deference constituting court culture.[16] In keeping with Holinshed's account of the relationship between Edward and his favourite Piers Gaveston in the *Chronicles*, Marlowe depicts Gaveston, in the words of Holinshed, as 'so high in his doings' and disdainful of the peers.[17] Yet Holinshed makes no mention of Gaveston's attire. He neither identifies Gaveston as wearing foreign clothes, nor associates him with impertinent practices of dress. Marlowe, however, revises and updates Holinshed's version of events by attending to Gaveston's sartorial sensibility, which he politicizes by identifying as the sign of an irreparable rift in Edward's court. While those who exhibited aspects of the Italian vice may not have been a source of dissent in the fourteenth-century court of the real-life Edward, those who distinguished themselves as 'marvelous monsters' in 'fashion' and 'condition' were of great concern to members of the late sixteenth-century court of Elizabeth.[18]

Marlowe avoids any one-to-one correspondence between the courts of the fictional Edward and the actual Elizabeth, but certain new modes of display on parade at the late sixteenth-century English court inform Marlowe's representation of Edward's milieu.[19] In the final years of Elizabeth's reign, as John Stow notes in his *Survey of London*, the queen's court was no longer regarded as an isolated enclave as it had been in previous eras. Stow himself muses on the number of young 'Gentlemen of all shires [who] do flie and flock to this Citty [London]' to take part in court culture.[20] Rather than constituting a realm apart, the court, like the city around it, was understood to offer an occasion for the intermixing of those from various backgrounds. One contemporary 'marvel[s]' at the 'misorders' at Court, where 'a young gentleman will venture himself into the company of ruffians,' emulating 'their fashions, manners, thoughts, talks, and deeds,' becoming 'ever like' them.[21] The increasingly diverse and evermore competitive atmosphere at court resulted in a 'politicization of areas of social behaviour which, for the aristocrat or gentleman in his locality, would be governed largely by personal taste.'[22] An influx of young hopefuls inspired a backlash, whereby elites adhered even more strictly to codes of display and patterns of behaviour through which '*common* tastes' could be elaborated.[23] In this delimited social context good taste was experienced and expressed as stylistic coherence, and those who disdained the court's codes of collective identification also denigrated its collective values.[24]

The noticeable upswing in the number of un-pedigreed petitioners seeking positions at court produced anxiety among the established elite and recently integrated aspirants, about the stylistic incoherence of a new breed of hanger-on. For moralists and magistrates alike, those who wore foreign apparel were associated with 'leisure, decadence, and disease,' as well as with the dissolution of those virtues associated with English cloth such as 'charity, hospitality, and humility.'[25] Extravagantly attired young men were not singled out, however, merely for wearing Italian silks, velvets, and furs, but for wearing these imported items in an ostentatious manner. As Thomas Overbury notes when the Italianified Englishman appears at court, his body is 'speaking fashion'; while his clothes boldly announce an Italian sensibility, his gait 'cries: Behold me.'[26] Altered in apparel and attitude alike, Overbury explains, the Italianified Englishman 'disdains all things above his reach,' and conveys his 'censure [of] all things' by exhibiting exaggerated 'countenances and shrugs.' Using the court as an arena for showcasing his newfound impudence, Overbury describes this young man as 'salut[ing]' his betters, 'without resaluting,' and 'offer[ing] courtesies, to shew *them*, rather than himself, humble.'[27]

Even as *Edward II* charts the barons' progressively negative responses to the flamboyant Gaveston, and later to the indecorous Baldock and Spencer Junior, the play acknowledges the vitality of an emerging sensibility that certain ambiguously positioned young men, notably those young court hopefuls who regularly attended the theatre, continued to cultivate. Through the shared recognition of an aesthetic based on excessive sartorial display, a penchant for non-reproductive erotic practice, and an impudent manner, Marlowe's play suggests, some bonded, even as they offended others. For this reason, *Edward II* does not simply condemn those who challenged the stable structure of recognition at court. By dramatizing the hazards and the allure but, most significantly, the symbolic centrality of a new brazen mode of display, Marlowe's play represents the Italian vice as a locus of collective identification for those who were not recognized by the established culture of taste and so produced their own.

2 *Artifizioso*

Readers typically take Gaveston's detractors at face value and, by not questioning the validity of the barons' depictions of him as 'base' (1.132, 4.291, 4.239), a 'slave' (2.25, 4.265), and a 'peasant' (2.30, 4.14, 4.82), assume that their characterizations are accurate rather than vindictive. Yet Marlowe is particularly sensitive to Gaveston's ambiguous status as at once an insider and an outsider to the world of elite privilege. According to Holinshed, the historical Gaveston was 'a goodly gentleman and a stoute,' the son of a French knight in Edward I's service and, while not an heir apparent, from gentle origins.[28] In keeping with Holinshed, Marlowe begins *Edward II* by showing that even before he arrives at Edward's court, Gaveston already identifies with the peers in regard to his sense of entitlement. In the opening scene we learn that Gaveston has been leading a life of service and that he finds the 'base stooping' it requires unbefitting his stature (1.18). Having been invited by Edward to 'share the kingdom' (1.2), Gaveston casts off his lowly status with the ease of one accustomed to a better way of life. This is illustrated by his hasty rejection of the assistance of the two 'poor men' who seek his patronage and offer to aid him in the practical areas of horse-keeping and soldiering (1.24). Already a nobleman in his own mind, Gaveston has little use for such quotidian services and, in keeping with the trend of English country lords, hires only the traveller, who will perform a decorative function by enlivening his dinner hour with witty conversation and entertaining tales (1.31–2). Even the barons intuitively recognize Gaveston as a threat that erupts from within rather than one that encroaches from without. Mortimer Junior indicates as much when he describes Gaveston as 'a canker' imperceptibly festering inside the social body (6.18). The ultimate sign of the French-born Gaveston's alienation from a staid English court culture and his familiarity with innovative continental trends is his Italian sensibility.

Gaveston's description of the masque he wishes to produce for Edward frames the action of the play and offers a window onto the distinctive foreign aesthetic he plans to introduce to England. Aware of 'emminent and conspicuous Theatre' as a key component of monarchical authority, Gaveston lays claim to the power of spectacle and asserts his prerogative to use it to influence the political climate of the court.[29] He muses:

> Therefore I'll have Italian masques by night,
> Sweet speeches, comedies, and pleasing show;
> And in the day when he shall walk abroad,
> Like sylvan nymphs my pages shall be clad,
> My men like satyrs grazing on the lawns
> Shall with their goat-feet dance an antic hay;
> Sometime a lovely boy in Dian's shape.
> With hair that gilds the water as it glides,
> Crownets of pearl about his naked arms,
> And in his sportful hands an olive tree,
> To hide those parts which men delight to see,
> Shall bathe him in a spring, and there hard by,
> One like Actaeon peeping through the grove,
> Shall by the angry goddess be transformed,
> And running in the likeness of a hart,
> By yelping hounds pulled down, and seem to die.
> Such things as these best please his majesty. (1.54–70)

While 'pleasing his majesty' would have been understood to members of Marlowe's audience as the phrase used to describe one's willingness to make oneself pliable to the whims of the monarch, Gaveston envisions his relationship to the king not in accordance with the traditional dynamic between pliant courtier and demanding sovereign, but rather along the lines of the titillating interactions between the seductive Bacchus and the doting Pentheus. Gaveston's plan, it appears, is not to please the king but to arouse him. Towards this end, he imagines ruling over a retinue of pages and servants, whom he will commandeer to 'draw' Edward (7.53), a word meaning to 'allure' and 'entice,' as well as to 'pervert' through conversion. By having Gaveston use the word 'draw,' Marlowe implicitly evokes the specter of Pentheus who, like Actaeon, was torn from limb to limb after becoming compelled to seek exalted heights and climb atop a towering tree from where he could freely indulge his transgressive 'peeping' of the sacred rituals below. Foreshadowing the violent end awaiting Edward, the word draw also subtly reminds the audience of the most widely used form of torture visited upon those accused of treason. Traitors had their limbs drawn or stretched to the breaking point. Finally, draw was a hunting term, and the word's association with the slow tracking movement of a hound towards its prey further implicates Gaveston and Edward in the primal drama of chase and conquest.[30]

Gaveston is a seductive figure who wrests 'drawing' from the authority of the state, and his delight in the masque's culmination, in which Actaeon is transformed into a deer that is then savagely dismembered by his own hounds, demonstrates his plan to use violence as a means of aesthetic expression. He offers viewers a shocking apotheosis in which the barriers between human and animal, pleasure and pain, and life and death merge and dissipate. It is not only the final moments of Gaveston's masque, however, that are marked by the dramatic violation of the boundaries discriminating the beautiful from the terrible. Making all of Edward's world *his* stage, Gaveston intends to transform the court into a theatre of unbounded eros with half-naked young men, 'like sylvan nymphs ... clad,' and other youths costumed like satyrs, as well as a boy cross-dressed as Dian. This 'lovely boy' with arms festooned with 'crownets of pearls' telegraphs Gaveston himself, who will soon enough be seen jetting through the court 'larded with pearl' (4.415). Determined to erode the borders separating life and art, private and public, and nature and artifice, Gaveston mobilizes a campaign to overwhelm Edward by overtaking him everywhere and anywhere, even those places he 'walks abroad.' In Gaveston's vision, figures from classical myth do not cater to but surprise Edward 'on the lawns,' 'in a spring,' and 'through the grove.'

In planning his debut, Gaveston chooses to instrumentalize the very medium upon which the early modern English court relied to reflect itself back to itself as the seat of civility. For late Tudor and early Stuart monarchs the court masque visually and thematically promoted poise, balance, and harmony in association with the motifs of antiquity, and it was through this form of entertainment that the monarch sought to tutor aspirants in 'subdu[ing] or at least mask[ing] their aggressive and competitive drives' through dissimulation and assimilation.[31] The fictive world of the masque was adequately contained by the monarch, who, by remaining on the periphery, redirected its participants back into the world of the court at the end of the performance. Orazio Busino, chaplain to the Venetian Embassy, in his description of the masque he witnessed at the court of James I, relays the satisfying sense of closure the audience experienced when the masquers 'had overcome the sloth and drunkenness of Bacchus with their prowess' and moved out of the demarcated playing area to embrace and kiss the monarch.[32] Through the institution of the masque, a court always endangered by 'the fierce competition for favors' could demonstrate the victory of order over the libidinous energies that simmered beneath the surface of graceful interchange.[33]

Unlike the English masque, which in the hands of Ben Jonson and Inigo Jones adhered to Aristotelian principles of mimetic coherence and classical rules of symmetry, the spatial rhetoric of Gaveston's masque employs the stylistic elements of *maneria*, the cinquecento artistic trend in Italian architectural and visual arts characterized by ornamentation, hybridity, and artifice.[34] *Maneria* was a visual mode characterized by 'the ruthless dethronement of aesthetic doctrines based on principles of order, proportion, balance, and economy of means,' and entailed a rejection 'of rationalism and naturalism in the rendering of reality.'[35] An oppositional form that irreverently reinscribed that to which it was reacting, the key components of a mannerist aesthetic were defiance, exaggeration, and insincerity. Art historian Arnold Hauser explains that this aesthetic may be discerned by its 'piquancy,' by which he means a predilection for 'the strange, the overstrained ... the pungent, the bold, [and] the challenging.' Its virtuosity lay in its 'compulsive deviation from the normal,' since the mannerist work of art, Hauser emphasizes, is 'always a piece of bravura, a triumphant conjuring trick, a firework display with flying sparks and colors.'[36] Anticlassical and antinatural 'mannerism is not normative,' insofar as it demonstrates an unapologetic flamboyance that does not seek to mask its stylistic exuberance.[37]

Scribbled in Inigo Jones's sketchbook are his dismissive comments about the continental trend in art and architecture that promoted *artifizioso* over *sprezzatura*. Disapproving of the hyperbole of *maneria*, he argues that just as 'outwarly every wyse man carrieth a graviti in Publicke Places ... so in architecture, ye outward ornaments oft [ought] to be sollid, proporsionable according to the rulles, masculine and unaffected.'[38] Aiming to create visual forms that would inculcate in their onlookers 'virtues of sobriety' and the desire to lead 'a well-ordered life,' Jones strove to produce forms 'purged of all the licentious ornament of Michelangelo and his mannerist followers.'[39] Not surprisingly, he devoted his energies to reining in the court masque, which as a theatrical genre served as the 'most comprehensive manifestation of mannerism' on the continent.[40] Even though *intermedio* were in high fashion at the Medici court, where grand spectacles offered audiences a smorgasbord of visual marvels through the presentation of opulent stage costumes and elaborate scenery, Jonson and Jones collaborated to tame the disruptive elements of this 'audacious' art form.[41] In the 1611 masque *Oberon, The Faery Prince*, for instance, Jonson transforms the satyr Silenus, an obese older man with a penchant for young boys, into a harmless pedagogue and master of the revels. Along similar lines, the young boys, who are described as bejewelled with fairy bracelets, pearls, garlands, ribbons, and posies, do not stand out as objects of decadent desire but become seamlessly absorbed into the conventional symbolism of the masque.[42]

A reading of mannerism in the context of a late sixteenth-century English court culture that abhorred displays of affectation illuminates the unorthodox potential of this particular aesthetic, which in the wrong hands could be manipulated to inspire a breakdown of decorum. With its typical theme of metamorphosis the masque provided a compensatory fantasy by which it substituted the opportunity for actual social advancement with the spectacle of magical transformation. As explicated by one contemporary, 'the miseries of the courtier's life' could be displaced through recourse to artful rhetoric, such as 'similitude, examples, comparisons from one thing to another, apte translacions, and [a] heaping of allegories.'[43] By unleashing an irreverent form of conspicuous display that highlights the sensuality of same-sex eroticism, the allure of Italian style, and the blurring of off- and onstage spaces, Gaveston's performance amplifies the connection between sexual appetite and desire for alteration, both of which are explicitly linked to sartorial extravagance. The metamorphosis Gaveston commissions, unlike the masques of Jonson and Jones, is not dictated by the principles of mimesis, which encouraged proper subject formation through identification with the return to order that ended the performance. Rather, through its refusal to reconcile aesthetic activity with didactic purpose, Gaveston's masque is driven by the energies of performativity, which inspired the *reformulation* of the subject through an expropriation of social ritual. A mannerist aesthetic such as Gaveston's, according to one critic, was the predominant symptom of 'an illness of the social body' and signalled a 'mentality of crisis.'[44]

Not long after Gaveston issues his opening salvo, in which he describes the spectacle he plans on commissioning at court, he moves from the role of director to that of actor as his own theatrics become the focus of the barons' censure. The criticisms the barons level against Gaveston address his intimacy with the king, but it is Gaveston's overweening confidence in his own sensibility, which he wields as a weapon against a court that he openly disdains, that awakens their ire. While Isabella, Edward's queen, registers distress that Edward 'regards [her] not' but 'dotes upon the love of Gaveston' and 'claps his cheeks and hangs about his neck, / Smiles in his face and whispers in his ears' (2.50–3), and Lancaster expresses a similar concern about an atmosphere in which 'arm in arm, the King and he doth march' (2.20), the issue at hand comes down to the general perception that 'the guard upon his lordship waits, / And all the court begins to flatter him' (2.21–2). Warwick hones in on the true source of the barons' distrust of Gaveston when he describes him impudently 'leaning on the shoulder of the King,' while 'he nods and scorns, and smiles at those that pass' (2.23–4). Already incensed by Gaveston's accrual of undeserved titles, by which he has been elevated to the 'Lord High Chamberlain, Chief Secretary to the state and [the king], Earl of Cornwall, [and] King and Lord of Man' (1.153–5), the barons persist in focusing on his haughtiness. The Earl of Lancaster, for instance, seems more outraged by Gaveston's insouciance than by the news that Edward has sent the Bishop of Coventry to the Tower and awarded Gaveston his property. Mortimer Senior's preoccupation with Gaveston's insolence crystallizes the barons' impression of him, as he pointedly reminds them, 'see what a scornful look the peasant casts' (4.14), moving members of the court to join forces with the Archbishop of Canterbury to effect his banishment.

Deciding to bring Gaveston back to the kingdom with the sole purpose of arranging his murder, the barons subject themselves to more scorn upon his reentry to the court. At the reception welcoming his return, Gaveston appears as contemptuous as ever towards the commoners, the clergy, and now the very nobles who facilitated his recall. In this scene he loudly refers to the peers as 'base leaden earls that glory in [their] birth' and advises them to 'go sit at home and eat [their] tenants' beef' (5.74-8). By associating them with the lead of cheap alloy coins, rather than the pure gold that constituted those coins called 'nobles' (6n74), Gaveston emphasizes not only that the barons are of common stock but also that they appear dull to the eye. His reference to beef augments their conventionality. Like the satiric target of Ben Jonson's Macilente, who bitterly refers to the man who is 'poor and meanly clad' and thus 'beef-witted,' the 'fellow that knows nothing but his beef' is a man known to be uncouth in his tastes.[45] For Gaveston, the barons' provincial palates reflect their uninspired sartorial preferences.

The final insult occurs when Gaveston literalizes what the barons have feared all along, namely, that he intends to outdo or to 'over-peer' them (4.19). Positioning himself on high on an upper balcony, Gaveston stands proudly arm in arm with Edward as he peers down upon those that walk below. As Mortimer Junior explains:

> While others walk below, the King and he
> From out a window laugh at such as we,
> And flout our train and jest at our attire.
> Uncle, 'tis *this* that makes me impatient. (4.417–20, emphasis mine)

In a subtle but ominous reenactment of the Actaeon myth Gaveston plans to stage, Marlowe shows us that it is Gaveston and Edward's peering or peeping that proves the coup de grâce in the cold war between them and the barons. By flaunting his intimacy with the king whom he makes an accomplice in his mockery, Gaveston in this moment confirms Mortimer Junior's characterization of him as a bloated pustule that has become 'swoll'n with venom of ambitious pride,' and which promises to be 'the ruin of the realm and us' (2.31–2). After being scorned by the haughty Gaveston who looks down upon him from his balcony perch, Mortimer Junior vows to take extreme measures to 'purge' the realm of 'such a plague' (4.270).

By representing Gaveston as 'laugh[ing]' and 'jesting' at the barons' attire, Marlowe elicits a range of significations that would have reverberated with his audience, most notably the attitudes and behaviour of the Inns of Court man who was known to distinguish himself by his flamboyant attire and his contempt for the apparel of others. This young student, according to Sir Thomas Overbury, sports 'a pair of silk stockings, and a beaver hat' and struts down the street 'laugh[ing] at every man whose band sits not well, or that hath not a fair shoe-tie, and ... is ashamed to be seen in any man's company that wears not his clothes well.'[46] John Earle describes the Inns of Court man similarly as censoring others 'for that hainous Vice being out of fashion.'[47] These young men are not unlike Ben Jonson's gallant whose 'fashion is not to take notice of him that is beneath him in clothes,' and who 'stabs any man that speaks more contemptibly of the scholar than he.'[48] The figure of the sumptuously attired young student cum court aspirant not only shadows Gaveston but also haunts Marlowe's Baldock and Spencer Junior.

According to Holinshed, Gaveston peopled Edward's kingdom with other young men who 'were like to himself' and 'furnish[ed] his court with companies of jesters, ruffians, [and] flattering parasites.'[49] While Marlowe does not show Gaveston inviting his compatriots to join him, he does connect Gaveston with the scholar Baldock and the court aspirant Spencer Junior, the two young men whom Edward 'adopt[s]' (11.144) as his new favourites after Gaveston is murdered. Our introduction to Baldock and Spencer Junior immediately follows Gaveston's mockery of the barons' attire, and in their conversation about the importance of sartorial flamboyance to court politics, these hangers-on articulate the terms of the unspoken philosophy underwriting Gaveston's derisive attitude towards the established elite. Figures located squarely in the sixteenth-century world of Marlowe's queen and her court, Baldock and Spencer Junior show themselves to be like those second sons whose life goal was 'to winne them[selves] new friends, and obtayne the acquaintance of noble men, whose credit and estimation with the prince may honor and countenance them.'[50]

Strategizing how to win the favour of an influential lord and plotting how best to ensure a rapid course of advancement, Spencer Junior reveals the inner workings of a court that is surprisingly similar to Elizabeth's. Unlike the fourteenth-century court of Edward II, the court culture Spencer Junior describes seems to be decreasingly oriented towards rewarding lineage and progressively invested in granting advancement to those who aggressively curry favour. Spencer Junior stresses to Baldock the importance of fastening onto an assertive lord, preferably one who 'hath the favour of a king,' since 'with one word' he can advance them 'while [he] lives' (5.8-9). He also emphasizes that he and Baldock should stop serving their respective lords, who, in observance of tradition, encourage their docility and train them only in pleasing their betters. In keeping with the model of Gaveston's relationship with Edward, Spencer explains to Baldock that he will from henceforth no longer be a 'follower' but a 'companion' to his patron (5.12–14). In a description that echoes Mortimer Junior's characterization of Gaveston as 'jet[ting]' through the court, Spencer Junior instructs Baldock to 'court it like a gentleman' (5.32). He advises him to

> Cast the scholar off
> And learn to court it like a gentleman.
> 'Tis not a black coat and a little band,
> A velvet-caped cloak, faced before with serge,
> And smelling to a nosegay all the day,
> Or holding of a napkin in your hand,
> Or saying a long grace at a table's end,
> Or making low legs to a nobleman,
> Or looking downward with your eyelids close,
> And saying, 'Truly, an't may please you honour,'
> Can get you any favour with great men.
> You must be proud, bold, pleasant, resolute,
> And now and then, stab, as occasion serves. (5.31–43)

Most importantly, Spencer Junior explains, Baldock must abandon all sartorial and behavioural restraint, lest he become like one of those pathetic students who, having failed to secure a powerful patron, are relegated to a life serving in a nobleman's household as a tutor.[51] Spencer Junior insists that only by casting off his plain, black academic attire – trimmed with cheap woolen materials – and by cleansing himself of the overly-sweet, ingratiating scent of nosegay can Baldock release himself from an entire repertoire of subservient protocols such as 'making low legs to a nobleman, Or looking downward with your eyelids close, And saying, "Truly, an't may please you honour." There is no favour to be gained, Spencer Junior insists, by being polite or bland in matters of either style or sexuality. In addition to adopting a manner that is 'proud, bold, pleasant, and resolute,' one should, he avers, be prepared to 'stab, as occasion serves,' a fencing metaphor with decidedly homoerotic overtones.[52] This trope, which links ambition with erotic violence, recalls Gaveston's depiction of Actaeon whose transgressive climbing and illicit peeping epitomize the dangerous delights of boundary violation.

Baldock needs little convincing to repudiate the pose of obeisance since casting off his 'curate-like' ensemble offers the exhilarating prospect of taking on an indecorous manner marked by sartorial ostentation, unrestrained eros, and uncharitable stabbing. While Baldock claims to 'hate such formal toys' (5.44), or contrived plans for social ascension, he readily agrees that one must 'use' such contrivances to move ahead and is well aware that the Byzantine order, which he has been observing dutifully, yields little in the way of advancement. He admits to Spencer Junior that the old style of reverence was appreciated by his now-deceased lord, who was himself so staid and punctilious that 'he would take exceptions at my buttons, and, being like pins' head, blame me for the bigness, which made me curate-like in my attire' (5.47–9). Baldock even goes so far as to confess that while serving his former master, he secretly regarded his deference as mere show, since he always knew himself to be 'inwardly licentious enough / And apt for any kind of villainy' (5.50–1). By the time Edward falls into the grips of the 'smooth-tongued scholar Baldock' (18.66), Baldock has gained enough confidence in his newfound strategy of advancement to lecture the king himself on how to adopt a 'haught resolve,' impressing upon him that arrogance 'becomes your majesty,' who should not be like a 'schoolboy' to the barons nor 'awed and governed like a child' (11.28–9). Gaveston's Italian aesthetic, Marlowe shows, has ushered in a new phase of court politics in which mercenary sexuality and vaunting ambition, once effectively managed, are now unleashed. Through the promotion of flamboyant display and sensual homoeroticism, Gaveston has transformed the court, and even its surrounding environs, into a battlefield from which he can launch a sustained attack on courtly conventions of deference.

3 *Inglese Italianato*

The new style infiltrating Edward's court on the stage could be detected at Elizabeth's court off the stage. The expectation that the queen would inevitably favour some courtiers remained at the foundation of the patronage system. Yet young men who were of good birth, poor estate, and average talent were perceived as using their bodies and the clothes they wore to exploit the traditional routes by which suitors obtained access to the mind and body of the monarch. As Mark Thornton Burnett explains, in Elizabeth's later years 'an alternative system of promotion' grew up at court.[53] While 'many of Elizabeth's favorites would have been hampered by their lack of gentle credentials,' in the aging queen's court, where the excessive display of her supplicants was more of a compliment to her diminishing allure than a threat to her authority, her 'sometimes whimsical policies' of favouritism proved hopeful to those without sufficient background.[54] Established elites certainly were aware of the changing constituency at court. By offering audiences an account of the fall of Edward II that puts style at the centre of civil conflict, Marlowe's play suggests that some members of Elizabeth's court were also deeply disturbed by what they perceived to be an influx of new men.

Roger Ascham is one of the period's most outspoken critics of the deleterious effects of Italian manners on English court culture. Purposely misconstruing Castiglione's influence, as well as the implications of his ideal of *grazia*, Ascham complains in *The Schoolmaster* that newly translated Italian comportment manuals instructed young men to demonstrate an unconscionable boldness:

> For if a young gentleman be demure and still of nature, they say he is simple and lacketh wit ... if he be innocent and ignorant of ill, they say, he is rude and hath no grace, so ungraciously do some graceless men misuse the fair and godly word GRACE.
>
> But if ye would know what grace they mean, go, and look, and learn among them, and ye shall see that it is, first, to blush at nothing ... then followeth to dare to do any mischief, to contemn stoutly any goodness ... To do thus in court is counted of some the chief and greatest grace of all. (41–2).

Ascham devotes a substantial portion of his guide for English youth to describing the offensive characteristics of the Italianified Englishmen peopling the court who, 'fawn, flatter ... [and] have some trim grace in a privy mock' (42). According to Ascham, these men have contaminated its atmosphere with

> the religion, the learning, the policy, the experience, the manners of Italy. That is to say, for religion, papistry or worse; for learning, less, commonly, than they carried out with them; for policy, a factious heart, a discoursing head, a mind to meddle in all men's matters; for experience, plenty of new mischiefs never known in England before; for manners, variety of vanities and change of filthy living. (67)[55]

Because of their influence, the court has become, Ascham stresses, 'a place most dangerous for youth to live without great grace, good regard, and diligent looking to' (60). Here, 'reverence is neglected, duties [are] confounded ... and disobedience doth overflow the banks of good order, almost in every place, almost in every degree of man' (44).

As a case in point, in an attempt to denigrate the earl of Oxford's manoeuvers to gain favour, Cambridge professor Gabriel Harvey describes him as the court '*Speculum Tuscanismi*,' proclaiming that 'since *Galateo* came in, and *Tuscanisme* 'gan vſurpe, Vanitie aboue all: Villainie next her.'[56] Detailing the untoward influences of Italian courtesy manuals on Oxford's behaviour, Harvey explains that Oxford is 'no man, but Minion,' who uses his time at court to flaunt notorious Italianified affectations, such as the '*cringing side necke, Eyes glauncing, Fisamie [physiognomy] smirking,* with *forefinger kisse* and braue *embrace to the footwarde.*' This Italianate courtier is, Harvey proclaims, 'glorious in shew, in deede most friuolous, not a looke but *Tuscanish* alwayes,' since after but one year abroad he is able to tutor others in how to be 'queynte in araye [and] conceited in all poyntes.'[57]

Harvey himself was not immune to such criticism, and he was the subject of a vicious anecdote circulated by his former student Thomas Nashe. According to Nashe, on his presentation to the queen, Harvey 'came ruffling it out huffty tuffty in his suite of veluet ... There did this our *Talatamtana* or Doctor *Hum, thrust* himselfe into the thickest rankes of the Noblemen and Gallants.'[58] In yet another redaction of 'pleasing the prince,' Nashe notes that when Harvey approached Elizabeth and bowed to kiss her hand

> it pleased her Highnes to say ... that he lookt something like an Italian ... and [he] quite renouncst his naturall English accents & gestures, & wrested himselfe wholy to the Italian *puntilios*, speaking our homely Iland

> tongue strangely, as if he were but a raw practitioner in it, & but ten daies before had entertained a schoole-master to teach him to pronounce it.'[59]

Accusations levelled against those who putatively displayed Italianate manners highlight not only the practitioner's sartorial flashiness but also his social boldness, as evidenced by his 'brave embrace' or tendency to 'thrust' himself into a crowd of his 'betters.'

While Nashe may have been amused by the pleasure the queen took in her supplicant's exaggerated modes of display, Hubert Languet reflects on his recent visit to court and is noticeably distressed. He describes himself as compelled to 'speak plainly' of its decadent atmosphere. In a letter to Philip Sidney, he does not focus on the Italianified Englishman per se but does take note of a new mode of embodiment promoted by young men seeking position at court:

> The habits of your court seemed to me somewhat less manly than I could have wished, and most of your noblemen appeared to me to seek for a reputation more by a kind of affected courtesy than by those virtues which are wholesome to the state, and which are most becoming to generous spirits and men of high birth.[60]

Languet concludes his missive by warning Sidney to remain vigilant 'lest from habit [he] should be brought to take pleasure in pursuits which only enervate the mind.'[61] Here he describes a court where recognition and promotion no longer seem to follow from having the traditional credentials of gentility or even from employing conventional courtly strategies like *sprezzatura*. By identifying this new mode of conduct as 'less manly' than what he had expected, Languet suggests that sumptuous display at the Elizabethan court has become reduced to mere theatricality. His comments seem to confirm the phenomenon whereby the decorative details of courtly apparel and the elaborate scripted manners of the courtier signalled his feminization, his decreased political importance, and his 'increasingly parasitic' function in government.[62] Yet the brunt of Languet's criticism is aimed at those court aspirants who, because they are not of 'high birth,' attempt to compensate for their insufficient background with demonstrations of affectation.

As historians have suggested, members of a new generation of court aspirant 'exercised their power and office with less probity' than their predecessors, and Elizabeth's court, in the last decade of her reign, was plagued by a devolution of 'standards of official morality.'[63] Indeed

Elizabeth's court was peopled by young men who, as victims of primogeniture, made up the 'crue' that 'pinch their bellies to poliʃh their backs [and] kepe their mawes emptie, to fill their purʃʃes.'[64] Those who were renowned for being rich in apparel but poor in assets flocked to Elizabeth's court with the hopes of purchasing or otherwise obtaining 'an office of some countenance and credite.'[65] A significant portion started out at the universities and the Inns of Court, which served as an unofficial finishing school for the sons of members of the merchant and minor gentry classes. Like Marlowe's Spencer Junior and Baldock, they 'fetch[ed] from Oxford, not from heraldry' (6.241). These young men seldom stayed more than a year or two at the universities and rarely took a degree, since their primary aim was to come away with 'a few tokens of higher education.'[66] Because of the central role of the universities and Inns of Court in the purveyance of cultural capital, those who inhabited a university milieu, albeit even for a brief period, often regarded garnering a reputation at court as the most fruitful route to advancement.[67]

These young students who migrated to court were also associated with the conspicuous cultivation of an Italian aesthetic. In 1570, for instance, Harvey expressed chagrin about what he perceived to be the superficiality of higher education and bemoaned the inordinate amount of time Cambridge students devoted to studying Italian courtesy manuals. He registers distress about what he describes as the 'vogue for Aretino,' the Italian poet whose 1527 *Sonetti Lussuriosi* or *Lascivious Sonnets* were accompanied by Giulio Romano's erotic engravings, which showcased anal intercourse.[68] While some, like Harvey, deplored the general decay of learning, the most consistent area of censure among university officials focused on students' outrageous dress, which according to university and Inns of Court by-laws typically included 'fancy hose, excessive ruffs, and swords and rapiers.'[69] A 1578 Cambridge decree penned by Burghley criticizes the sartorial excesses of 'sundry young men,' those being 'the children of gentlemen and men of wealth,' as well as those others who 'by their example' are drawn 'to change and cast away their modesty and honest frugality.' In 1602 Sir Robert Cecil, the chancellor of Cambridge, reported that young men 'now go in their silks and velvets, liker to courtiers than scholars.'[70] Even the Kings College student Christopher Marlowe was not above 'cast[ing] the scholar off' and was arrested in 1572 for sporting a slashed, velvet doublet.[71] Described by one twenty-first century critic as 'a working-class boy with a high-class university education that somehow did not get him the kind of life he thought it would,' Marlowe, like Gaveston, Spencer Junior, and Baldock, tried to secure a place in the service of a powerful lord, whom he hoped to impress with his education, as well as with his 'shrewdness, unscrupulousness, [and] willingness.'[72]

4 The Politics of Taste

In Holinshed's account, Piers Gaveston is depicted as generally leading the king into practising 'heinous vices,' 'disordered doings,' 'wantonness,' 'voluptuous pleasure,' and 'righteous excess,' yet Marlowe earmarks sartorial extravagance as the specific vice to which Gaveston introduces the king (2:547). Significantly, Mortimer Junior dismisses Holinshed's catalogue of sins and, in a statement that once again situates the action of the play squarely in the late sixteenth century, he publicly acknowledges that the 'mightiest kings' have had their 'minions' (4.402). Mortimer Junior's primary concern is Edward's sumptuous display – ordinarily the prerogative of the monarch – which over the course of the play comes to register as excessive when it becomes paired with what the barons regard as Edward's scornful attitude (6.214). In Marlowe's estimation, all goes awry when Edward co-opts the semiotics of spectacle by wresting the signs of sumptuousness from a system of patronage that served an established order and by mobilizing them instead in the service of a foreign aesthetic fuelled by various forms of unruly desire. Just as Gaveston promoted an offensive mode of exhibitionism, Edward too comes to demonstrate a disturbing gravitation towards inordinate display.

At the beginning of the play, Marlowe represents Edward as dutifully observing court propriety, exemplified by the proper form of political theatre. He willingly participates in 'solemn triumphs' and 'public shows' that feature his barons, such as the traditional 'bear[ing] the sword' ceremony in which the peers lead the king in a stately procession as they showcase their prerogative to display the symbol of state justice (4.351–2). Edward ably exercises restraint when, after naming Warwick as Chief Counsellor, he refuses pomp and fanfare. By having Edward assure Warwick and onlookers that his 'silver hairs will more adorn my court / than gaudy silks or rich embroidery' (4.347–8), Marlowe shows Edward to be well-versed in and compliant with the sobrieties of state ceremony, which he initially seems to honour.

These ceremonies stand in direct contrast to the decadent spectacles that lead to a dissolute court atmosphere and, more broadly, that come to compromise the integrity of the realm. Before Gaveston tainted the kingdom with his 'idle triumphs, masques, [and] lascivious shows' (6.154), the court, associated with its barons and their proper command of state ceremony, communicated the moderation of a martial culture. In the later half of the play, Edward stands accused of compromising the virility of the realm by bringing forth a retinue of masquers. The barons describe the king's soldiers as 'march[ing] like players / with garish robes, not armor' (6.180–1). Likened to the flamboyant and disdainful Gaveston, Edward himself is described as appearing on the battlefield 'bedaubed with gold,' seated high on horseback. Here Edward comes to be perceived as peering down on those below, while 'laughing at the rest / Nodding and shaking ... [his] spangled crest / Where women's favours [hang] like labels down' (6.182–4). Critics have argued that Edward's sartorial extravagance signals his lapse into femininity and that his veering from the tenets of normative masculinity is the key to his inability to rule.[73] Yet when we consider the barons' criticism of Edward in light of their response to Gaveston's insolent, Italian style, what comes into sharp relief is that the source of their outrage is not Edward's deviation from gender norms. Rather the barons recognize that their own codes of distinction become evacuated of meaning when their king empties out the signs of his entitlement by committing them to unorthodox performances.

Edward's insouciance is best comprehended as cumulative insult, which includes his scorn for his barons' repeated warnings, his rejection of Isabella's emotional and erotic overtures, and, most important, his immoderate use of the realm's revenue, including its land, titles, and jewels. When in the tradition of the court, Mortimer Junior and Lancaster call upon Edward to provide the ransom for the release of Mortimer Senior, who has been captured by the Scots, Edward denies their request. The barons perceive the king's violation of this long-standing tradition as a complete disregard for decorum. Levelling the irrational accusation, 'Your minion Gaveston hath taught you this' (6.146), Lancaster identifies Edward's failing in his office as an attempt to sabotage court order. Mortimer Junior also associates Edward's boldness with Gaveston's irreverence and, echoing his earlier assertion that Gaveston 'riot[s] it with the treasure of the realm / While soldiers mutiny for want of pay / ... / He wears a lord's revenue on his back' (4.406–8), decides that the 'prodigal gifts bestowed on Gaveston / Have drawn [the] treasure dry and made [Edward] weak' (6.155–6). In her rousing speech to the troops, Isabella also attributes the cause of civil strife to Edward's extravagance and irreverent attitude towards his office:

> Misgoverned kings are cause of all this wrack;
> And Edward, thou art one among them all,
> Whose looseness hath betrayed thy land to spoil
> And made the channels overflow with blood. (17.9-12)

In referring to Edward's 'looseness,' Isabella suggests that kings themselves must be ruled when their intemperance leads them to senselessly dissipate coin and seed, which portends the destruction of the patrilineal line.[74]

Edward's disregard for his people and his privilege is, however, Marlowe shows, the sign of a pandemic that has overtaken the court and threatens to contaminate the entire realm. Spencer Junior, having worked his way into Edward's favour, is characterized by the barons as 'wanton' (18.59), a 'base upstart' (12.20), and 'a putrefying branch / That deads the royal vine' (11.162–3). One of the 'pernicious upstarts' (11.165) Edward has taken into his confidence and awarded with honours (11.49), Spencer Junior, like Gaveston before him, is neither pliant to the will of the monarch nor obsequious to the authority of the barons. Instead, he boldly embraces Edward in front of the enemies' herald (11.177) as a direct challenge to what he regards as *their* 'display' of 'pride' (11.172). A disrespect for the status hierarchy in general and for authority in particular is evident, moreover, in Edward's own son, who impudently refuses his father's request to act as a messenger to France, prompting Isabella's comment, ' Ah, boy, this towardness makes thy mother fear / Thou art not marked for many days on earth' (11.79–80). Isabella too is associated with forceful stabbing as she is not above using her erotic appeal to seduce Mortimer Junior to achieve her political aims. The ambitious lovers are described by one of the barons as those who 'do kiss while they conspire' (18.22). Isabella's status as a foreigner anticipates her treasonous tendencies; she is described as 'a French Strumpet' (4.145), an insult that echoes the barons' characterization of the French Gaveston as a 'Greekish strumpet' (9.14).[75] Even Edward's subjects' revolt is represented as the people's attempt to 'brave' or to brazenly outface the king (11.86). The country is under siege on multiple fronts, and the encroaching Danes are described as 'haughty,' while the Scots are reported to have been moved to 'sleer' or 'sneer' at the excessive king of England. They have even devised a jig mocking the country that he has led to 'high disgrace' (6.185–6).

Marlowe deepens the connection between such widespread disrespect and sartorial extravagance by representing the barons' 'curb[ing]' (20.16) of Edward as a process of retributive divestiture. In his attempt to convey the gravity of the situation, Mortimer Junior engages the king's own investment in sartorial display and ominously points out, 'Thy court is naked, being bereft of those / That makes a king seem glorious to the world – / I mean the peers whom thou shouldst dearly love' (6.171–3). The revelation comes too late to Edward that without their peers, kings are 'but perfect shadows in a sunshine day' (20.27). The peers, it turns out, and not extravagant attire, are the indispensable accoutrements of monarchy. Edward's resignation to the dire nature of his situation is made evident by his weary request that his keeper open the execution warrant and 'tell thy message to [his] naked breast' (20.130). At this moment, the play comes full circle, having begun with the sumptuously attired Edward and Gaveston 'rent[ing] and [tearing]' the ecclesiastical garments of the bishop (2.35), whose headdress they cast into the gutter (1.186), and ending with Edward imagining his breast bared (20.130), his heart rent (20.140), his hair and beard shaved (22.36), and his head stripped of its 'glittering crown' (20.60).

In the end, though, Marlowe garners sympathy for Edward, and indirectly for Gaveston, by emphasizing that Gaveston's, Spenser Junior's, and Baldock's 'stabbing,' while mercenary, does not ultimately perpetrate the same kind of violation of Edward's body as the punishment commissioned by the barons.[76] *Edward II* suggests that the grave consequence of the flagrant exhibition of an Italian sensibility is not necessarily that it corrupts the practitioner, but that it singles him out as the target of retaliatory violence. Like the actual peers of Edward II's court who, according to Holinshed, ordered an Oxford student, a 'naughty fellow called John Poidras,' to be 'drawn, hanged, and bowelled' for his ambitious stabbing by which he 'thrust[ ] himself into the king's hall' to declare himself an unacknowledged heir to the throne, Marlowe's peers meet threats to the established order with equally extreme measures (2:587). Apparently, once the competitive violence underwriting court politics is no longer contained by the conventions of 'hospitality, generosity, and politeness,' there are no more 'gestures of peace in an environment otherwise structured by violence.'[77] The barons can only respond to what they perceive as an unmasking of their compensatory strategies with a demonstration of brute force. The illusion of decorum has been punctured, and Edward's barons show themselves to be the social conservatives that they are. They fight not for dismantling the office of the monarchy but for restoring the establishment, with the hope that Mortimer Junior and Isabella will reinstate the working hierarchy of the realm and its codes of decorum. Until these codes are reinstalled, there is, after all, no existing structure by which they may be recognized.

Yet by having Edward and Gaveston's shared appreciation for exaggeration and artfulness, as well as their pride in this sensibility, carry over into the symbolic elements of Edward's murder, Marlowe renders Edward's final moments an impressive instance of theatre. In this respect the stylized aspects of his assassination triumph over Mortimer Junior and the barons insofar as they link Edward, Gaveston, Baldock, Spencer Junior, and Lightborne to Marlowe himself. Marlowe bookends the play, at one end, with Gaveston's description of the Italian masques he will perform to initiate Edward into self-abnegating pleasure and, at the other end, with Lightborne's equally sensual description of how he will induce Edward to his death. Edward's execution is thus fashioned in accordance with Gaveston's 'lascivious shows' (6.154), making Lightborne a 'fitting' assassin not because of his decision to anally penetrate Edward, as critics have argued, but because of his pronounced sense of the aesthetic.[78] Edward is murdered, according to Holinshed, by being suffocated with 'heavy featherbeds or a table (as some write) being cast upon him,' as his assassins 'kept him down and withall put into his fundament, an horne, and through the same they thrust up into his body a hot spit ... the which passing up into his entrails, and being rolled to and fro, burnt the same.'[79] By substituting the Italianate Lightborne for Holinshed's anonymous, rough murderers, Marlowe culminates the play by implicitly contrasting the barons' overt acts of aggression with the destructive yet alluring capabilities of Lightborne.

It is more than coincidental that Edward's assassin understands homicide as an art, one in which he was expertly trained, he explains, in Naples. Lightborne brags of his ability to subtlety insert poison into men's orifices (23.30). Unlike Mortimer and the barons, he prides himself on his elegance and does not assault his victims. Rather, he employs 'tricks' (23.38) and his 'gear' (24.28), a word that referred both to male genitalia and to stage costumes.[80] He entices men to smell poisoned flowers (23.30). He seduces them into swallowing fine linen, which he then 'thrust[s] through the throat' (23.31). Alternatively, he gently pierces their windpipe with 'a needle's point' (23.32). Or, 'whilst one is asleep,' he takes 'a quill / And blow[s] a little powder in [their] ears' (23.33–4). In an even more erotically charged image, he 'open[s] his [victim's] mouth and pour[s] quicksilver down' (23.35).

Emphasizing the virtuosity and preciosity of his plan for Edward, Lightborne effects his own *artifizioso*, as he proudly calls attention to his innovation. He boasts, 'ne'er was there any so finely handled as this king' (23.39–40), and in envisioning the particular mode of murder he plans for Edward, he relishes that it is 'braver still' than any of his other methods (23.36). In choosing the adjective 'braver,' the word used in the period to describe not only courage but also a way of wearing one's clothes, Lightborne reinscribes Mortimer Junior's use of the word in his instructions to 'do it bravely' (23.27). To be brave was not only to be fearless but also to be sartorially fabulous, as one braved it out or jetted in one's clothes by wearing one's ostentatious ensemble in an exaggerated manner. A brave was a young man or a gallant known for his social impudence and sartorial excesses. Lightborne, whose name – the English translation of Lucifer – recalls Ascham's *Inglese italianato* cum 'devil,' promotes an exaggerated self-consciousness by which he asserts his *style qua Italian style*.[81] While it would be politic to quickly collect his reward and flee the scene of the crime, Lightborne cannot resist lingering to ask Maltraver and Gourney afterwards, 'Tell me, sirs, was it not bravely done?' (24.115). This final vaunt proves fatal, since Gourney responds by stabbing him to death (24.116).

Bravery was also the term for a sumptuous theatrical display, such as a court masque, and through the character of Lightborne, Marlowe offers his audience the dark apotheosis of the performance envisioned by Gaveston at the play's start.[82] 'Comedies [and] pleasing shows' (1.55) are not, however, what Lightborne brings to the incarcerated Edward but 'tragedy,' which Edward sees 'written in [his] brows'(24.74). Yet, like Gaveston, Lightborne employs the medium of theatricality to achieve his ends. The pleasure Gaveston, Lightborne, and Edward take in exaggeration and spectacle ties them, moreover, to a theatre that, in the words of Stephen Gosson, operated subtly, like the 'devil' who 'speaks when we hear him not, strikes when we feel not, and woundeth sore when he raiseth no skin, nor rents the flesh.'[83] In language that reverberates with Lightborne's description of his methods, Gosson claims in *The School of Abuse* that the satanic stage player violates his victim's 'privy entries,' such as his ears (B7). Actors, he explains, ply theatricality like sugar that 'slip[s] down' the throat, since 'that which delighteth never troubleth our swallow' and before we know it, we have ingested 'poison [that] creeping on secretly without grief chokes us at last' (D8v-E1).

Coda: Wilde Style

Because Christopher Marlowe refuses to contain or diffuse the homoerotic impulses of his characters, as one critic observes, we sense in this playwright's work 'a way of putting homosexual desire into discourse that differs radically from anything we have encountered before.'[84] This chapter has shown that while Marlowe's *Edward II* may not introduce us to 'the possibility of a homosexual subjectivity' in a modern sense,[85] it does explore a homoerotic sensibility. By showing how male same-sex desire in the fictional court of Edward II converged with and was shaped by broader concerns with corporal propriety, Marlowe represents Edward's relationship with his favourites as generating a series of political offences that coalesce around the issue of style. In this respect, *Edward II* confronts us with both the ruptures and the continuities between early modern and modern conceptions of male same-sex desire as integral to social identity.[86]

Speculating that Oscar Wilde's enemies found him particularly abhorrent because of the ways that he conjoined aesthetic defiance and erotic transgression, scholars have championed Wilde as the first public figure to self-consciously link erotic preference to a distinctive corporeal and sartorial mode of expression. Indeed, one could argue that for Wilde, homosexuality was at once a social and a sexual identity. *Edward II* suggests that long before Wilde came on the scene, masculine dissidence could be articulated in terms of alternative modes of embodiment. Even as Elizabethan authorities periodically attempted to police sartorially excessive servants, students, and apprentices, the ideological appropriation of Italy continued to serve as a source of identification for those gentle born, socially disenfranchised young men who existed alongside of but who did not identify with the dominant culture. Acknowledging that certain young men persisted in cultivating an Italian aesthetic, Thomas Nashe observes, 'It is nowe a priuie note amongst the better sort of men, when they would set a singular marke or brand on a notorious villaine, to say, he hath beene in *Italy*.'[87] Italian courtesy manuals were translated into English, after all, so that aspirants could ameliorate their demeanour. In the eyes of some, English manners were the epitome of bad taste, indeed, 'counted barbarous' by many.[88]

5 Plotting Style in Ben Jonson's London

The Cittie is the mappe of vanities,
The marte of fooles, the *Magazin* of gulles,
The painters shop of Antickes: walke in Poules,
And but obserue the sundry kindes of shapes.

Everard Guilpin, *Skialetheia*.[1]

1 Urban Conduct ca. 1600

After centuries of being discounted as an 'abortive drama,' Ben Jonson's amorphous *Every Man Out of His Humour* has come into critical favour.[2] Most notably, Jonson's 'inartistic' herding of bodies on stage, whereby he offers his audience 'as little integrity of plot as a massive street brawl,' is now seen as a bold departure from theatrical convention.[3] This reassessment of *Every Man Out* grows out of a more nuanced understanding of how it utilizes '*plot*,' a technical term that in the early modern period referred to spatial logistics.[4] Jonson was the first English playwright to use the word to describe the scope of dramatic action, and the disjointed nature of *Every Man Out*, arguably, reflects an author who engages plot to effect spatial mapping and to convey narrative meaning.[5] While critics are now coming to understand the experimental aspects of Jonson's stage technique, they have yet to address the cultural implications of his sense of space as social practice. Jonson's innovative play inaugurates a new form of urban drama nurtured by a theatre moved to respond artistically and commercially to the rise of London as the capital of not only England but soon to be of all Western Europe.[6] Space in *Every Man Out* is not an abstract medium but is materialized through the particular ways Jonson's characters inhabit public sites and neighbourhood locales easily recognizable to his late sixteenth-century audience.

One out of a handful of plays set entirely in the contemporary London of its audience, *Every Man Out* is one of the first plays to showcase patterns of '*behavioral urbanization*' that organized individuals' 'modes of identity-formation, systems of belief, [and] habits of deportment and civility' in accordance with new demographic and infrastructural developments.[7] The enhanced awareness of the symbiosis of city and self that was coming to be displayed on the early modern stage was also taking hold off the stage, as demonstrated by an explosion of advice literature instructing the reader on how to carry oneself in urban space, where to position oneself relative to strangers, at what venues to appear and which ones to avoid. In a fluid, anonymous milieu, comportment conveyed crucial information not only about status but also about the values to which one ascribed and the communities with which one identified. As prescriptions of proper urban conduct attempted to accommodate increasingly complex economic, social, and physical arrangements, codes of inclusion and exclusion, as one historian emphasizes, became 'far more radical and more anxious, than the straightforward sense of rank and degree characteristic of the rural life and society of lordship.'[8]

Turn-of-the-century comportment manuals urged young men to attend closely to what they wore and how they wore their clothes in urban settings. It was not, for example, atypical for a master to impress upon his servant that in the city men will 'look deeply into your usage, behavior and carriage, and in your manner of going in your apparel. And according as they find it to be mixed with sobriety, so shall you find credit.'[9] One commentator counsels his reader to cultivate a 'port and state of the body' that is 'bolt upright' and 'framed to comeliness,' and he discourages the projection of a demeanour 'nicely affected [or] curiously counterfeited' as practiced by 'players and disguised masquers.'[10] This writer stresses that those men 'who by a kind of upstart and stately gait hopeth rather to win credit, estimation, and authority' do not convey the gravitas of fiscal solvency but the exhibitionism of prodigality.[11]

Advice writers who instructed young men in the codes of civic conduct, as well as the young men who read these manuals, implicitly understood the city as a venue that was competitive with the household and the court as an arena of male display. Yet even as some obtained status by exhibiting social capital through the modelling of proper urban comportment, or by demonstrating cultural capital through the execution of courtly grace, others garnered an alternative kind of status by flaunting *subcultural capital* through showing themselves to be 'in the know.'[12] The city gallant was a figure that stood in stark contrast to the householder practised in social authority, the courtier versed in the art of civil conversation, and even the creditworthy city dweller able to communicate 'an honest commendable and vertuous kinde of living in the world.'[13] The gallant or the 'Phantastick,' as Richard Brathwait explains, was, instead, skilled at 'strut[ting]' down the street, believing that 'the eyes of the whole city are fixed on him as the very pattern which they esteem worthy [of] imitation.'[14]

Also known as the 'Affected Man,' the immoderate young man was known to be 'extraordinary ... in ordinary things.'[15] Renowned for 'go[ing] a straine beyond himselfe,' or exaggerating his behaviour even while performing the most mundane activities such as walking, this man 'over-does all things,' and 'every action of his cryes, *Doe yee marke mee?*'[16] Thomas Dekker in his mock conduct manual, which lampoons the legitimate advice offered to those who aspired to be urbane Londoners, counsels his reader to 'set off your estimation' by 'put[ting] off to none, unless his hatband be of a newer fashion than yours and three degrees quainter ... for, in my opinion, that brain that cannot choose his felt well, being the head-ornament, must needs pour folly into all the rest of the members and be an absolute confirmed fool *in summâ totali*.'[17] While most young men would continue to cultivate corporal moderation in hopes of gaining recognition among legitimate city dwellers, other men, instead, broadcast the quaintness of their apparel and their ability to evaluate another's in order to obtain membership in a subcommunity that valued an alternative form of social authority based not on status but on style.

By staging how those who flouted prescriptions of proper urban comportment used the objects and spaces made newly available to them in an urban context as the material of histrionic self-expression, *Every Man Out* plots the transformation of a theatre traditionally conceived as a *theatrum mundi* into a *theatrum civitatis*. For Jonson's young male characters, as well as for the young men in his audience, the theatre was not *of* the city. Rather, the city itself was an expansive stage on which its star player, the gallant, strutted his style. *Every Man Out* explores the processes by which gallants make the city a stage in three successive phases, each of which projects a vision of the progressively expanding influence of the theatre on early modern London. In the first phase, young men turn St Paul's Cathedral into a 'presuppos[ed]' stage (3.1.2). In the second phase, these same young men wear their street clothes in such a way that they take on the aura of stage costumes. In the third and final phase, Jonson's gallants expand the zones of leisure activities primarily associated with the early modern theatre, the pawning of clothes and the smoking of tobacco, by remapping these dubious pursuits onto the city beyond the walls of the playhouse.

Because Jonson's play identifies itself as a 'comical satire,' the audience is prepared for the ample mocking of its characters.[18] Indeed, in tracking the irreverent spatial and corporal practices certain young men employ as they render London an unbounded playing space, *Every Man Out* ably parodies them. Yet by representing their outrageous behaviour as the means by which they distinguished themselves from established city dwellers, *Every Man Out* also credits the theatre as the arbiter of a new urban style. In this respect Jonson's play functions as a persuasive argument for the centrality and the relevance of a form of entertainment that could have become easily overshadowed by an increasingly vital and rapidly expanding metropolis. Young men attended plays like *Every Man Out* expressly to see people like themselves portrayed on stage, and the theatre kept itself commercially and culturally viable by paying close attention to the evolving attitudes and habits of its young male attendees. Even if they could not set mainstream trends, Jonson and his fellow playwrights had a stake in promoting the playhouse as a site where the key material markers of subcultural style, like satin suits and tobacco, were advertised and disseminated.

2 Uncivil Dramaturgy

The impressive ability of Jonson's characters to exploit the theatrical potential of urban space is saliently illustrated in the extended Paul's Walk scene, the 'physical center and emblematic hub of the play,' which in the Holme's folio of 1600 constitutes almost all of act 3.[19] An example of what Helen Ostovich has described as *Every Man Out*'s hallmark 'flagrant theatricality,'[20] this scene surpasses all others with respect to the number of incidents that it showcases and the number of bodies that it packs on the stage. By establishing multiple groups of actors who move between the activities of watching and performing, as well as by setting up simultaneous onstage acting arenas, Jonson offers viewers a chaotic dramatization of the events that transpire inside St Paul's Cathedral. This melee both evokes and undermines the offstage ideal of the cathedral as a site reserved for official ceremony.

One the most renowned structures in all of early modern Europe, to which, according to one early modern commentator, visitors from all over the world flocked to stand 'gazing about,' London's massive cathedral was a proud monument to the harmonious joining of England's sacred and secular traditions.[21] State and local officials heralded the expression of civic heritage in the built environment and regularly employed St Paul's as the public stage of pageantry. Processions commissioned by guild authorities commemorated the achievements of prominent Londoners, such as Sir Thomas Gresham, the financier who constructed the Royal Exchange, and Alexander Nowell the dean of St Paul's. In these performances characters representing city luminaries dramatized the myths, motifs, and ideas underwriting the principals of local order.[22] The Crown also used the cathedral as a staging ground from which to celebrate its magnificence and authority. Monarchs and ambassadors came to this 'fayre building of stone' to 'beholde the shewes of [the] Citty' that culminated at St Paul's.[23] In one such 'triumphant shewe,' described by John Stow, Londoners celebrated the inauguration of the Lord Mayor, who paraded to the church 'in long garments, embrodered about with gold, and silks of diuerse colours' through a cityscape that was itself sumptuously 'adorned with silkes' and dressed up 'with Lamps, Cressets, and other lights, without number.'[24] Peripatetic ceremonies such as the queen's procession and the Lord Mayor's pageant, harnessed spectacle to the imagined endurance of a hierarchic society. These dramatizations offered observers an object lesson in the proper use of sartorial splendour for the conferral and continuance of legitimate forms of power.

With its showcase of gallants, Jonson's Paul's Walk scene bears a closer relationship to the Paul's revels and to the unofficial parades that transpired daily in the middle aisle of the cathedral than to those official performances that encouraged observers to regard themselves as members of an ordered society. In addition to state-sponsored and locally commissioned ceremonies, the cathedral provided a home to a boys' choir who used the small playhouse adjacent to the church's chapter house to perform before an exclusive audience of gentleman scholars. The specialized nature of the Paul's boys' repertoire reflected the fact that the plays in which they performed were penned by a group of law students that one critic has characterized as 'an inbred milieu of young men,' whose 'orthodox ideals and ambitions mingled easily with licentious conduct.'[25] Paul's plays were known for their distinctive aesthetic by which they validated disorderly conduct, mock solemnity, and hyperbole. Writers for the Paul's players, such as Middle Temple student and satirist John Marston, used these performances as occasions to foster 'the fashion for railing.'[26] Marston and his compatriots typically wrote scripts that would 'chiefly appeal to the gallants and law students whose enthusiasm for railing in print was halted by the bishops and their book-burning in 1599.'[27] Despite their purported aim to expose the hypocrisies of the histrionic characters they portrayed, these plays inevitably valorized acerbic, witty young men who distinguished themselves by their cleverness and contempt for their less urbane peers.[28]

The association of St Paul's Cathedral with an irreverent genre of student entertainment would not have been lost on Jonson's audience, since a sizable portion was composed of university and Inns of Court students. Jonson announces his personal connection to these students in the play's dedication, where he reminds them that he understands their taste intimately. He explains, 'I understand *you*' and 'not your houses,' in order to assure these young men that his play will not merely include references to the content of their legal studies, but in both its tone and mode of presentation it will reflect their particular aesthetic, one that he too came to appreciate as a result of having 'had friendship with diverse in [their] societies.'[29] Acknowledging the predominance of Inns of Court students and their influence on the style and subject matter of the plays performed at the Globe Theatre, playwrights Thomas Dekker and Thomas Middleton note that their offerings are always 'fit for the times and Termers,' or those young men who frequented the Globe after the termination of the Paul's boys.[30]

By appealing to those young male viewers who regarded themselves to be at once observers of and participants in the theatrical events that defined their experience of London, Jonson commissions his own *uncivic* procession, by which he effectively dismantles the boundary separating the playing space and the audience. Through the use of intricate framing devices, including a formal Greek chorus or Grex that comments on the action of the play for its entirety, Jonson conflates the fictive world of the play peopled by excessive gallants with the world of the audience made up of those inclined towards ostentatious presentation. Members of the Grex, for instance, remain stationed throughout the course of the play among the real life gallants who typically purchased seats in the upper galleries hanging over the stage proper. This fraternizing with audience members would seem to compromise the chorus's detached stance as well as its promise to maintain a critical perspective towards pretentious city gallants such as the ones among whom they sit.

The character Asper exemplifies the fractured allegiances of Jonson's performers. The stage player who assumes the role of Asper portrays the play's author, but the character Asper is also an actor, who then takes on the role of a disaffected university student, who in turn resembles one of the many young men peopling Jonson's audience. In the Induction, Asper vows to 'scourge those apes' (Ind. 155) who promote a 'fantastic strain' (Ind. 114) by setting up a mirror 'as large as is the stage whereon we act, where they [the disapproving audience] shall see time's deformity anatomized' (Ind. 117–19). Yet despite Asper's commitment to use the play to mock gallants by imitating their excesses on stage, the Walk scene mirrors only the paradoxes involved in showcasing the behaviour of a group of performative young men to an audience of performative young men who were themselves known to imitate the actors and characters they observed at plays like Jonson's – such as the gallant who is depicted in popular tracts as attending the theatre with his 'table-book' or notebook in hand.[31] Even Asper, who prides himself on remaining on the sidelines to 'behold such prodigies' (Ind. 10) and who comments on the 'ragged follies' (Ind. 15) he witnesses, appreciates that he too is 'observed' by a 'throng'd round' (Ind. 49) and becomes inspired to 'fling his body' into the 'Thespian spring' to play the part of the discontented scholar Macilente (Ind. 68). Perhaps in a last ditch attempt to perform some kind of educative function, the chorus warns the offstage viewers that *they* will be watched by the characters in the play. To drive home the point, Asper instructs members of the chorus to pause the action of the play whenever they 'espy a gallant of this mark, who (to be thought one of the judicious) sits with his arms thus wreathed, his hat pulled here, cries mews and nods, then shakes his empty head' (Ind. 157–61).

By having the chorus set up the Walk scene by first explaining to the audience that the stage is now the middle aisle of St Paul's, only to then ask viewers to regard this facsimile of St Paul's as a 'presuppose stage' (3.1.2), Jonson frames the action that follows with an inside joke between his actors and the men in the audience who were themselves known for appropriating the sacred/civic space of the church.[32] The progression of this extended scene, which is loosely organized around the activities of watching and walking, inspires its offstage audience to assume the familiar role of St Paul's regulars as they are compelled to enact at the Globe the very same behaviour they would at the church: that of observing various characters in the act of observing other characters. Those who enter the scene meld into crowds and then disperse as they 'walk together,' 'walk aside,' and then station themselves along the supposed middle aisle to watch others promenade (3.1.29). In another area of the stage, pairs and threesomes cluster together at what is identified as the 'west end' of the cathedral, where they linger to 'look upon the bills' or ads for service posted on the pillars there (3.1.90). All the while, other characters set themselves up in yet another part of the stage cum cathedral cum stage, where they perfect the various poses they will show off in 'the *Mediterraneum*' (3.1.91). To make his audience's vicarious visit to the cathedral complete, Jonson begins the scene with two random 'Paul's men,' who may very well have stepped out of the audience. These superfluous characters have not appeared previously, have no connection with any of the other characters, and will not return again. Moreover, they seem to have innocently wandered on stage, as both maintain that they are not in a play but in the actual cathedral where they have come 'by chance' to 'walk a turn or two' (3.1.39-40). Their inability to discern the physical environs of the Globe Theatre, as well as their comfort level with a throng of observers, amplifies how parading down the middle aisle of St Paul's for some was an experience that was virtually indistinguishable from visiting the playhouse.

By demonstrating the persistence with which certain young men refused to delineate between traditional civic ceremony and subcultural exhibitionism, Jonson exposes the fissures within an urban ideology that aimed to identify St Paul's Cathedral as 'the ceremonial heart of the metropolis.'[33] From the thirteenth century on, Paul's Churchyard, which contained the pulpit of St Paul's Cross, operated as a centre of communal assembly, public oratory, and official sermonizing. The churchyard was where 'folk-motes were gathered together, Bulls and Papal edicts were read, heretics were denounced, heresies abjured, excommunications published, great political changes made known to the people, [and] penances performed.'[34] To address a congregation from St Paul's was 'to address the city and through it the nation.'[35] Despite the efforts of royal dignitaries and the Lord Mayor to render the cathedral an urban site associated exclusively with the issuance of prescriptions for social order, by the end of the sixteenth century the church was overrun by young men whose regular attendance, ironically, defied not only the crown and city fathers but also university principals and household and guild masters. Indeed, the period's satiric literature suggests that the largest building in London was second only to the playhouses in offering an unrivalled place to observe a range of urban behaviours, particularly those revolving around the display of apparel. Paul's Walk, Thomas Dekker explains in *The Dead Tearme*, is the first place the aspiring gallant must visit upon arriving in London, since there he can observe 'what brauing with Feathers, what bearding with Muſtachoes, what caſting open of cloakes to publiſh new clothes.'[36] In *The Black Book*, Thomas Middleton's Lucifer pays a visit to Paul's with the express purpose 'to see [the] fashions.'[37]

This trend was not lost on John Earle who characterizes a visit to St Paul's as an experience that takes up the entire day, and which, for this reason, puts it on par with 'the other expence[s] of the day,' such as 'Playes, [the] Taverne, and a Bawdy-House.'[38] Not surprisingly, the authorities regarded 'loitering persons' as akin to 'vagabonds' and 'masterless men' insofar as they too were guilty of misdemeanours typically associated with placelessness.[39] In a 1558 proclamation intending to address the growing problem of social unrest, Queen Mary includes a separate clause targeting those who 'roam and loiter suspiciously in places.'[40] (2:92). In 1601 Elizabeth expands the scope of her regulatory purview, which encompassed masterless men and wanderers (particularly, newly returned, unemployed soldiers), to include 'the great multitude' of people who 'lie privily in corners and bad houses, listening after news and stirs, and spreading rumors and tales ... and gather to our city and the places confining about the same.'[41] Her administration appended provisions to a number of proclamations that called for social order that specifically address the disruptive activities associated with Paul's men. Reference is made in the preamble of one decree to those young men who 'walk up and down [the middle aisle], or spend the time in the same, in making any bargain or other profane cause, and [who] make any kind of disturbance during ... divine service.' The law threatened these men with 'pain of imprisonment and fine.'[42]

The early modern sense of the verb 'to loiter' did not merely objectively describe the physical activity of standing around but also conveyed a cultural judgment about wasting time, since the word referenced a state of moral lassitude.[43] A 1530 description of the young man who 'loitereth about like a masterless hound' emphasizes that lack of supervision enables loitering, and implies, in turn, that those who 'loiter [away] the time' are not simply careless but also indolent.[44] Paul's men confounded the meaning of stasis, as suggested by Thomas Harman in his poem:

> A Stock's to stay sure, and safely detain,
> Lazy lewd Loiterers, that laws do offend,
> Impudent persons, thus punished with pain,
> Hardly for all this, do mean to amend.[45]

The loiterer, Harman observes, undermines the punitive aim of one of the state's primary means of disciplining subjects who defied the prescriptions of proper place. A 'material, legal, and ideological machinery of placement,' the stocks used detention as a means by which to reinsert recalcitrants back into the social order.[46] Yet clearly the stocks posed little threat to those who defiantly chose to hold their ground by hanging out in the wrong place, at the wrong time.

3 Apparel Performed

Advice writers discouraged exhibitionism and advocated, instead, what they defined as appropriate urban demeanour. Towards this end, they promoted gesture over gesticulation, the derogatory term that referred to excessive bodily movement, which came into wide usage in the late sixteenth century.[47] Thomas Wilson in *The Arte of Rhetorique* echoes Cicero's maxim that 'the gesture of man is the speech of the body,' and he stresses the importance of corporal harmony:

> Gesture is a certaine comely moderacion of the countenance and all other partes, of a mannes bodye, aptle agreeynge to those thinges, which are spoken ... the hedde to bee holden upright, ... the armes not much caste abroade, but comely sette out, as tyme, and cause shall beste require.[48]

Similarly, Stefano Guazzo advocates understated bodily gesture, which for him also entails holding one's head upright when speaking and ensuring that 'the woordes agree to the jesture, as the daunce doeth to the sownde of the instrument.' Guazzo warns against 'rude, lowtishe lookes' and 'wrying the bodie aside ... too sower a countenaunce, [and] of gazing about,' as well as inappropriate expressions of intimacy towards one's companions, like 'whispering in any others eare,' 'laughing without occasion,' 'shewing [oneself] greeved at the speakers wordes,' or expressing 'amaze' [ment] to 'him that speaketh.' Above all, one must guard against too much 'libertie of ... jestures,' Guazzo explains, and restrain oneself from conveying 'a player like kinde of lightnesse' in one's comportment.[49] The young man who is depicted as 'light' is typically condemned by advice writers for forswearing rational discretion and bodily control, both of which are confirmed by a demonstration of 'profanenesse, riotousnesse, drunkennesse, lewdnesse ... [and] unthriftinesse.'[50]

Gesticulation, which conveyed self-love and inconstancy, was both the cause and the sign of immoderation. Thomas Wright avers that artificial and exaggerated movements should be avoided at all costs, since 'too much gesticulation' may be perceived as signalling 'lightness.'[51] He also goes on to disparage young men who become light because they are overly concerned with their apparel. These men are always 'fiddling about their garments, either prying for moths, binding of garters, pulling up their stockings, that scarcely when they go to bed they are apparelled.'[52] Men who are constantly engaged in the project of self-fashioning are inclined to

> cast their heads now hither, now thither, as wantonly as lightly, which springeth from folly and inconstancy ... Some gaze upon themselves, how proper bodies they bear, how neat and proportioned legs sustain them, and in fine, almost are enamoured of themselves, so they are pleased with their own persons; but this gesture displeaseth commonly, and proceedeth from pride and vain complacence in going. [53]

James Cleland associates gesticulation with exaggerated posture, which for him is exemplified by those who bend their body backwards when they walk. He complains that

> many are so monstrous in their manner of going that they must needs either be nodding with their head, shaking of their shoulders, playing with their hands, or capering at every step with their feet, rolling from side to side like a Turkey Cocke. As they go through the streets, you shall not see them go forward one step without looking down to the rose upon their shoes, or lifting up their hand to set out their band, as if it were in

print, or setting up the brim of their hat, or doing some such apish toy: whereof I council you to be aware, if you would not be mocked with them.[54]

While Jonson had his pick of sources from which to draw in representing his gallants-in-training, he did not choose to follow the instructions of those who advocated measured posture, which in an anonymous, urban milieu connoted fiscal solvency and moral consistency. Rather, by aligning his fictional gallants with real life Paul's men, Jonson pressures the generic possibilities of theatrical production to stage certain men appropriating the symbolic aspects of civic culture through the manipulation of its material elements. In the second half of the Paul's Walk scene, the gallants use resplendent attire to complete the transformation of the middle aisle into a subcultural stage. Here the gallants' extravagant behaviour serves as an inspiration for Thomas Dekker, who in his satiric manual recommends exaggerated display as the basis of urban comportment.

Unlike those who deplored gesticulation and 'a monstrous manner of going,' Dekker provides precise guidelines in *The Guls Horne-book* on how to unleash the theatrical potential of London by moving through the city in ways that call attention to oneself. After the playhouse, the venue where one could best realize one's own dramatic potential was, of course, the monumental St Paul's. Dekker outlines how to exploit the grandeur of the church by using the 'Mediterranean' as a catwalk for 'publishing [one's] suit' (34). He recommends ambling down the middle aisle in a flamboyant manner and completing one's promenade by 'striking a pose' (34). A 'turn in the walks' is essential for those who intend 'to keep their decorums,' Dekker emphasizes, 'in fantasticality' (34). Simply hanging out in the middle aisle will not in and of itself guarantee ample recognition; he carefully anatomizes how one should use one's body in this impressive setting so as to best ensure that one's apparel assumes a disproportionate focus. Towards this end, he stresses the importance of 'fashion[ing] [one's] legs to [one's] silk stockings,' which will entice 'all the Inns of Court [men] to rejoice to behold [your] most handsome calf' (34). He also instructs his gallant on how to conspicuously 'mount the steps into the choir' and how to position himself in such a way so as to best enable the 'singing-boys' to 'prefer the fashion of [his] doublet' (36). Dekker, moreover, implores his gallant to interrupt the choir performance by suddenly leaping from his seat and dramatically 'draw[ing] forth a perfumed embroidered purse' under the pretext of making a donation (36). Once 'this noble and notable act' has been completed, Dekker recommends 'vanish[ing] presently' to prepare to 'appear again in the walk' (36).

Well versed in the corporal details of showmanship, Dekker is firm that one can only create the necessary aura by limiting one's promenading to those moments at which one is confident that he can successfully compete with the surrounding distractions while maintaining complete control of his persona. For this reason, Dekker advises conceiving of oneself as a character in a play who performs his part and then disappears from view. Those who do not understand the allure of inaccessibility, he explains, 'cheapen' themselves (34). Realizing that some will not be able to resist taking 'four turns' in the walk, Dekker advises these men to 'make yourself away' after that, since 'too long walking' makes a suit 'stale' to spectators (35). A brief after-dinner appearance can work to one's advantage, however, if one is able to model yet another ensemble, for instance, by 'translating [oneself] out of [one's] English cloth cloak into a light Turkey grosgrain [a coarse fabric of silk and wool] ... and then be seen for a turn or two' (35). Describing what would come to be known in the twentieth century as 'voguing,' Dekker breaks down the sequence of the Walk's promenade into its various movements, which include sauntering down the aisle, then violently 'sliding' one's cloak 'from [one's] shoulder' as if ''twere in anger,' and then finishing with a flourish by 'suddenly snatch[ing] at the middle of the inside, if it be taffeta at the least, and so by that means the costly lining is betrayed' (34).

Just as Dekker guides his gallant in how best to model his clothes so that they take on the properties of sumptuous stage costumes, Jonson has his characters wear their stage costumes in ways that magnify the role of apparel in the production of gratuitous spectacle. Immune to the mockery they incur from the chorus and from other characters, Jonson's gallants successfully revise the relationship among clothing, space, and the body by confronting onlookers with not simply clothes worn but with apparel performed. Fastidious Brisk, a 'neat, spruce, affecting courtier,'[55] professes to be an aficionado on debuting in the 'Mediterranean' (3.1.91). As Jonson shows, Fastidious's expertise resides in his appreciation of the sartorial *how* over and above the sartorial *what*. As much is indicated by his immodest declaration that he is renowned for his 'judicious wearing of apparel,' since they who 'so commend and approve [his] apparel' are amazed by the way he wears his clothes, which, in his own estimation, is 'above wonder!' (2.2.244–5). Fastidious demonstrates an impressive understanding of the kind of attention one needs to devote to the cultivation of a properly exaggerated carriage. The position and angle of one's hat, for instance, he avers, are crucial, since the hat alone will not 'bear you out' or carry the day (3.1.96–7). He advises taking 'especial care to wear your hat that it oppress not confusedly this your predominant or foretop,' since when you make your first appearance, 'you may, with the once or twice stroking up your forehead thus, enter with your predominant perfect; that is, standing up stiff' (3.1.97–102). In order to achieve this effect, he recommends gum water or the whites of eggs to guarantee the desired stiffness of the front lock.

Feeding the visual appetite of viewers both on and off the stage (thus, thwarting the proposed aim of his play to cure our excesses by starving our humours), Jonson portrays his characters as overwhelmed by sartorial spectacle. In the words of the antitheatricalist Stephen Gosson, this insatiable mode of perception, which may be characterized by the phenomenon whereby 'the longer we gaze, the more we crave,' is endemic to the theatre.[56] In *Every Man Out* it seems that one can only view clothes with an acquisitive eye, which leads one to regard the male bodies wearing them as desirable objects that also may be obtained. As a case in point, the sartorially extravagant Inns of Court student Fungoso, who counts himself a gentleman despite his yeomanry background (2.1.291), suffers from the 'disease of the flux of apparel' (4.5.127), a condition marked by frequent vestimentary transformation.[57] Like Dekker's gallant who is advised to move through London accompanied by a tailor who remains on the lookout for 'the stuff, colour, and fashion of any doublet or hose,' Fungoso keeps a tailor by his side at all times.[58] Fungoso's exclusive object of attention is the fabulous Fastidious, and his devotion to the pretentious courtier inspires within him the desire to procure every single one of his outfits. Upon first meeting 'the fresh, Frenchified' Fastidious (2.1.7), Fungoso appears transfixed. After remaining in a dazed state for the entirety of a chaotic scene that crescendos around him, he is forced to speak and, while still 'staring at Fastidious' (2.1.403), can only manage to declare, 'By Jesu, it's a very fine suit of clothes' (2.1.404). He then launches into extravagant praise, commending Fastidious's 'excellent suit' (2.1.411), as well as the way that it 'neatly becomes him' (2.1.412). Accused of having his mind 'carried away with somewhat else' (2.1.419), Fungoso admits that until he laid eyes on Fastidious, he was 'never so pleased with a fashion, [all the] days of [his] life!' (2.1.422). As Fungoso fixates on 'such a suit, such a hat, such a band, such a doublet, such a hose, such a boot, and such a – ' (he is cut off) (2.1.422–5), he convinces himself that if he can purchase any one of these items, he will be 'made forever' (2.1.456).

Later in the scene, Jonson highlights the slippery slope between the desire to be someone and the desire to be *with* someone. Fungoso's fascination with Fastidious's suits leads imperceptibly to an obsession with the wearer. Fungoso admires Fastidious's 'blush-colored' or pink satin suit (3.1.280) and instructs his tailor to make him one out of 'such stuff' and 'without a difference' (3.1.284). Yet Fungoso is not satisfied with having his tailor perform the task of anatomizing Fastidious's-various parts. Relishing the opportunity to take an inventory himself, Fungoso is moved to compose a *blazon* by which he offers a paean to Fastidious's dressed body. Here, he goes a step beyond merely cataloguing Fastidious's various sartorial accessories and reveals his fascination with the more intimate items of Fastidious's couture, as he lavishes praise on those pieces that bear a close relation to specific body parts, like the 'wing, the sleeve, the skirt, belly and all' (3.1.285).[59] No less attentive to the details of how Fastidious models his attire, Fungoso explains to his tailor that he does not want him simply to replicate the pattern of Fastidious's suit but also to 'mark how it [his skirt] hangs at the knee' (3.1.296) and to note how Fastidious's collar sits on his neck (3.1.301). Like a thwarted lover, Fungoso's preoccupation with Fastidious and his apparel are only intensified by the futility of his desire. Despite his best efforts to approximate Fastidious's glamour, Fastidious's newest suit becomes his oldest one once Fungoso has obtained and assembled its various parts. After indebting himself to the point of insolvency to raise the cash necessary to recreate Fastidious's latest ensemble, Fungoso swoons in distress when he discovers that Fastidious has once again purchased yet another outfit (4.5.124).

Throughout *Every Man Out*, Jonson confirms antitheatricalists' worst fears by reminding his audience that the playhouse is a *theatron* or a 'beholding place' that stimulates desire by creating the experience of sensory overload for its visitors. In the Paul's Walk scene, he shows that the cravings elicited by watching boys are not necessarily contained within the world of the play or even within the confines of the playhouse.[60] In addition to condemning the promiscuous changing and exchanging of clothes among actors and audience members alike, those who railed against the theatre accused adult actors of trafficking in boys.[61] By depicting his gallants as attempting to enhance their prestige in the eyes of their peers by appearing in the Walk accompanied by a boy, Jonson acknowledges that for some men the body of the boy, like certain items of apparel, announced one's inclusion in a community of shared taste. The always-fashionable Fastidious flaunts his boy Cinedo, whose name is an anglicized version of the Latin *cinaedus*, the term for an effeminate, passive partner in a same-sex pair.[62] Cinedo is described by one bystander as a highly prized accessory that 'would show well upon a haberdasher's stall at a corner shop rarely' (2.1.17–18), and the Paul's Walk observers confirm the boy's function as a necessary decorative item like a hat, a pair of gloves, or a ruff. Jonson has his characters emphasize the purposelessness of the boy, who exists for mere show, by having Fastidious enthusiastically praise him for performing the underwhelming task of reporting the imminent arrival of another character. When someone suggests rewarding the boy with a 'French crown' (2.1.126), a reference to both a French, gold coin and a bald spot produced by the 'French pox' or syphilis, for the hard work he has performed, Fastidious insists that his boy does not need to be tipped because he 'wants no crowns' (2.1.129). Another bystander opines, however, that the boy of such a promiscuous master would inevitably not be wanting in crowns because he would be infected with syphilis (2.1.130). This wry comment serves to refocus the gallants' and the audience's attention on the true function of the boy: to circulate as an object of exchange, to complete his man's couture, and, when necessary, to provide erotic pleasure. Even the country rube Sogliardo, who has earlier announced his 'humour' or predilection for adult men over boys (1.2.145), gets caught up in the sartorial competition transpiring around him and becomes 'resolute to keep a page' (1.2.158). Having come to London to cultivate the 'carriage and behaviour' of a city gallant (1.2.49), his plan to procure a boy (1.2.144) falls in line neatly with the other activities that he aims to pursue, such as selling off his land for cash, purchasing costly apparel, smoking tobacco, affecting a state of melancholy, behaving badly at the theatre by sitting 'o' the stage and flout[ing] ... a good suit' (1.2.66), and amassing an insurmountable amount of debt.

Illustrating to the audience their own complicity in the guilty pleasure of watching young men strut it out in sumptuous clothes, Jonson sets up a double triangle of desire that implicates both off- and onstage observers. Within the world of the play, spectators in the chorus bond with other onstage male characters through their mutual enjoyment of watching young men parade before them. In a continued violation of the fourth wall that traditionally divides the audience from the actors, Jonson's chorus engages in a steady stream of comments to various offstage audience members about the onstage gallants. Here, Jonson constructs the activity of watching young men as a communal pursuit. Jonson's play, however, not only comments on but also stimulates the potentially unruly desires specifically associated with observing men perform their apparel. Moreover, *Every Man Out* broadens the context of this experience beyond the playhouse. By making St Paul's yet another, grander playhouse, Jonson draws an implicit comparison between watching boys at the theatre to the bustling activities of walking and watching that occurred daily on the streets of London. Thus the city itself, as Jonson's play suggests, may be regarded as an expansive stage for promenading gallants and a site of unlimited pleasure for their observers.

4 Uncivic Exchange

Jonson's characters use urban space as a medium of theatrical display, and throughout *Every Man Out* their irreverent sartorial practices are enabled by their participation in disreputable economic practices. Those who exhibit the physical signs of flux of apparel also embody the figurative disturbances associated with the theatre itself. The behaviours presented on the Jonsonian stage, such as loitering, promenading, and posing, evoke other scandalous pleasures that undermined state, ecclesiastical, and civic authorities. As advice writer Henry Crosse points out, the notorious playhouse gallant does not consider himself of esteem, 'unless he be cut of the fashion and can swagger and brave it out, swear himself into smoke with pure refined oaths ... and take tobacco with a whiff and be oddly humorous.'[63] Indulging in tobacco was connected in the minds of some to sartorial flamboyance, and, as such, was yet another example of the tendency of male youths to reject expectations of fiscal prudence.[64] Yet those pleasures that members of the dominant culture associated with extravagance and waste, like smoking tobacco, were, Jonson's play suggests, crucial to the forging of subcultural networks that formed around such shared practices. By staging prodigal young men participating in ad hoc economies, notably those that flourished in London's Liberties where the Globe Theatre resided, Jonson charts the ways in which young men remap the coordinates of productivity and pleasure delineating London's legitimate and illegitimate enterprises.

Unlike the ideal London, imagined as a coherent social and economic grid designated by specific neighbourhoods and the commodities produced and sold there, the real London consisted of overlapping zones of reputable and disreputable forms of commerce, which in turn generated licit and illicit profits. *Every Man Out* emphasizes that the playhouse was one of many spaces in the early modern city where activities that countered industriousness and hierarchic order were sustained. By stressing that the same group of young men spent their days moving from St Paul's Cathedral to the broker's stall, from there to the inn or ordinary, and from the ordinary to the playhouse, Jonson reveals these men to be the nodal points connecting London's myriad notorious locales. These various urban sites, Jonson shows, offered young men commensurate experiences, as they encouraged among visitors the practice of 'shifting.'

The word 'shift,' like the word loiter, was the term used in early modern England to describe a defiant placelessness.[65] Historians have commented on the impressive number of unfixed agents who are depicted in popular pamphlets as peripatetic opportunists.[66] A tactic of the marginal, 'to shift' was a way of making do by improvising and by creatively adapting one's position or attitude. A shift was also the cant or slang term for a young rogue or a petty criminal who relied on artifice to achieve his ends. According to one early modern commentator, 'the undoing of a number of good gentlemen, citizens, tradesmen and such like' was the direct result of a vast 'army' of 'shifters' that had descended upon London.[67] In the period, the verb 'to shift' also meant to change clothes and connoted the use of apparel for strictly theatrical purposes. For instance, players' dressing rooms were referred to as shifts. Shifting also described the act of wasting resources, as one would 'shift' one's time or money.[68]

In acts 4 and 5, Jonson provides an extended dramaturgical riff on the word 'shift' by having various characters enact different valences of the term. The character Shift, for example, who makes his debut in the Paul's Walk scene, successfully exploits every possible occasion to generate a profit as he assumes various disguises to lure in unsuspecting gulls. Described as 'a threadbare shark' whose 'profession is skeldring and odling,' or begging and cheating, with 'his bank Paul's, and his warehouse Pict Hatch,' an area notorious for second-hand clothing brokers and prostitutes, Shift regularly posts bills at the west end of St. Paul's Cathedral composed in the different voices of his various personae.[69] In one ad Shift, under the pseudonym of Signor Whiff (3.1.489), appeals specifically to those 'younger brothers' or 'young gentleman of the first, second, or third head, more or less' who desire to 'entertain the most gentlemanlike use of tobacco' (3.2.138–43). Offering to provide private lessons, which he ensures will take place at an ordinary where 'tobacco and pipes of the best sort shall be ministered' (3.2.152–3), Shift a.k.a. Signor Whiff entices his potential patron with the vaguely erotic promise of his 'sweet attendance' (3.2.154). His invitation elicits an enthusiastic response from one gallant who generously agrees to forgo the services of Signor Whiff and instead 'mark this fellow' for his gallant-in-training to 'use' (3.2.155).

In *Every Man Out*, the communal activity of smoking tobacco becomes an ideal material metaphor for homosocial/erotic bonding among the onstage gallants and the offstage audience. Swift becomes the 'good Pylades' (4.3.234) to his charge Sogliardo, whom he refers to as his loyal 'Orestes,' and he does indeed bring his devoted friend 'to the whiff' (3.1.464). For the remainder of the play, this so-called villainous Ganymede (4.3.82) and his Jove hole up, 'all private,' in a rented room at the Horn's Ordinary, where they are reportedly binging on tobacco, and, by implication, engaging in other sordid activities. Although these two remain out of sight they continue to occupy a central place in the action of the drama. We hear periodic reports, for instance, from the gallants who have set up a peep show, whereby 'some dozen and twenty' of them take turns 'kneeling down and peering through a keyhole ' at the two men (4.3.82).

Swift and Sogliardo, we are told, are engaged in 'the making of the *Petun* [A South American name for tobacco and the moulding of tobacco into fantastic shapes] and the *Receipt Reciprocal* [a form of French inhalation through the nose and mouth at once and the passing of the pipe from one smoker to another],' as well as busily pursuing 'a number of other mysteries, not yet extant [or seen in public]' (4.3.87–9). Specializing in techniques that involve methods of rapid inhalation and sustained exhalation, Shift tutors his trainee in gulping in and gushing forth larger and larger quantities of smoke. Shift, for example, has Sogliardo 'sit in a chair, holding his snout up like a sow under an apple tree, while th' other opens his nostrils with a poking-stick to give the smoke more free delivery' (4.3.90–5). Excelling in the arts of 'the rare corollary and practice of the Cuban Ebullition, Euripus, and Whiff,' whereby one may 'take in here in London and evaporate at Uxbridge, or farther, if it please him' (3.1.145–8), Shift pushes Sogliardo to expand his nasal orifices and lung capacity to absurd proportions. The joint pursuit of enhanced penetrability implies the physical intimacy between these men, a closeness that is augmented by their shared world of smell. As Robert Burton observes, scent is an *intercorporeal* experience, since the act of smelling requires that through 'outward sense,' we draw the external environment into our body via 'fume, vapour, or exhalation.'[70] The popularity of 'taking tobacco' among groups of young men was regarded suspiciously by authorities, such as the vice chancellor of Cambridge who in 1607 issued the complaint

> There is too much practice grown in these latter years amongst scholars of the university (not heard of in former better times) in ... taking tobacco in taverns and shops too commonly and immodestly frequented, to the dishonour of God, great scandal of the university at home and abroad, waste of expence besides hurt of body and mind, and evil example from those that profess learning and sobriety.[71]

Henry Crosse warns that tobacco compromises the integrity of the male body and notes that only those who have refused to be 'dieted with moderation' smoke, and, as a result, become 'unfruitful, fit for nothing ... effeminated, corrupted, and weakened.'[72] In staging groups of men taking vapours, Jonson offers playgoers both a titillating visual and olfactory experience. In yet another breach of the barrier separating the world of the play from that of the audience, the players' tobacco smoke permeates the playhouse and enters the viewers' nasal passages. Offering an embodied metaphor for the experience of Jonson's play itself, which in its inordinate length, frequent of bursts of chaotic activity, and over-packed staging compels audience members to take in more and more, Jonson's smoking gallants palpably demonstrate that their subculture is as potent and varied in its stimulants as the city itself.

Just as Jonson attends to the expenditures of those who shift or waste their time and money on taking tobacco, he also devotes these final scenes to tracking the shifting of people and goods that sustain elaborate relations of credit. The clothes the gallants model throughout the play are the products, after all, not of the industry of cloth-makers, feather-makers, tailors, and seamstresses, for example, but of the 'labour' of pawning. By highlighting the mechanics of this other 'industry,' Jonson continues to tie the theatre, an all-male institution that was itself implicated in a debt economy, to an illicit market that extended beyond the bounds of the playhouse. By including the surrounding outlying liberties in his representation of London, Jonson shines a light on a shadow world whose flexible economic and social topographies frustrated official efforts to fix young male inhabitants in a static grid. Jonson's play thus highlights the cross-pollination between markets in second-hand clothes and the theatre. He shows that those young men who frequented 'extraterritorial zones of production and exchange'[73] were connected not only by the maverick commercial practices in which they engaged but also by their rejection of the social ideals of the established citizenry.[74]

Fungoso engages in his own skilful shifting as he moves fluidly between the worlds of St Paul's Cathedral, the playhouse, the Inns of Court, and the broker's stall, as he sells or pledges his books, such as the 'parcel of law books (some twenty pound's worth)' that he exchanges 'for little more than half the money they cost' (2.1.445–6). He secures the necessary funds to compensate his tailor by manipulating his less-than-well-to-do father into believing that he needs 'five or six pound' to purchase the textbooks of 'Plowden, Dyer, Brooke, and Fitzherbert' required for his legal studies (2.1.449–50). Once he gets the loan, Fungoso does not, however, buy these or any other textbooks, but goes directly to the broker to redeem a suit of clothes he has pledged as security for yet another purchase. After he reclaims this suit, he then promptly sells it off to another broker in order to generate the cash to pay for the even newer suit that his tailor has made for him. Later in the play, when it occurs to Fungoso that his latest outfit will not be an accurate facsimile of Fastidious's unless he is able to accessorize his boots with spurs, he searches for his scholar's gown, the only item that he has left to pawn (2.2.191). When he realizes that he has already pledged his gown, he finds a way to borrow more money so that he can redeem it from 'Fetters Lane,' before going off in search of another broker to whom he may resell it at a higher price (4.2.139). In the final act, Fungoso's compatriots abandon him at the Mitre tavern, and since he is unable to pay the bill, he is forced to offer his ornately attired person as security against the amount due (5.3.297). Reduced to a walking, talking 'pawn for the reckoning' (5.3.356), Fungoso is, however, only temporarily detained in the Counter before he is redeemed by his brother-in-law.

In the unorthodox economy of this play, debt is not a constraint on consumption but rather, in the words of one character, 'more for [one's] credit' (1.2.93) since it serves as yet another example of a clever way of making do or shifting. Debt, Jonson shows, inspires men to adapt to even the most difficult circumstances. Providing an opportunity to transmute the seemingly incontrovertible form of capital, the debtor's bond, into a sign of subcultural capital, ingenuity, these gallants render what would otherwise be a source of shame into a source of pride. To amass debt one character explains to a gallant-in-training is 'an excellent policy,' since one's 'creditor observes you with no less regard than if he were bound to you for some huge benefit and will quake to give you the least cause of offence, lest he lose his money' (1.2.109, 113–15). Here the dangers of dependency that define credit relations off the stage are reversed such that the borrower is guaranteed not degradation but obsequiousness (1.2.117). The character Sogliardo, for instance, who has sacrificed all his assets to become a gentleman (1.2.7–8) discovers that the more he borrows, the more he appears credit-worthy, and that the more he is perceived by strangers as a man of worth, the more he is treated as if he were credit-worthy. When the merchant Deliro discovers that one character, Puntarvolo, has forfeited all his lands and taken out bonds of fifty, one hundred, and two hundred pounds (4.2.53–5) to adorn himself in the accoutrements of a gentleman, the other gallants are not appalled by his elaborate pretence but impressed by the false knight's resourcefulness. Indeed one bystander is moved to exclaim, 'Damn me, I could eat his flesh now: divine sweet villain!' (4.4.88). The admiration generated by performative display founded on the illusion of substance and based on the reality of debt is captured by another character's enthusiastic declaration to one of the shrewdest con artists of the group, 'I love thee above the love of women' (4.4.104). Later he declares his ultimate expression of affection when he resolves to 'bite off' this man's 'nose' (5.4.38). Here eating and biting are not associated with the predatory creditor who practised so-called biting usury, but with the desire of one man to bond with another.[75] Debt, moreover, validates an alternative form of manhood, in which men identify the male body not as a repository of monetary worth but as a receptacle of delicious sweetness.

Even debtor's prison, where all social and economic enterprise defining the networking of urban life would ordinarily be curtailed, becomes another stage on which the gallant can perform exhibitions of resplendence. While the gallants engineer Fungoso's release, Fastidious is not so fortunate. When it comes to light that he has purchased his suits on expired bonds worth twenty, twenty-five, and thirty pounds, he is apprehended (4.1.100). Legal actions are taken against Fastidious, including one for 'three thousand mark' and two others adding up to 'five thousand pound together,' as well as another for one hundred pound and 'six score pounds for a diamond' (5.4.554-60). Incarcerated without any hope of imminent release, Fastidious maintains his elan and decides to make the Counter his new base of operation. As one character confirms, once Fastidious is set up in the 'twopenny ward,' he may occupy a private room, have his own bed, and enjoy the privilege of coming and going as he pleases (provided he pays the turnkey his standard fee).[76] From this urban venue, Fastidious plans to shift by continuing his courtship of a wealthy countess, whom he hopes will inevitably be seduced into financing his release.

As the man who produces a luxurious persona based on non-existent assets, the city gallant is at his most theatrical when he is able to make something out of nothing. His disregard for economic capital is exemplified by the advice given to one of the play's aspiring gallants who is informed of the magical properties of performative display, whereby one may transform otherwise useless land, goods, and cash into fabulous sartorial items. As one character explains, 'First, to be an accomplished gentleman, that is, a gentleman of the time ... 'twere good you turned four or five hundred acres of your best land into two or three trunks of apparel. You may do it without going to a conjurer' (1.2.41–7). The prodigal young man, a popular figure of advice literature, is epitomized off the stage as well practised in the art of dissipation, since for him it is an 'ordinary thing' to put 'a thousand oaks and an hundred oxen into a suit of apparel, [and] to wear a whole manor on his back. What with shoe-ties, hangers, points, caps and feathers, scarfs, bands, cuffs, etc., in a short space [his] whole patrimon[y] [is] consumed.'[77] Advice writer James Cleland similarly describes those young men who, wishing to leave the country for the city, 'put their lands . . . up into a little trunk, and hold it a point of policy to wear their lands upon their backs.'[78] Henry Crosse notes that some young men 'juggle their lands into gay apparel ... clap it up in a small room ... and hold it a point of policy to put their lands into two or three trunks of new clothes,[79] and Joseph Hall describes the gallant as the young man whose 'humour possess[es] him ... [to] wear all his land on his back.'[80]

The fiscal lightness of the gallant is represented in *Every Man Out* as a physiological condition defined by an inability to contain one's bodily fluids. Once again Jonson's play seems to be in conversation with Dekker, who, in *The Guls Horne-booke*, will come to describe the city gallant's body as a liquid entity, one 'overflowing with the corrupt humours of this age's phantasticknesse, or else being burnt up with the inflammation of upstart fashions' (18-19). Similarly, Jonson's Asper characterizes the parading peacocks before him as having porous bodies that cannot maintain their solidity. According to Asper, when one is out of one's 'humour,' or unable to achieve the necessary physiological stasis, one leaves a residue:

> Why, *humour* (as 'tis, *ens*) we thus define it
> To be a quality of air or water,
> And in itself holds these two properties:
> Moisture and fluxure. As for demonstration,
> Pour water on this floor, 'twill wet and run;
> Likewise, the air, forced through a horn or trumpet,
> Flows instantly away, and leaves behind
> A kind of dew; and hence we do conclude
> That whatsoe'er hath fluxure and humidity,
> As wanting power to contain itself,
> Is *humour*. So, in every human body,
> The choler, melancholy, phlegm, and blood,
> By reason that they flow continually
> In some one part and are not continent,
> Receive the name of humours. (Ind. 85–100)

Humours are, as Asper explains, fluids born of the heat and air found in matter that are at once part of the internal atmosphere of the body and the external environment. As the nebulous signs of corporal instability, the body plagued by humours is marked by an unlimited potential for changing form and substance. Not surprisingly, those suffering from humoural incontinence demonstrate an uncanny motility and an impressive talent for shifting.

Conclusion: Sumptuary Operations

The sumptuousness of Jonson's gallants' apparel and the exaggerated way these young men wear their clothes do not serve solely as metaphors for a 'general disposition' (Ind. 102) that is 'not continent' (Ind. 99), or a humoral condition expressed by a 'fluxure' that lacks the 'power to contain itself' (Ind. 94–5). While sartorial luxuriance attributed a general lack of restraint to the wearer, through its characters' exhibitions of humours Jonson's play points to the central role of the theatre in the material production of an urban type constituted by a series of 'sumptuary operations.'[81] At the theatre, the act of consuming is not simply that of procuring those items that would ensure one's inclusion in the city's established communities but also that of *using* objects in such a way that one may bodily transform civic place into subcultural space.

One of the most radical implications of *Every Man Out*'s staging of the city as an enormous theatre is its suggestion that certain young men have come to see themselves as first and foremost star players in an elaborate social drama, one in which their own role takes on disproportionate significance. The impertinence of servants towards their masters and the insolence of court aspirants towards members of the established elite was taking on a new form in an urban milieu. In the city such presumptuousness was no longer representative of a dynamic engendered by a particular social relation but was morphing into a more generalized attitude associated with an entire cohort. The brazen attitude accompanying the gallants' performative mode of dress is explicated by one character who counsels his gallant-in-training to cultivate a carriage that conveys 'an exalted presence' and to always communicate a 'mood' and 'habit' that broadcasts a scornful disposition (3.1.261–4). Fastidious Brisk asserts his own version of this nascent creed as he petulantly asserts:

> They say I am fantastical. Why, true. I know it, and I pursue my humour still in contempt of this censorious age. 'Slight, an a man should do nothing but what a sort of stale judgments about this town will approve in him, he were a sweet ass. I'd beg him, i'faith. I ne'er knew any more find fault with a fashion than they that knew not how to put themselves into 't. For mine own part, so I please mine own appetite, I am careless what the fusty works speaks of me. Puh! (3.1.286–95)

By using flamboyance as an unstable but necessary instrument of social performance, young men like Fastidious demonstrate the myriad means by which to bodily reject the norms of urban conduct as they engage a repertoire of irreverent spatial and sartorial practices that seem to have permeated the world beyond the household and the court. As Jonson shows, even the playhouse could no longer adequately contain the very modes of impertinent display that it had inspired. The theatre found itself forced to keep up with new sartorial attitudes and behaviours spawned among those who used their bodies and the clothes they wore to animate the theatrical potential of an increasingly vital city.

Epilogue: The Twilight of Sumptuousness, the Dawn of Style

In 1674 Samuel Vincent reissued Thomas Dekker's satiric pamphlet *The Guls Horne-booke* as *The Young Gallant's Academy, or, Directions How He Should Behave Himself in All Places and Company*. Preserving Dekker's original chapter headings, Vincent provides an overview of the optimal methods by which the young man may 'proclaim his good clothes' at those places he frequents, notably the ordinary, the tavern, and the playhouse.[1] In his chapter on the playhouse, Vincent faithfully reproduces Dekker's advice on how to make a conspicuous entrance so that one's 'eminence is gotten, by which means the best and most essential parts of a gentleman, as his fine clothes and peruke, are perfectly revealed' (57). Vincent also reiterates Dekker's menu of disruptive behaviours, including laughing, talking out loud, and 'mew[ing] at passionate speeches' (59), all of which promise to draw 'all eyes in the galleries [to] leave walking after the players and only follow you' (58). Vincent makes minor revisions along the way, adding a peruke to the gallant's costume and stationing him in 'the middle of the Pit,' where he pulls out his 'comb and manage[s] his flaxen wig with all the grace he can' (56), but the theatre remains unchallenged as the central arena from which to broadcast one's newest ensemble. While the theatre continued to provide a venue for sartorial display, more than half a century after Dekker's original publication, the disposition of the young man who attended the theatre seems to have changed. In his dedication, Vincent explains his intention to offer an anatomy of 'the behaviour and character of A *Fop*' (4), and here he deviates from his source by appending an original chapter entitled 'The Character of a Proud, Huffing, Self-Conceited, Foppish, and Lascivious Young Gallant' (73).

According to Vincent, the fop is the opposite of the 'true, noble, liberal, and staid gentleman' (87) who is neither 'too precise [nor] too lavish, but keeps a just medium and decorum in everything' (88). The well-respected man, Vincent confides, 'hates a Fop and avoids him as much as a Mariner doeth Scylla and Charibdis' (88). In marked contrast to the 'true, noble gentleman,' who devotes his leisure time to 'hunting, hawking, fowling, ... fishing,' and 'reading history' (95), the fop spends his days showing off his outfits. When on occasion, the 'staid gentleman' does attend the theatre, he watches the play attentively as an anonymous audience member. In sum, Vincent explains, the moderate man has a stellar reputation among all who know him as 'the Sterns-man of his own Destiny' (98). The fop, by contrast, is 'a silly huffing thing,' 'born and shaped for his clothes,' since his 'first care is his dress, the next his body' (73). His insubstantial nature is epitomized by 'his very essence,' which, Vincent emphasizes, is ' plac[ed] on his outside' (76). Even the fop's breath is artificial; he inhales and exhales perfume instead of air (76). Comparing him to a roving mannequin, Vincent describes the fop as 'a kind of walking mercer's shop that shows one stuff today, and another tomorrow' (75). Moreover, the fop 'imagines every place where he comes his theatre,' and walks through the city as an object and not the subject of the gaze. His eyes remain 'most fixed upon his own person' (81) as he ambles down the street. Although 'all his gay-glitter shows on him as if the sun shone in a puddle,' he is, Vincent assures us, an insubstantial 'Huff' (73).

Like his prototype the city gallant, the fop distinguishes himself by his sartorial excess. Described by John Evelyn as 'a fine silken thing,' in 'red, orange, and blue satin,' boasting 'as much ribbon on him as would have plundered six shops and set up twenty country peddlers,' the fop's ensemble stands out because of its sheer scale. Unlike the gallant, however, the fop is not associated with flaunting, the corporal sign of impudence or resistant pride. Rather, he is preoccupied with the relatively harmless activity of preening. The fop is depicted as an empty cipher, regarded by Evelyn as a bundle of gaudy clothes, such that the onlooker cannot distinguish whether there is a man 'clad with this garment' or 'a porter only carrying it.'[2] This 'whimsical empty fellow' is absorbed in 'modes and fashions,' and his primary occupation is 'ogling himself in a glass; primming his figure, and caressing his curls and toupee.'[3] His narcissism, such descriptions suggest, renders him impotent.

Flaunting has explored the attitudes and practices of those young men who were not rendered impotent but were empowered by braving, jetting, and rioting it out in sumptuous clothes, as they expressed their ambivalent position to late Elizabethan and early Jacobean society by simultaneously identifying with and reworking the sartorial codes upon which the dominant culture relied. Those who distinguished themselves by their monstrous manner of dress cultivated effeminacy as the basis of a defiant aesthetic. Here I have parted ways with those who have interpreted the charge of effeminacy levelled against sartorially extravagant young men as a combative rhetorical strategy mobilized by elites aiming to denigrate so-called upstarts.[4] Effeminacy, I have aimed to show, moved among a constellation of offences committed by those who did not seek to pass as or even to emulate their betters. Predominant perceptions of male youths as an unruly collective whose excesses regularly upset established traditions and values led authorities to characterize sumptuously attired young men as unable and unwilling to curb their appetite – for luxurious clothes, unproductive leisure pursuits, and disreputable erotic activity. Thus, the young men I have discussed were regarded as threats to a social order based on an ideology of deference, an economic order founded on principles of productivity, and an erotic order based on reproductive heteroeroticism.

In the late seventeenth century, a new ethics of male embodiment came to define the legitimate Englishman in opposition to the decorative Englishman. It was during this period that flaunting gave way to preening. Unlike those men who had a century earlier rioted it out in luxurious ensembles, the non-elite young men of Vincent's day who were preoccupied with clothes were not perceived as socially disruptive but as socially irrelevant. According to seventeenth-century social commentators such as Evelyn, authority was always expressed by *inconspicuous* display. Evelyn points out that in a society in which 'his majesty shall fix a standard at court,' there is 'no need for sumptuary laws to repress and reform the Lux which men so much condemn in our apparel.' In keeping with his vision of a sober society, Evelyn exhorts all 'great persons of England' to choose 'virile and comely' ensembles and to eschew 'extreme' apparel, arguing that moderate ensembles proclaim the perdurance of social authority.[5]

As Evelyn hoped, the monarch did come to promote sartorial inconspicuousness. Embodying Evelyn's call for a national style that was 'constant,' 'comely,' and 'of use' Charles II introduced the vest in 1666.[6] The vest, according to fashion historians, ushered in not simply a new wardrobe item for men but also a radically revised the relation between the male body and standards of display. For this reason, Charles II is credited with initiating the 'great masculine renunciation.'[7] Indeed, the king's demonstration of masculine authority as grounded in corporal expressions of sobriety overturned the long-standing association between sumptuousness and elite male status. The vest communicated the republican virtue of manly simplicity, and the plainness of elite couture stood in direct contrast to the subservient, effeminate 'tyranny' of fashion associated with the decadent court culture of Charles's predecessors.[8] As a symbol of the new regime, the vest promoted a vision of legitimate manhood as graceful, virile, and useful:

> Graceful, because [this] new social identity was formed around a practice of refined simplicity rather than sartorial splendor; virile, because they [members of the court] were about to deflect criticism of being effeminate fops; and useful, because they were wearing garments which were 'advantageous to the drapers of the kingdom.'[9]

Evolving notions of the relation between manly virtue and responsible expenditure also spawned a revolution in manners. Non-elite men were encouraged to emulate the new sober aesthetic promoted by members of the court.[10] Moreover, many who were in sympathy with the Puritan agenda willingly embraced a sartorial mode that bespoke 'the modest, civill, and commendable custome of ... [the] Nation.'[11]

While the image of the sober statesmen prevails to this day, modern scholars who have heralded the unqualified success of 'the great masculine renunciation' may be unwittingly contributing to its ideological mystification. Despite the success of this shift in style, certain men, through widely variant modes of embodiment, continued to appropriate and to revise the terms of male display. The fissures within the great masculine renunciation can be detected in the cultural work performed by the theatre. Stephen Greenblatt and Katherine Eisaman Maus have attributed the shift from boy actors to female actresses on the early modern English stage to changing ideas about the incommensurability of the sexes.[12] Over the course of the seventeenth century, the Galenic model of male and female anatomical homology that held sway for much of the sixteenth century was becoming displaced by new theories of physiological distinction.[13] Discoveries in the nascent fields of biology and medicine reinforced burgeoning social ideas about gender disparity. Yet the influence of emerging ideas about the absolute difference between men and women does not explain why a culture that had traditionally perceived boys as antithetical to adult men, and which had identified effeminacy as a quality endemic to *all* youths, came to regard effeminacy as the distinct quality of *some* men.

The appearance of the actress on the English stage coincided not only with new theories of gender difference but also with burgeoning prejudices towards those with class privilege. The links between shifts in perceptions of the gendered body and changes in the ideas about the classed body have still to be explored. For instance, how did new attitudes towards the elite influence the late-seventeenth theatre's representations of men as avid participants in a burgeoning commercial society? The plays staged in this period reveal a preoccupation with the effects of consumer appetite on the male body, an entity that is portrayed, despite the new gender essentialism, as capable of evincing an impressive range of feminine attributes. The Restoration theatre offered audiences a steady parade of sartorially excessive male figures distinguished by their pretensions to aristocratic sensibility, which disqualified them from participation in masculine civic culture. Objects of farce, such as the decorative beau, coxcomb, fribble, macaroni, jessamy, pretty fellow, and the exquisite eventually all became subsumed into the figure of the preening fop.[14]

Through its elaboration of the fop, the Restoration theatre intervened into an evolving discourse about the male body and improper modes of display.[15] In 1676 George Etherege's Sir Fopling Flutter made his debut in the *Man of Mode*, in which he appeared in a 'very fine dress of tasseled pantaloons, tight coat, and heavily fringed gloves scented with orange water,' with 'shoes from Piccar' and 'periwig from Chedreux.' In addition to sporting an international ensemble, Sir Fopling Flutter brags of having studied dance with a private master in France and kisses his male acquaintances upon greeting.[16] A 'Silly *Gloworme*' 'tricked up in *Gauderies*,' like Samuel Butler's 'modish man' who will not be seen 'varying in the least article of his life, conversation, apparel, and address from the doctrine and discipline of the newest and best reformed modes of the time,' the fop is represented on the English stage as self-promoting, conspicuous, and feminine.[17] His loss of manly status is directly connected to his obsessive attention to the sartorial, which is further confirmed by other putatively non-masculine behaviours, such as his avoidance of traditionally male recreations and locales, his excessive socializing with women, his conspicuous consumption of delicacies imported from Italy, and his cultivation of French manners.[18]

As scholars have emphasized, foppery was not merely a theatrical convenience but 'a real social phenomena' that represented an alternative mode of male behaviour off as well as on the Restoration stage.[19] Historian Michael Kimmel understands the fop as a response to an economic climate marked by the heightened visibility of women. The fop, Kimmel argues, was born of a culture-wide 'crisis of masculinity' engendered by a series of economic downturns that altered the organization of the English family and delimited occupational opportunities for middle-rank men.[20] These circumstances resulted in a backlash against real and perceived increased instances of female participation in public life. Philip Carter interprets the emergence of the fop differently and sees the significance of this figure in largely symbolic terms. The fop, for Carter, is the symptom of a society confused by ambivalent ideals of culturally legitimate expressions of public manhood. In an age in which social and political standing were attached to the correct balance between polite sociability and manly virtue, the fop, Carter argues, 'provided information on the distinction between men of admirable refinement and those guilty of ceremony, affectation, and excessive polish.'[21] Serving a corrective function, the fop inexorably stood as the negative exemplar of luxury and superficiality.

Randolph Trumbach, who concurs that the fop was more than a theatrical invention, emphasizes neither the material underpinnings nor the symbolic valence of this figure. Trumbach identifies the fop as a positive figure insofar as he served to link the early seventeenth-century extravagant man and the sodomite molly, who was also singled out for his conspicuous display and who, in the later half of the eighteenth century, was associated with gender dissonance and homoerotic activity.[22] While sodomy had been condemned as an evil indulged in by a variety of men, it gradually came to be regarded as the sign of a particular sort of man, who, as a result, was disqualified from assuming a public role in civic culture. In the post-Restoration era members of the Societies for the Reformation of Manners devoted an inordinate amount of regulatory energy to persecuting effeminate mollies.[23] According to Ned Ward, a promoter for the societies, mollies could be identified by their display of 'all the little vanities that custom has reconciled to the female sex, affecting to speak, walk, tattle, curtsy, cry, scold, and to mimic all manner of effeminacy.'[24] Alan Bray offers a crucial corrective to the historical narrative that attributes the steady increase in the prosecution of mollies to heightened fears of same-sex erotic practice. He suggests that what troubled authorities in the period was not homosexual activity per se but the birth of a viable, visually apparent, distinct subculture 'expressed and therefore recognized' by its outsiders and its own members alike through its members' 'clothes, gestures, language, particular buildings, and particular public places – all of which could be identified as having specifically homosexual connotations.'[25]

The end of the regulation of clothing in early seventeenth-century England may have marked the twilight of the specific oppositional subculture of style that I have been examining, but it also heralded the dawn of an unprecedented number of subcultural groups whose members forged community through their identification with alternative forms of masculinity. Between the late seventeenth and early eighteenth centuries, the population of London more than doubled from 200,000 in 1600 to well over 500,000 in 1700. Concomitantly, new forms of global exchange, commodity production, and consumption practices enabled new modes of expression by which ambivalently positioned men could articulate their social disaffection and sexual dissidence.[26] Importantly, London itself was evolving into a series of neighbourhoods, each with its own distinctive subcommunities, which afforded young men various opportunities to form connections beyond the leisure sites of the previous generation like taverns, ordinaries, St Paul's, and even the playhouses.[27] Sartorial exhibitionism was increasingly on display at London's coffeehouses, parks, promenades, and pleasure gardens.[28] Emergent figures like the molly indicated that men who chose to distinguish themselves by their sartorial excesses could exploit their culture's denigration of aristocratic sumptuousness by translating class defiance into gender transgression. Masculine modes that favoured exaggeration, performativity, and artifice continued into the late nineteenth century, as the dandy appeared on the scene to proclaim sincerity to be 'simple philistinism.'[29] The merging of sartorial flamboyance and theatricality in the persona of Oscar Wilde indexes another crucial moment at which an alternative masculinity was formed out of the reinscription of aristocratic style as gender dissonance.

While the stakes of oppositional dressing have changed and continue to change, the fraught relationship between social order and corporal deference endures. As those who occupy positions of authority continue to rely upon conventions of display and rules of bodily demeanour to proclaim their privilege, as well as upon the deference of others, those seeking to challenge authority will continue to look to their bodies and the clothes they wear as the means by which to mock and alter established codes of conduct. Particular kinds of collective experiences and shared tastes still enable certain people to form solidarities, affording even those who are in relatively weak positions the opportunity to claim some degree of autonomy through the manipulation of the signs of the dominant culture. In any social hierarchy in which agreed-upon roles need to be performed in accordance with expectations of proper behaviour, seemingly minor acts of bodily resistance can be – and often are – extremely disruptive. The final sentences of this book must therefore not only conjure the fop, the dandy, and Oscar Wilde but also subcommunities of young men, like the Zooties, the Hippies, and the Punks. These young men, like the flaunting apprentice, the braving servant, and the rioting gallant, reinscribed their societies' prevalent assumptions about the proper expression of position and place and desire and deference by using their bodies and the clothes they wore to transform marginality into insurgency.

Notes

1. 'Style is the man': Defiant Aesthetics and the Culture of Male Youth

1 The phrase '*stylus virum arguit*' first appears in the 1624 (the second) edition of Robert Burton's *Anatomy of Melancholy*; *Oxford English Dictionary* s.v. 'style.' George Chapman, Ben Jonson, and John Marston, *Eastward Ho*, 1.1.26–9; 1.1.123. I have modernized the spelling and punctuation where I have used early printed sources.

2 Up until the eighteenth century, all London apprentices were sworn in under an Oath of Indenture; see Margaret Gay Davies, *The Enforcement of English Apprenticeship, 1563–1642* (Cambridge: Cambridge University Press, 1956).

3 Dick Hebdige, 'Posing ... Threats, Striking ... Poses: Youth, Surveillance, and Display,' in Gelder and Thornton, *The Subcultures Reader*, 404.

4 Earle, *Microcosmography*, 70.

5 *Oxford English Dictionary*, s.v. 'style.'

6 Ben Jonson, *Timber: Or, Discoveries*, in *Ben Jonson: The Complete Works*, 8:615.

7 Thomas Middleton and Thomas Dekker, *The Roaring Girl*, in Bevington et al., *English Renaissance Drama*, Epistle, lines 1–2.

8 Ibid., lines 2–11.

9 Dekker, *The Guls Horne-booke*, 34; *Oxford English Dictionary*, s.v. 'publish.'

10 Books, like playtexts, were dressed in decorative frontispieces to encourage sales. See Paul J. Voss, 'Books for Sale: Advertising and Patronage in Late Elizabethan England,' *Sixteenth Century Journal* 29 (1998): 733–56. On the sumptuary politics of bookbinding and the use of books as clothing accessories, see Helen Smith, '"This one poore black gowne lined with

white": The Clothing of the Sixteenth-Century English Book,' in Richardson, *Clothing Culture*, 195–209.

11 Ann Rosalind Jones and Peter Stallybrass, 'Fetishisms and Renaissances,' in Carla Mazzio and Douglas Trevor, eds., *Historicism, Psychoanalysis, and Early Modern Culture* (New York: Routledge, 2002), 20–36. See also Margreta de Grazia, Maureen Quilligan, and Peter Stallybrass, Introduction, in Margreta de Grazia et al., eds, *Subject and Object in Renaissance Culture*, 1–17.

12 In particular, Patricia Fumerton, *Cultural Aesthetics: Renaissance Literature and the Practice of Social Ornament* (Chicago: University of Chicago Press, 1991); Lisa Jardine, *Worldly Goods: A New History of the Renaissance* (New York: Doubleday, 1996); Patricia Fumerton and Simon Hunt, eds., *Renaissance Culture and the Everyday* (Philadelphia: University of Pennsylvania Press, 1999); Jones and Stallybrass, *Subject and Object in Renaissance Culture*; and Korda, *Shakespeare's Domestic Economies*.

13 *Oxford English Dictionary*, s.v. 'fashion'; s.v. 'art.'

14 Roland Barthes characterizes style as the 'aberrant message' that 'surprises the code' and as a 'citational process,' in 'Style and Its Image,' in *The Rustle of Language*, trans. Richard Howard (New York: Hill and Wang, 1986), 94. See also Georg Simmel, 'The Problem of Style,' *Theory, Culture, and Society* 8 (1991): 66–7.

15 Fashion Studies classics include Thorstein Veblen, *The Theory of the Leisure Class: An Economic Study in the Evolution of Institutions* (New York: Macmillan, 1899); Georg Simmel, 'Fashion,' *International Quarterly* 10 (1904); repr., *American Journal of Sociology* 62 (May 1957): 541–58; Flugel, *The Psychology of Clothes*; Roland Barthes, *The Fashion System*, trans. Matthew Ward and Richard Howard (1967; repr., New York: Hill and Wang, 1983); Guy Debord, *Society of Spectacle* (1967; repr., Detroit: Black and Red, 1983); and Renée König, *The Restless Image: A Sociology of Fashion*, trans. F. Bradley (London: George Allen and Unwin, 1973). More recent scholarship in this area tends to emphasize dress as a socially situated practice: see Richardson, *Clothing Culture*; Joanne Entwistle and Elizabeth Wilson, *Body Dressing* (Oxford: Berg, 2002); Stella Bruzzi and Pamela Church Gibson, eds., *Fashion Cultures: Theories, Explorations, and Analysis* (London: Routledge, 2000); and Joanne Entwistle, *The Fashioned Body: Fashion, Dress, and Modern Social Theory* (London: Polity, 2000).

16 By the mid-sixteenth century, cloth made up 86 per cent of England's export market. See J.L. Bolton, *The Medieval English Economy, 1150–1500* (London: Dent; Totowa, NJ: Rowman and Littlefield, 1980), 195. See also Robert Brenner, *Merchants and Revolution: Commercial Change, Political Con-*

flict, and London's Overseas Traders, 1550–1653 (Princeton: Princeton University Press, 1993); and C.G.A. Clay, *Economic Expansion and Social Change: England 1500–1700*, 2 vols. (Cambridge: Cambridge University Press, 1984).

17 This phrase was coined by Roland Barthes in *The Fashion System*. On the shift from the situated phenomenon of the marketplace to the placeless market process, see Agnew, *Worlds Apart*; and Bruster, *Drama and the Market in the Age of Shakespeare*. For recent studies that revise the notion of the placeless market, see Natasha Korda, 'Labors Lost: Women's Work and Early Modern Theatrical Commerce,' in Peter Holland and Stephen Orgel, eds., *From Script to Stage in Early Modern England* (New York: Palgrave, 2004), 195–8; and Jonathan Gil Harris, *Sick Economies: Drama, Mercantilism, and Disease in Shakespeare's England* (Philadelphia: University of Pennsylvania Press, 2004). My own thinking on early modern markets has also been influenced by Boulton, *Neighbourhood and Society*; Muldrew, *The Economy of Obligation*; and Ceri Sullivan, *The Rhetoric of Credit: Merchants in Early Modern Writing* (London: Associated Press, 2002).

18 Edward Misselden, *The Circle of Commerce* (London, 1623), as quoted in Muldrew, 141; Thomas Mun, *A Discourse of Trade* (London, 1621), as quoted in Kuchta, *The Three-Piece Suit*, 12.

19 For a discussion of fashion trends in the early modern period, see Fernand Braudel, *Capitalism and Material Life: 1400–1800* trans. Miriam Kochan (New York: Harper and Row, 1973); Joan Thirsk, 'The Fantastical Folly of Fashion: The English Stocking Knitting Industry, 1500–1700,' in N.B. Harte and K.G. Ponting, eds., *Textile History and Economic History* (Manchester: Manchester University Press, 1973), 50–73; N. McKendrick et al., eds., *The Birth of a Consumer Society: The Commercialization of Eighteenth-Century England* (Bloomington: University of Indiana Press, 1982); Chandra Mukerji, *Graven Images: Patterns of Modern Materialism* (New York: Columbia University Press, 1983); John Brewer and Roy Porter, eds., *Consumption and the World of Goods* (London: Routledge, 1993); and Lisa Jardine, *Worldly Goods*.

20 This approach is epitomized by Alison Lurie, *The Language of Clothes* (New York: Random House, 1981); Grant MacCracken, 'Clothing as Language: An Object Lesson in the Study of the Expressive Properties of Material Culture,' in Barrie Reynolds and Margaret A. Stott, eds., *Material Anthropology: Approaches to Material Culture* (Lanham, MD: University Press of America, 1987), 103–33; M. Barnard, *Fashion as Communication* (London: Routledge, 1996); Patrizia Calefato, 'Dress, Language, and Communication,' in Patrizia Calefato, *The Clothed Body*, trans. Lisa Adams (Oxford: Berg, 2004), 5–15; and Barthes, *The Fashion System*. This

assumption also underwrites analyses of clothes in early modern culture in Marjorie Garber, *Vested Interests: Cross-Dressing and Cultural Anxiety* (London: Routledge, 1992) and Whigham, *Ambition and Privilege.*

21 Stephens, *Satirical Essays, Characters, and Others*, book 2, character 4, 'A Common Player.'

22 Hughes and Larkin, *Tudor Royal Proclamations*, 2:187.

23 Manley, *Literature and Culture*, 372–409.

24 G.R. Elton describes sumptuary laws as 'very peculiar' and 'quirky,' in *The Parliament of England, 1559–1581* (Cambridge: Cambridge University Press, 1986), 273. N.B. Harte refers to this body of law as 'one of the most curious of all episodes in the history of social organization,' in 'State Control of Dress,' 133.

25 The social emulation theory may be credited to Veblen, *The Theory of the Leisure Class*, and Simmel, 'Fashion.' For an extended application of the emulation thesis, see Garber, *Vested Interests*, 21–36; Kuchta, *The Three-Piece Suit*, 17–51; and Whigham, *Ambition and Privilege.*

26 Anna Bryson discusses the importance of young men's sartorial management in the period's courtesy literature in *From Courtesy to Civility.*

27 Hughes and Larkin, *Tudor Royal Proclamations*, 2:462, emphasis mine.

28 A.L. Beier and Roger Finlay, 'The Significance of the Metropolis,' in Beier and Finlay, *London 1500–1700*, 11–15. E.A. Wrigley and R.S. Schofield also demonstrate that in the period between 1576 and 1621 there was a noticeable increase in the number of young men in London, *The Population History of England and Wales, 1541–1871: A Reconstruction* (Cambridge: Cambridge University Press, 1981), 215–19, 443–50. John Gillis refers to second, third, and fourth sons as the 'superfluous' or 'surplus' children of the elite. He notes that in periods of population growth, such as between 1550 and 1630 (when the population of England doubled), younger sons suffered the most since demographic pressures resulted in stricter settlements on inheritance and greater competition for limited resources. See his *Youth and History*, 21.

29 Dekker, *The Guls Horne-booke*, 8, 11; Dekker, *Work for Armorours, or, The Peace is Broken* (London, 1609), in *The Non-Dramatic Works of Thomas Dekker*, 4:119.

30 Dekker, *Work for Armorours*, 4:120.

31 Earle, *Microcosmography*, 70.

32 My investigation of early modern English youth has been informed by the findings of Keith Thomas, 'Age and Authority in Early Modern England,' *Proceedings of the British Academy* 62 (1976): 1–46; Gillis, *Youth and History*; Ben-Amos, *Adolescence and Youth in Early Modern England*;

Fletcher, *Gender, Sex and Subordination in England*; Griffiths et al., *The Experience of Authority in Early Modern England*; and Braddick and Walter, *Negotiating Power in Early Modern Society*.

33 Griffiths, *Youth and Authority*, 6. See also Peter Rushton, '"The Matter in Variance": Adolescents and Domestic Conflict in Northeast England, 1600–1800,' *Journal of Social History* 25.1 (1991): 89–107.

34 As in Griffiths, *Youth and Authority*, 76. See also S.T. Bindoff, 'The Making of the Statute of Artificers,' in S.T. Bindoff et al., eds., *Elizabethan Government and Society* (Oxford: Oxford University Press, 1961), 86–94.

35 Griffiths, *Youth and Authority*, 76.

36 Earle, *Microcosmography*, 3.

37 Cited in Griffiths, *Youth and Authority*, 34.

38 Hughes and Larkin, *Tudor Royal Proclamations*, 2:191.

39 See McIntosh, *Controlling Misbehavior in England*, 110.

40 Michael Mitterauer asserts that in the early modern period, the 'leisure activities of young people' were 'completely under the control of the householder,' cited in Griffiths, *Youth and Authority*, 114. Ilana Krausman Ben-Amos argues that the transient nature of youths' lives in early modern England undermined the formation of youth subcultures; see *Adolescence and Youth*, 20. Barbara Hanawalt makes a similar claim in her *Growing up in Medieval London: The Experience of Childhood in History* (New York: Columbia University Press, 1993), 137.

41 Griffiths, *Youth and Authority*, 174.

42 *The English Courtier and the Country Gentleman*, 15.

43 A.L. Beier and Roger Finlay, Introduction, in Beier and Finlay, *The Making of the Metropolis*, 21. See also S.R. Smith, 'The London Apprentices as Seventeenth-Century Adolescents,' *Past and Present* 61 (1973): 155–6, and A.L. Beier, 'Social Problems in Elizabethan London,' *Journal of Interdisciplinary History* 9 (1978): 204–5. On early modern youth culture as part of popular culture, see R.W. Malcolmson, *Popular Recreations in English Society, 1700–1859* (Cambridge: Cambridge University Press, 1973) and Bernard Capp, 'English Youth Groups and *The Pinder of Wakefield*,' *Past and Present* 76 (August 1977): 127–33.

44 I am using the term 'subculture' as defined by the founding members of the Birmingham Centre for Contemporary Cultural Studies. In 1964, members of CCCS wrested the concept of subculture away from the field of criminology and the study of juvenile delinquency and initiated investigations into the ways in which members of a given society could demonstrate resistance to dominant values and expectations through acts of cultural appropriation. The analyses of CCCS members were strongly

influenced by the then-current work of British Marxists such as Raymond Williams, E.P. Thompson, and Richard Hoggart, as well as by the scholarship of continental theorists like Louis Althusser, Antonio Gramsci, and Roland Barthes. For a representative sampling of this work, see Hebdige, *Subculture and the Meaning of Style*; Hall and Jefferson, *Resistance Through Rituals*; and Angela McRobbie, ed., *Zoot Suits and Second-Hand Dresses: An Anthology of Fashion and Music* (London: Macmillan, 1989). For a critique of the CCCS and the concept of subculture, see Gary Clarke, 'Defending Ski-Jumpers: A Critique of Theories of Youth Subcultures,' in Simon Firth and Andrew Goodwin, eds., *On Record* (1981; repr., London: Routledge: 1990); and J.S. Epstein, ed., *Youth Culture: Identity in a Postmodern World* (Oxford: Blackwell, 1998).

45 Hall and Jefferson, *Resistance through Rituals*, 15.

46 For classic studies of youth subculture, see Howard S. Becker, *Outsiders: Studies in the Sociology of Deviance* (1963; repr., New York: Free Press, 1973); John Clarke and Tony Jefferson, 'Working Class Youth Cultures,' in Geoff Mungham and Geoff Pearson, eds., *Working Class Youth Culture* (London: Routledge, 1976), 138–59; Michael Brake, *The Sociology of Youth Culture and Youth Subcultures* (London: Routledge, 1980); and Vered Amit-Talai and Helena Wulff, *Youth Cultures: A Cross-Cultural Perspective* (London: Routledge, 1995).

47 Sinfield, *Faultlines*, 37.

48 Shepard, *Meanings of Manhood*, 1.

49 Those who have begun to explore the history of masculine identity formation and the historicity of maleness include Harry Brod, *The Making of Masculinities: The New Men's Studies* (London: Unwin Hyman, 1987); Jeff Hearn and David Morgan, eds., *Men, Masculinities, and Social Theory* (London: Unwin Hyman, 1990); Josh Tosh, 'What Should Historians Do with Masculinity? Reflections on Nineteenth-Century Britain,' *History Workshop Journal* 38 (1994): 179–202. On manhood in early modern England see Hitchcock and Cohen, *English Masculinities*; Elizabeth Foyster, *Manhood in Early Modern England: Honor, Sex, and Marriage* (New York: Longman, 1999); Kuchta, *The Three-Piece Suit*; Shepard, *Meanings of Manhood*; King, *The Gendering of Men*; and Bruce Smith, *Shakespeare and Masculinity*.

50 Shepard, *Meanings of Manhood*, 2.

51 Common Council Act of 1582, as in Griffiths, *Youth and Authority*, 225.

52 Alan Bray and Michel Rey, 'The Body of the Friend: Continuity and Change in Masculine Friendship in the Seventeenth Century,' in Hitchcock and Cohen, *English Masculinities*, 73.

53 Hitchcock and Cohen, Introduction to *English Masculinities*, 10.

54 See Margaret Hunt, 'Afterword,' in Goldberg, *Queering the Renaissance*, 359–79. According to Alan Bray, a distinctive male homosexual identity and concomitant subculture first distinguished itself in the late seventeenth century (*Homosexuality in Renaissance England*). Randolph Trumbach has argued that the figure of the effeminate molly was spawned by an all-male homosexual subculture that emerged in the eighteenth century. See Randolph Trumbach, 'London's Sodomites: Homosexual Behavior and Western Culture in the Eighteenth Century,' *Journal of Social History* 1 (1977): 1–33; 'Sodomitical Subcultures, Sodomitical Roles, and the Gender Revolution of the Eighteenth Century: The Recent Historiography'; and 'Gender and the Homosexual Role in Modern Western Culture: The 18th and the 19th Centuries Compared,' in Dennis Altman et al., eds., *Homosexuality, Which Homosexuality: Essays from the International Scientific Conference on Lesbian and Gay Studies* (London: Gay Men's Press, 1988), 149–69. See also Rictor Norton, *Mother Clap's Molly House: The Gay Subculture in England, 1700–1830* (London: Gay Men's Press, 1992). For a discussion of sexuality and subculture, see E. Ross and R. Rapp, 'Sex and Society: A Research Note from Social History and Anthropology,' *CSSH* 1 (1981): 51–72; Gregory A. Sprague, 'Male Homosexuality in Western Culture: The Dilemma of Identity and Subculture in Historical Research,' *Journal of Homosexuality* 10.3/4 (1984): 29–43; and Sinfield, *Faultlines*, 37, 290–9.

55 Notably, Digangi's *The Homoerotics of Early Modern Drama*.

56 See Jeffrey Masten, *Textual Intercourse: Collaboration, Authorship, and Sexualities in Renaissance Drama* (Cambridge: Cambridge University Press, 1997); Alan Stewart, *Close Readers: Humanism and Sodomy in Early Modern England* (Princeton: Princeton University Press, 1997); Mary Bly, *Queer Virgins and Virgin Queans on the Early Modern Stage* (Oxford: Oxford University Press, 2000); and Stephen Guy-Bray, *Homoerotic Space: The Poetics of Loss in Renaissance Literature* (Toronto: University of Toronto Press, 2002).

57 On the 'stylization' of sexual conduct, see Michel Foucault, *The Use of Pleasure*, volume 2 of *The History of Sexuality*, trans. Robert Hurley (1984; repr., New York: Vintage Books, 1990), 187–246; and *The Care of the Self*, volume 3 of *The History of Sexuality*, trans. Robert Hurley (1984; repr., New York: Vintage Books, 1988), 39–68, 124–32, 189–210. See also Halperin, *How to Do the History of Homosexuality*; and David Halperin, 'Forgetting Foucault: Acts, Identities, and the History of Sexuality,' *Representations* 63 (1998): 93–120.

58 Foucault, *The Use of Pleasure*, 92.

59 Bourdieu, *Distinction*, 173.

60 Jones and Stallybrass, *Renaissance Clothing*, 179.
61 Lenton, *The Young Gallants Whirligigg*, C4v.
62 Court Records of the Merchant Taylors Guild for 1592, as in Chambers, *The Elizabethan Stage*, 4:309.
63 Ben Jonson, Dedicatory Epistle in *The New Inn*, ed. Michael Hattaway (Manchester: Manchester University Press, 1984), 8–10.
64 *Office of Christian Parents*, as in Shepard, *Meanings of Manhood*, 24. On youth and the early modern theatre, see Charles Whitney, 'Out of Service and In the Playhouse: Richard Norwood, Youth in Transition, and Early Response to *Dr. Faustus*,' *Medieval and Renaissance Drama in England* 12 (1999): 166–89; and Charles Whitney, '"Usually in the werking Daies."' 433–58.
65 Archives of the Merchant Taylors Company, 1574, as in Chambers, *The Elizabethan Stage*, 2:75.
66 Here I part ways from several studies from which I have benefited greatly, such as Leggatt, *Citizen Comedy in the Age of Shakespeare*; Leinwand, *The City Staged*; and Twyning, *London Dispossessed*.
67 Jonson, *Every Man Out of His Humour*, ed. Ostovich 4.5.127.

2. Monstrous Manner: Clothing Law and the Early Modern Theatre

1 Dekker, *The Guls Horne-booke*, 26.
2 Gosson, *Plays Confuted in Five Actions*, 197.
3 Stephen Gosson, *The School of Abuse*, 39.
4 The provision that the owner of the Rose Theatre, Philip Henslowe, included in his players' contracts prohibiting them from leaving the playhouse in their costumes suggests that it was not uncommon for actors to wear the clothes provided to them as costumes off the stage. Jones and Stallybrass cite the Article of Agreement drawn up between Philip Henslowe and actor Robert Dawes, in which Dawes is prohibited from leaving the theatre with 'any [of the company's] apparel on his body' on the forfeiture of 'forty pounds.' See Jones and Stallybrass, *Renaissance Clothing*, 195. E.K. Chambers also discusses the agreement actors signed pledging not to leave the playhouse in clothes that they had worn on stage, in *The Elizabethan Stage*, 1:348.
5 *Oxford English Dictionary*, s.v. 'jet.'
6 Ibid.
7 Burton, *The Anatomy of Melancholy*, The Third Partition, 98.
8 Guilpin, *Skialetheia*, Epigram 38, 'To Licus,' 49.
9 Hughes and Larkin, *Tudor Royal Proclamations*, 2:193.
10 Ibid.

11 Ibid., 2:381.
12 Gillis, *Youth and History*, 21.
13 Seaver, 'Declining Status in an Aspiring Age,' 146.
14 Griffiths, *Youth and Authority*, 355.
15 Hughes and Larkin, *Tudor Royal Proclamations*, 3:4 and 3:3.
16 Fabio Cleto, 'Introduction: Queering the Camp,' in Cleto, *Camp*, 25.
17 City Corporation Records, *Reportorium* (London, 1565), as in Hooper, 'The Tudor Sumptuary Laws,' 441.
18 Hughes and Larkin, *Tudor Royal Proclamations*, 2:189–90.
19 Ibid.
20 Vaughan, *The Golden-Grove*, Book I, G4.
21 Ibid., G5.
22 As in Shepard, *Meanings of Manhood*, 29. In 1617 William Jones, in his *A Wonder Worth the Reading*, claimed that a pregnant woman who wore great ruffs gave birth to a monstrous progeny with 'a piece of flesh of two fingers thick round about, the flesh being wonderfully curled like a Gentlewoman's attire'; see Susan Vincent, *Dressing the Elite: Clothes in Early Modern England* (Oxford: Berg, 2003), 129–30.
23 *Oxford English Dictionary*, s.v. 'monstrous.'
24 John Lyly writes of a man who is 'so monstrous to love a bull,' *Euphues, or, The Anatomy of Wit* (London, 1579), as in *OED*. The epistemological and connotative connections between the monstrous and the obscene are explored by Patricia Parker in 'Fantasies of "Race" and "Gender": Africa, *Othello* and Bringing to Light,' in Margo Hendricks and Patricia Parker, eds., *Women, 'Race,' and Writing in the Early Modern Period* (New York: Routledge, 1994), 84–100.
25 Laws regulating subjects' consumption of food and purchase of imported items had been an integral part of England's legal corpus since 1336. The first statute devoted solely to the regulation of apparel was enacted in 1463. This Act of Apparel argued that the 'excessive and inordinate arrays' worn by subjects had excited 'the great displeasure of God,' but the bill was ultimately ratified on the grounds that the state had a responsibility to abate the enriching of 'strange realms and countries' (*Rot. Parl.*, vol. 5 [n. d.], as in Baldwin, *Sumptuary Legislation*, 101). Throughout the fifteenth and into the first half of the sixteenth centuries, Parliament sporadically passed apparel laws, but Elizabeth was the first and last monarch to consistently bypass Parliament and promulgate proclamations that focused exclusively on dress. On English clothing laws, see Humphrey Dyson, *A Booke Contayning All Such Proclamations as Were Published During the Reign of the Late Queen Elizabeth* (London, 1618);

Evelyn, *Tyrannus*; Hooper, 'The Tudor Sumptuary Laws'; Baldwin, *Sumptuary Legislation*; Sylvia Miller, 'Old English Laws Regulating Dress,' *Journal of Home Economics* 20 (1928): 89–94; Harte, 'State Control of Dress and Social Change'; Frederic Youngs, *The Proclamations of the Tudor Queens* (Cambridge: Cambridge University Press, 1976). For an overview of sumptuary legislation throughout the world, see Hunt, *Governance of the Consuming Passions*.

26 Only three of the twelve clothing proclamations Elizabeth issued include an *abbreviat* or schedule for women's apparel. There is no mention made of female attire in any of the proclamations' formulaic preambles. Moreover, the law makes no reference to cross-gender dressing. Elizabethan clothing proclamations were as limited in respect to implementation as they were in scope. Royal proclamations could only confirm the provisions of preexisting statutes, and they could not violate a ratified law or override the precepts of common law or the custom of the realm. While Elizabeth's decrees include a list of penalties for infractions, enforcement measures, and exempted persons, as proclamatory edicts they could only prescribe fines and short-term incarceration as penalties. As such, these edicts were considered innovative legislative responses to immediate problems and were expected to have a prescribed duration; typically, all the monarch's proclamations died with him or her. While several apparel bills were introduced into Parliament during Elizabeth's reign, none were passed.

27 In the reign of Henry VIII, Parliament ratified four and repealed one statute regulating apparel. Henry VIII issued only three proclamations regulating dress in his thirty-eight years of rule. During the brief reign of Philip and Mary, Parliament ratified one Act of Apparel.

28 On 'Committees for Excesses of Apparel,' see Griffiths, *Youth and Authority*, 227. On dispatch assistance in London, see Hooper, 'The Tudor Sumptuary Laws,' 441.

29 Hughes and Larkin, *Tudor Royal Proclamations*, 2:136 and 2:187.

30 Ibid, 2:137–8 and 2:281.

31 Baldwin, in *Sumptuary Legislation*, regards the preservation of visible rank distinctions and the check on personal extravagance as the primary goals of early modern English clothing legislation. N.B. Harte, following suit, argues that the explanation for this legislation 'has to be sought in the interaction of the social thought of the time and changes in the levels of income' ('State Control of Dress,' 138). He stresses that the traditional social order was threatened by the expansion of the number of stations available within the established hierarchy and the increase in the number

of opportunities for mobility between various strata. More recently, David Kuchta has also interpreted these laws as aiming to curtail illegitimate forms of social emulation in his *The Three-Piece Suit*, 34.

32 Jonathan Barry, Introduction, in Barry and Brooks, *The Middling Sort of People*, 13.

33 Analysing the various social trajectories offered by status, income, and power, Lawrence Stone demonstrates that a new generation benefited from opportunities in trade, law, and government, as well as from the inflation of honours that enabled greater numbers of people to purchase titles; see 'Social Mobility in England.' See also Alan Everitt, 'Social Mobility in Early Modern England,' *Past and Present* 33 (1966): 70–2.

34 Bourdieu, *Distinction*, 165.

35 'Sort' meant 'of a certain kind,' and while the word appeared in English vernacular as early as the fourteenth century, it was not until the last quarter of the sixteenth century that it was deployed exclusively as an official term of social description (Wrightson, 'Sorts of people,' 31). During this period the language of 'sorts' begins to appear with notable frequency in state and local documents, where 'sort' is typically qualified by the comparative adjectives 'meaner' or 'better'; see Keith Wrightson, '"Sorts of People" in Tudor and Stuart England,' in Barry and Brooks, *The Middling Sort of People*, 28–52.

36 Elyot's *Castel of Health*, Lemnius's *The Touchstone of Complexions*, and Vaughan's *Directions for Health* all categorize youth in this age range. Hart, author of *KΛINKH, or, The Diet of the Diseased*, distinguishes between 'youths' aged fourteen to twenty-one and 'staid youths' aged twenty-one through thirty-five. Bullein in *The Government of Health* puts youth at an age ranging from fifteen to twenty-five. For an overview of these sources and their discussions of youth, see Shepard, *Meanings of Manhood*, 55.

37 Griffiths, *Youth and Authority*, 31.

38 Guild, *A Yong Mans Inquisition*, C2v-C3.

39 Lemnius, *The Touchstone of Complexions*, G4; X2v; K4v.

40 Ibid., X3v-X4.

41 Brathwait, *The English Gentleman*, B1.

42 Ibid.

43 Lemnius, *Touchstone*, X4.

44 Samuel Gardiner, as in Shepard *Meanings of Manhood*, 25; Lenton, *The Young Gallants Whirligigg*, B3.

45 Lenton, *The Young Gallants Whirligigg*, C2–C2v.

46 Nashe, *The Anatomy of Absurdity*, C4v.

47 Lemnius, *Touchstone*, X3–X3v.
48 Griffiths, *Youth and Authority*, 222.
49 Ibid., 226. See also Lane, *Apprenticeship in England*, 192–3; and Christopher Brooks, 'Apprenticeship, Social Mobility, and The Middling Sort, 1550–1800,' in Barry and Brooks, *The Middling Sort of People*, 80.
50 The title of the 1559 Ordinance is *Articles Agreed Upon by the Lords ... for a Reformation of their Servants in Certain Abuses of Apparel*, as in Harte, 'State Control of Dress,' 145–6. Guilds also legislated against apprentices keeping trunks and chests in hopes that these provisions would make it difficult for young men to amass and store a wardrobe; see Lane, *Apprenticeship in England*, 208. For instance, in 1577 the Court of Alderman inquired into apprentices 'harboring cloathes in comon ines or other places' (as in Griffiths, *Youth and Authority*, 225n223). In 1611 an ordinance of the Common Council of London forbade apprentices from having 'anie chest, presse, truncke, deske, or other place to laie upp or keepe anie apparrell or goods, saving onelie in his master's house or by his master's license' (ibid., 222).
51 As in Ian W. Archer, 'Shakespeare's London,' in *A Companion to Shakespeare,* ed. David Scott Kasten (London: Blackwell, 1999), 46.
52 J. Dunlop and R.D. Denman, *English Apprenticeship and Child Labour: A History* (London: T. Fisher Unwin, 1912), 188; Griffiths, *Youth and Authority*, 227.
53 As in Baldwin, *Sumptuary Legislation*, 231.
54 City of London Records Office, as in Griffiths, *Youth and Authority*, 223.
55 As in Baldwin, *Sumptuary Legislation*, 231. This ordinance is also cited in Lane, *Apprenticeship in England*, 207, and Griffiths, *Youth and Authority*, 225–6.
56 Ibid.
57 As in Baldwin, *Sumptuary Legislation*, 231.
58 Ibid., 231–2.
59 City of London Records Office, as in Griffiths, *Youth and Authority*, 226.
60 As in Baldwin, *Sumptuary Legislation*, 232.
61 London Curriers Company Records, cited in Lane, *Apprenticeship in England*, 207.
62 As in Griffiths, *Youth and Authority*, 225.
63 As in Hooper, 'Tudor Sumptuary Laws,' 446.
64 As in Baldwin, *Sumptuary Legislation*, 233–4.
65 Ibid.
66 Ibid., 234.
67 See Greaves, *Society and Religion in Elizabethan England*, 512–13.
68 Ibid., 513.

69 On James's repeals, Hughes and Larkin, *Stuart Royal Proclamations*, 1:253–7.

70 City of London Records Office, as in Griffiths, *Youth and Authority*, 226. Sumptuary bills were introduced into the House of Commons in 1604, 1610, 1614, 1621, 1626, 1628, 1656, and 1662. Not one of these bills was enacted into a statute. See Joan Kent, 'Attitudes of Members of the House of Commons to the Regulation of "Personal Conduct" in Late Elizabethan and Early Stuart England,' *Bulletin of The Institute of Historical Research* 46 (1973): 41–65.

71 See Brooks, 'Apprenticeship, Social Mobility, and The Middling Sort, 1550–1800,' in *The Middling Sort of People*, 80.

72 Newcastle Merchant Adventurers Records, as in Griffiths, *Youth and Authority*, 77.

73 Ibid., 228.

74 Merchant Adventurers Records, cited in Burnett, *Masters and Servants*, 42.

75 City of London Records Office, as in Griffiths, *Youth and Authority*, 226.

76 As in Lane, *Apprenticeship in England*, 207.

77 Margaret Pelling, 'Apprenticeship, Health, and Social Cohesion in Early Modern London,' *History Workshop Journal* 37 (1994): 54n43.

78 Liverpool Town Books, as in Griffiths, *Youth and Authority*, 77.

79 On bed sharing and assize court transcripts reporting cases of sexual activity between men in educational or professional situations, see Bray, *Homosexuality in Renaissance England*, 67–80; Bray, 'Homosexuality and the Signs of Male Friendship in Elizabethan England,' in Goldberg, *Queering the Renaissance*, 40–62; and Alan Bray and Michel Rey, 'The Body of the Friend: Continuity and Change in Masculine Friendship in the Seventeenth Century,' in Hitchcock and Cohen, *English Masculinities*, 65–85. See also DiGangi, *The Homoerotics of Early Modern Drama*; and Bruce R. Smith, *Homosexual Desire in Shakespeare's England*, 84–7.

80 Tim Hitchcock, 'Sociability and Misogyny in the Life of John Cannon, 1684–1743,' in Hitchcock and Cohen, *English Masculinities*, 25–44; Bray and Rey, 'The Body of the Friend,' in *English Masculinities*, 65–85; and Alan Bray, *The Friend*, 78–140.

81 Peter Burke, 'Popular Culture in Seventeenth-Century London,' in Reay, *Popular Culture in Seventeenth-Century England*, 34; Griffiths, *Youth and Authority*, 161; and Seaver, 'Declining Status in an Aspiring Age,' 147.

82 Shepard, *Meanings of Manhood*, 95.

83 Gurr, *Playgoing in Shakespeare's London*, 184, 65–70; Griffiths, *Youth and Authority*, 113–75.

84 Whitney, '"Usually in the werking Daies,"' 436. See also Griffiths, *Youth and Authority*, 219–21.

85 Chambers, *The Elizabethan Stage*, Appendix D, 4:267.
86 Ibid., Appendix D, 4:273–4.
87 Ibid., Appendix D, 4:279.
88 Gurr, *The Shakespearean Stage*, 9.
89 Chambers, *The Elizabethan Stage*, Appendix D, 4:321.
90 As in Gurr, *Playgoing in Shakespeare's London*, 66.
91 Ibid., 67–9.
92 Henry Chettle, *Kind-Harts Dream* (London, 1592), as in Whitney, '"Usually in the werking Daies,"' 435.
93 Chettle, as in Chambers, *The Elizabethan Stage*, Appendix C, 4:244.
94 Nashe, *Pierce Penniless*, 64.
95 Earle, *Microcosmography*, 82.
96 See Gurr, *Playgoing in Shakespeare's London*, 67.
97 Chambers, *The Elizabethan Stage*, Appendix D, 4:282.
98 Gurr, *Playgoing in Shakespeare's London*, 119–20.
99 Archer, *The Pursuit of Stability*, 4.
100 'An Order to Cambridge Students,' as in Gurr, *Playgoing in Shakespeare's London*, Appendix 2, 240.
101 Fletcher, *Henry VIII*, Epilogue; Fletcher, *Wit Without Money*, 4.1, as in Gurr, *Playgoing in Shakespeare's London*, Appendix 2, 226–7.
102 Hornbooks were primers for young children that typically contained the letters of the alphabet and the Lord's Prayer. They were bound with a thin sheet of horn and mounted on a square piece of wood with a handle.
103 Jonson, *Every Man Out of His Humour*, 1.2.49–56.
104 Guilpin, *Skialetheia*, Epigram 53, 'Of Cornelius,' 53–4.
105 Ben Jonson, *The Devil is an Ass*, in *Ben Jonson: The Complete Works*, 6:178.
106 John Marston, *Histriomastix*, in *The Plays of John Marston*, 2:274; Overbury, *Characters*, 141.
107 Guild, *A Young Mans Inquisition*, N-N3; Crosse, *Vertue's Commonwealth*, P2v-P3.
108 *Newes from the North* (London, 1579; 1585), as in Chambers, *The Elizabethan Stage*, Appendix C, 4:202.
109 Brathwait, *The English Gentleman*, CC2.
110 Nashe, *Pierce Penniless*, 65.
111 1592 Lord Mayor's Petition, as in Chambers, *The Elizabethan Stage*, Appendix D, 4:307.
112 1592 Court of Merchant Tailors Guild Minutes, ibid., 4:309. See also 1582 Article 62 of City Orders, ibid., 4:291.
113 1597 Lord Mayor's Petition, as in Chambers, *The Elizabethan Stage*, Appendix D, 4:322.

114 Ibid., Appendix D, 4:287.
115 Rappaport, *Worlds within Worlds*, 240.
116 Whitney, '"Usually in the werking Daies,"' 435.
117 Lenton, *The Young Gallants Whirligigg*, B4v.
118 Stubbes, *Phillip Stubbes' Anatomy of the Abuses in England*, 145.
119 As in Chambers, *The Elizabethan Stage*, Appendix D, 4:317.
120 The Lord Mayor in a 1583 correspondence to Walsingham, as in Chambers, *The Elizabethan Stage*, 4:294; William Harrison, *A Description of England*, as in Gurr, *Playgoing in Shakespeare's London*, Appendix 2, 234.
121 As in Chambers, *The Elizabethan Stage*, Appendix D, 4:304.
122 Sermon delivered by John Stockwood at St Paul's Cross (London, 1578) and sermon delivered by Thomas White at St Paul's (London, 1577), as in Chambers, *The Elizabethan Stage*, Appendix C, 4:200; 4:197.
123 *Pappe with a Hatchet* (London, 1589), as in Chambers, *The Elizabethan Stage*, Appendix C, 4:232.
124 Thomas Middleton, *No Wit, No Help, Like a Woman's* (London, 1611), Prologue, as in Gurr, *Playgoing in Shakespeare's London*, Appendix 2, 245.
125 Nashe, *Pierce Penniless*, 65.
126 See Bristol, *Big-time Shakespeare*, 37.
127 Ibid., 39.
128 Boulton, *Neighbourhood and Society*, 89.
129 Foakes, *Henslowe's Diary*, 32.
130 Boulton, *Neighbourhood and Society*, 90.
131 Foakes, *Henslowe's Diary*, 37.
132 Courtbooks of the Court of London at Bridewell, as in Griffiths, *Youth and Authority*, 225.
133 Ibid.
134 Ibid., 335.
135 Guildhall Library Records, as in ibid., 335–6.
136 Lenton, *The Young Gallants Whirligigg*, C4v.
137 Robert Greene, *Francesco Fortunes, or, The Second Part of Greene's Never Too Late* (London, 1590), as in Chambers, *The Elizabethan Stage*, Appendix C, 4:237.
138 Ben Jonson, *Underwood*, l.106–10, in *Ben Jonson: The Complete Works*, 8:165.
139 On destructive expenditure and the symbolic economy of elite largesse, see Richard Halpern, *The Poetics of Primitive Accumulation*, 264–9. For a discussion of second-hand clothing markets and the production of taste, see Andrew Ross, 'Uses of Camp,' *Yale Journal of Criticism* 2.1 (1998): 1–24.

140 The phrase is Vivienne Westwood's, as in Hebdige, *Subculture and the Meaning of Style*, 107.
141 Andrew Britton, 'For Interpretation: Notes Against Camp,' in Cleto, *Camp*, 140.
142 Dekker, *The Guls Horne-booke*, 52.
143 Ibid., 55. The feather has a particular association with excess and effeminacy. Barnabe Riche in *Farewell to Military Profession* (1581) complains that 'newfangled' gentlemen have become like Venetian courtesans. He registers particular repulsion for a gallant who parades before him with 'a great fan of feathers' whom he condemns for holding 'such a bauble in his hands,' as in DiGangi, *The Homoerotics of Early Modern Drama*, 135.
144 The phrase 'the clothes make the man' is associated with Polonius's statement that 'the apparel oft proclaims the man' in *Hamlet*, 1.3.73.
145 Hughes and Larkin, *Tudor Royal Proclamations*, 2:454, 2:462, emphasis mine.
146 Dekker, *The Guls Horne-booke*, 28.
147 Ibid., 36.
148 'An Homily Against Excess of Apparel' (London, 1588), in *Sermons or Homilies Appointed to be Read in Churches*, 305.
149 Crosse, *Vertues common-wealth*, L.
150 *Oxford English Dictionary*, s.v. 'masculinity,' s.v. 'manhood,' and s.v. 'manliness.' See also, Josh Tosh, 'The Old Adam and the New Man: Emerging Themes in the History of English Masculinities, 1750–1850,' in Hitchcock and Cohen, *English Masculinities*, 231–2.
151 Mun, *A Discourse of Trade*, L2–L2v.
152 Fletcher, *Gender, Sex, and Subordination in England*, 83–99, 411.
153 John Marston, *The Scourge of Villainy*, 'A Cynicke Satire,' l. 22, 1.27, 1.34, and 1.36, in *The Poems of John Marston*, 140–1.
154 Barnaby Rich, *My Ladies Looking Glass*, as in Shepard, *Meanings of Manhood*, 29.
155 Edward Sharpham, *The Fleire*, as in Manley, *Literature and Culture*, 431.
156 John Clarke, Stuart Hall, Tony Jefferson, and Brian Roberts, eds., 'Subcultures, Cultures, and Class: A Theoretical Overview,' in Hall and Jefferson, *Resistance Through Rituals*, 71.

3. Livery and Its Discontents in *The Taming of the Shrew*

1 Anonymous, *Witt's Recreations* (London, 1641), Epigram 579, 'On Spurco of Oxford,' in *Ben Jonson: The Complete Works*, 11:273n2059.
2 The two notable exceptions are David Evett, who observes that *The Shrew*

includes more sets of masters and servants than any other dramatic text of the period, in '"Surprising Confrontations" – Ideologies of Service in Shakespeare's England,' in *Renaissance Papers*, ed. Dale B.J. Randall and Joseph A. Porter, Papers Published for the Southeastern Renaissance Conference (Rochester, NY: Boydell and Brewer, 1990), 68; and Moisan's, '"Knock me here soundly."'

3 For discussions of *The Shrew*'s sensitivity to changes in early modern domestic economies, see Korda, *Shakespeare's Domestic Economies*, especially 52–76; Ann C. Christensen, 'Of Household Stuff and Homes: The Stage and Social Practice in *The Taming of the Shrew*,' *Explorations in Renaissance Culture* 22 (1996): 127–45; Boose, '*The Taming of the Shrew*, Good Husbandry, and Enclosure'; Karen Newman, 'Renaissance Family Politics and Shakespeare's *Taming of the Shrew*,' in *Fashioning Femininity*, 33–51; and Carol F. Heffernan, '*The Taming of the Shrew*: The Bourgeoisie in Love,' *Essays in Literature* 12 (1985): 3–15.

4 David Starkey discusses the early modern concept of magnificence and emphasizes that while it could be expressed in various ways, its 'supreme and chosen vehicle' of expression was the household; see 'The Age of the Household,' 255. Peter Stallybrass and Ann Rosalind Jones in *Renaissance Clothing* emphasize that household livery signified servitude whereas guild livery signalled freedom. For a discussion of the term 'livery,' see Peter Stallybrass, 'Worn Worlds: Clothes and Identity on the Renaissance Stage,' in Stallybrass et al., *Subject and Object in Renaissance Culture*, 289–321.

5 Complaints of flamboyantly dressed retainers and servants were a staple of the period's satirical literature; see Joanna Crawford, 'Clothing Distribution and Social Relations, 1350–1500,' in Richardson, *Clothing Culture*, 158. While the Crown made more than twenty legislative attempts, from the mid-fourteenth to the late fifteenth centuries, to regulate expenditure on liveried retainers, the monarch dropped livery as a distinct category of legislative concern after Henry VIII issued what would be the final proclamation attempting to curtail household expenditure on servants' apparel; see Hunt, *Governance of the Consuming Passions*, 114–16, and G.R. Owst, *Literature and Pulpit in Medieval England: A Neglected Chapter in the History of English Letters and of the English People* (Oxford: Oxford University Press, 1961), 281–3.

6 Neill, *Putting History to the Question*, 19.

7 I do not distinguish between servant and domestic, since, as Ann Kussmaul points out, in the late sixteenth century no distinction was made between productive and conspicuously idle servants. Moreover, the dif-

ferences among 'day-labourers,' 'menials,' 'domestics,' and 'servants' were not fully articulated by social category until the nineteenth century. Thus the meaning of the term 'servant' in this period extended to all of those who worked for others, and domestics were, most broadly, those who performed some kind of task in the home. See *Servants in Husbandry*, 5–7. On early modern England as a 'service society,' see Alan Macfarlane, *The Origins of English Individualism: Family, Property, and Social Transition* (Oxford: Basil Blackwell, 1978); Beier, *Masterless Men*; and Griffiths et al., *The Experience of Authority in Early Modern England*. On service as the hallmark experience of early modern male youth, see Peter Laslett and Richard Wall, eds., *Household and Family in Past Time* (Cambridge: Cambridge University Press, 1972); Amussen, *An Ordered Society*; Fletcher, *Sex, Gender, and Subordination in England*; and Griffiths, *Youth and Authority*.

8 I.M., *A Health to the Gentlemanly Profession of Servingmen*, 115. Hereafter referred to within the text as *Servingmans Comfort*. On the prevalence of gentle servants, see Amussen, *An Ordered Society*, 68, 158. Mark Thornton Burnett discusses the growing number of younger sons of minor gentry entering service and professional trades in *Masters and Servants in English Renaissance Drama and Culture*, 41–2. See also J.P. Cooper, *Land, Men, and Beliefs: Studies in Early Modern History* (London: Hambledon, 1983) and F.H. Mares, ed., *The Memoirs of Robert Carey* (Oxford: Oxford University Press, 1972). For early modern perceptions of the debasement of service, see Beier, *Masterless Men*, 22–8, and Alan Bray, 'Homosexuality and the Signs of Male Friendship in Elizabethan England,' in Goldberg, *Queering the Renaissance*, 40–61.

9 Ian Archer, 'Shakespeare's London,' in David Scott Kastan, ed., *A Companion to Shakespeare* (Oxford: Blackwell, 1999), 44. For 'superfluous' or 'surplus' children of the elite, see Gillis, *Youth and History*. Alan Macfarlane also discusses the social consequences of unequal inheritance in *The Origins*, 154–64.

10 Beier, *Masterless Men*, 22–8.

11 Shakespeare, *The Taming of the Shrew*: *Texts and Contexts*, ed. Dolan, Ind. 2.131. Hereafter referred to in the text as *The Shrew* and cited parenthetically by act, scene, and line number.

12 Heal, *Hospitality in Early Modern England*, 7. On the shift from a militaristic ideology of service, which emphasized protection of the person of the master, to a notion of service that tied domestic tasks to the display of luxury, see Dorothy Marshall, *The English Domestic Servant in History* (London: The Historical Association, 1949).

13 Earle, *Microcosmography*, 89

14 Ibid.

15 Henry Wotton, *The Elements of Architecture By Sir Henry Wotton: A Facsimile Reprint of the First Edition* (London, 1624), as in Viviana Comensoli, *'Household Business,' Domestic Plays of Early Modern England* (Toronto: University of Toronto Press, 1996), 72. Kate Mertes claims that as a rule the early modern household was 'actively hostile' to the presence of women workers and that it was not until the later half of the seventeenth century that women became a significant part of the household domestic staff. As long as service was considered a position of some prestige and regarded as an avenue for social advancement, women were largely discouraged from pursuing domestic positions. The proliferation of female domestics after 1700 accompanies the household's decline and the denigration of service as a profession; see *The English Noble Household*, 57–8. For an extended discussion of the rise of the female domestic, see also Heal, *Hospitality in Early Modern England*; and Burnett, *Masters and Servants in English Renaissance Drama and Culture.*

16 *The English Courtier and the Country Gentleman, or, Civil and Uncivil Life* (London, 1586), in W.C. Hazlitt, ed., *Inedited Tracts*, 34. Hereafter cited within the text.

17 Overbury, *Characters*, 108–9.

18 Fynes Morrison, *Itineraries*, as in Diana de Marly, *Working Dress: A History of Occupational Clothing* (New York: Holmes and Meier, 1986), 41.

19 Moisan, '"Knock me here soundly,"' 276.

20 Thomas Dekker's Sir Hugh Lacy describes his nephew, a gallant who squanders all his money on sumptuous clothing, as appearing as 'monstrous.' He is always flamboyantly attired with 'a scarf and here a scarf, here a bunch of feathers, and here precious stones and jewels and a pair of silk garters,' in *The Shoemaker's Holiday*, in Russell A. Fraser and Norman Rabkin, eds., *Drama of the English Renaissance: The Tudor Period* (New York: Macmillan, 1976), 1.1.17–35; 1.2.28–32. Petruchio's horse has the symptoms of the disease *farcins* that caused a swelling of the mouth. Peter F. Heaney suggests that this equine condition may be read as analogous to Petruchio's 'monstrous' and 'all consuming' ego, which portends his inability to properly manage his household; see 'Petruchio's Horse: Equine and Household Management in *The Taming of the Shrew,' Early Modern Literary Studies* 4.1 (May 1998): 1–12. [http://www.purl.oclc.org/emls/04–1/heanshak.html.]

21 See Boose, 'Scolding Brides and Bridling Scolds,' 192. Some critics have argued that in creating a spectacle, Petruchio attempts to match or to outdo Kate's histrionic behaviour. Barbara Hodgdon, for instance, con-

tends that this scene marks the moment when the play promotes a cross-coding of shrewishness onto the male body; see 'Katherina Bound, or, Play(K)ating the Strictures of Everyday Life,' *Publications of the Modern Language Association* 107.3 (1992): 538–53, and Valerie Wayne argues that 'Petruchio tames a shrew by becoming one,' in 'Refashioning the Shrew,' *Shakespeare Studies* 17 (1985): 171. Along similar lines, Joel Fineman reads 'Petruchio's lunatic behavior, even when it is itself nonverbal' as 'a derivative example of the shrewish voice of Kate,' in 'The Turn of the Shrew,' in Patricia Parker and Geoffrey Hartman, eds., *Shakespeare and the Question of Theory* (New York: Methuen, 1985), 142.

22 Natasha Korda explores Petruchio's explanation in some depth in *Shakespeare's Domestic Economies*, and my discussion is informed by her analysis of the word 'wear.' On men's anxieties about women spending money on clothing and the association of women's sartorial extravagance with pride and lasciviousness, see C. Brant and D. Purkiss, *Women, Texts, and Histories, 1575–1760* (Oxford: Oxford University Press, 1992).

23 As in Dolan's edition, *The Taming of the Shrew: Texts and Contexts*, Appendix, 251. For more examples of spendthrift and vain women, see Linda Woodbridge, *Women and the English Renaissance: Literature and the Nature of Womankind, 1540–1620* (Urbana: University of Illinois Press, 1986). Lisa Jardine also discusses wives squandering their husband's wealth on finery in *Still Harping on Daughters*, 151–4.

24 Vaughan, *The Golden-Grove*, book 3, chapter 58, Bb4.

25 McIntosh, *Controlling Misbehavior in England*, 13.

26 I.M., *Servingmans Comfort*, 138.

27 See Griffiths, *Youth and Authority*, 335, 224–34.

28 Mertes, *The English Noble Household*, 98.

29 As in Griffiths, *Youth and Authority*, 335.

30 Ibid. On items of clothing as securities, see Boulton, *Neighbourhood and Society*, 90.

31 Gouge, *Of Domestical Duties*, 374.

32 I.M., *Servingmans Comfort*, 108.

33 Gouge, *Of Domestical Duties*, 363.

34 Cleaver and Dod, as in Dolan, Appendix, *The Taming of the Shrew: Texts and Contexts*, 205.

35 Frances E. Dolan, 'The Subordinate(s')Plot: Petty Treason and the Forms of Domestic Rebellion,' *Shakespeare Quarterly* 43.3 (1992): 324.

36 I am using José Esteban Muñoz's term for a mode of interacting with dominant culture that entails neither assimilation nor opposition, but

rather enables the appropriation of its codes; see José Esteban Muñoz, *Disidentifications: Queers of Color and the Performance of Politics* (Minneapolis: University of Minnesota Press, 1999), 1–34.

37 My discussion of braving is indebted to Henry Louis Gates's notion of 'Signifyin(g).' 'Signifyin(g),' Gates writes, 'turns on the sheer play of the signifier. It does not refer primarily to the signified; rather, it refers to the style of language ... Again, one does not Signify some thing; one Signifies in *some way*' (*The Signifying Monkey*, 78). Gates explores related modes such as 'the dozens' (which means to censure in twelve or fewer statements), as well as later eighteenth-century meanings of the word such as to stun, to stupefy, or to daze with language (ibid., 68–88; 99–103).

38 *Oxford English Dictionary*, s.v. 'brave.'

39 Ibid.

40 Franco Zeffirelli gets this right in his 1967 film version of *The Taming of the Shrew* in which he milks for its full comic effect the first appearance of the newly attired Tranio, who is dressed more sumptuously than any other character in the play.

41 Bruce R. Smith, *Homosexual Desire in Shakespeare's England*, 54. For the sartorial and attitudinal implications of 'brave' as a stage direction, see Alan C. Dessen and Leslie Thomson, *A Dictionary of Stage Directions in English Drama, 1580–1642* (Cambridge: Cambridge University Press, 1999), 37.

42 Fitzgeffrey, *Satyres and Satyrical Epigrams*, D1v.

43 Anonymous, *A Diamond Most Precious, Worthy to be Marked*, as in Lena Cowen Orlin, *Elizabethan Households: An Anthology* (Washington, DC: The Folger Shakespeare Library, 1995), 46.

44 Richard Climsell, *A Pleasant New Dialogue: or, the Discourse between the Serving-man and the Husband-man* (London, 1640), as in Burnett, *Masters and Servants*, 94.

45 For a discussion of the use of the word 'curious' in reference to matters of style, see John Greenwood, *Shifting Perspectives*, 17. 'Curiousness,' as Karen Newman has shown, was also associated with an excess of significance that bespoke the effeminate decorousness of 'crowded ornament'; see *Fashioning Femininity*, 123. Ben Jonson employed sartorial tropes to describe the improper use of language and drew explicit connections among excess of apparel, social disorder, linguistic wantonness, and sickness of mind. Advocating a plain rhetorical style that he likens to dress without ornamentation, Jonson refers to those young men who are 'exceedingly curious,' as 'always kempt'd, and perfum'd'; with the 'every day smell of the Taylor.' Jonson declares that 'too much pickednesse is

not manly,' and that ostentatious language is 'affected and preposterous as our Gallants cloathes, sweet bags, and night-dressings: in which you would thinke our men lay in, like *Ladies*: it is so curious'; see *Discoveries*, in *Complete Works*, 8:607; 8:581.

46 See Henry Louis Gates on 'back at you' or 'in your face' as a standard signifyin(g) retort, in *The Signifying Monkey*, 66.

47 Simon Shepherd, '"What's So Funny about Ladies' Tailors?" A Survey of Some Male (Homo)Sexual Types in the Renaissance,' *Textual Practice* 6.1 (Spring 1992): 17–31. E.A.M. Colman also notes that tailors were typically represented as effeminate and lascivious, and he glosses a series of ententdres associated with the words 'prick' and 'yard,' in *The Dramatic Use of Bawdy Shakespeare* (London: Longman, 1974), 224. On tailors as dishonest and sumptuously attired, see Jane Ashelford, *Dress in the Age of Elizabeth I* (New York: Holmes and Meier, 1988), 77.

48 Mario DiGangi discusses the indeterminacy of the 'sexual' and the importance of considering seemingly non-erotic activities when investigating same-sex contacts that may have functioned to subvert the assumptions of reproductive sexuality; see *The Homoerotics of Early Modern Drama*, 11.

49 The word 'tailor,' derived from the old French 'tailler,' is etymologically linked to the word 'cut.' E.A.M. Colman glosses 'cut' as referring to the vulva and more generally to the vagina (*The Dramatic Use of Bawdy Shakespeare*, 190). For a discussion of the word 'cut' as a reference to the anus, see D.A. Miller, 'Anal Rope,' in Diana Fuss, ed., *Inside/Out: Lesbian Theories, Gay Theories* (New York: Routledge, 1991), 134–9. Another early modern association with the word 'cut' is 'crack,' the word for an ingle or the young boy who sexually served his older patron; see Wendy Wall, '"Household Stuff': The Sexual Politics of Domesticity and the Advent of English Comedy,' *ELH* 65 (1998): 24.

50 The notion that what occurs at Petruchio's country house replicates the environs of an all-male grammar school is suggested by Tranio's description of Petruchio's house as a 'taming school' (4.2.55). In a closed world of men and boys, pedagogical violence was seen as facilitating the rigid disciplining of the body as well as the mind, and beatings were integrated even into newer humanist systems of learning. Wall notes that 'the fetishized rod served as an almost ubiquitous emblem of order and knowledge' in the period (*Staging Domesticity*, 19), and Walter J. Ong points out that Latin was taught in connection with violent flogging designed to instil physical hardiness in young boys, in 'Latin Language Study as a Renaissance Puberty Rite,' in *Rhetoric, Romance, and Technology:*

Studies in the Interaction of Expression and Culture (1959; repr., Ithaca: Cornell University Press, 1971), 113–41.

51 Mark Thornton Burnett, '"The Trusty Servant": A Sixteenth-Century English Emblem,' *Emblematica* 6.2 (1992): 1–17.

52 See DiGangi, *The Homoerotics of Early Modern Drama*, 67–80.

53 Gouge, *Of Domestical Duties*, 335; emphasis mine.

54 Ibid., 364.

55 Ibid., 364, 374.

56 As in Burnett, *Masters and Servants*, 35.

57 Ibid.

58 Cleaver and Dod, *A Godly Form of Household Government*, as in *Taming of the Shrew: Texts and Contents*, ed. Dolan, Appendix, 205.

59 Gouge, *Of Domestical Duties*, 364.

60 Leonard Barkan, *The Gods Made Flesh: Metamorphosis and the Pursuit of Paganism* (New Haven: Yale University Press, 1986), 11.

61 Bruce R. Smith, *Homosexual Desire*, 192.

62 For an overview of the instructional literature depicting the household as a productive economic unit, see Amussen, *An Ordered Society*, 67–94. On the sexual activities of young men as a sign of the failure of household discipline, see Fletcher and Stevenson, eds., *Order and Disorder in Early Modern England*, 33, and S.R. Smith, 'The London Apprentices as Seventeenth-Century Adolescents,' *Past and Present* 61 (1973): 149–61.

63 The steep drop in the number of servants employed within elite households, such that live-in servants made up less than 10 per cent of the population by the early eighteenth century, speaks to the gradual dissolution of the household that revolved around its decorative male domestics (Beier, *Masterless Men*, 23–4). These changes were also reflected in eighteenth-century architectural innovations that removed servants from view and relegated them to separate quarters and back stairwells, as the young men no longer served as the visible emblem of the ceremonious household but, instead, joined 'an invisible machinery sustaining the visible and exclusive social world of the householder'; Bryson, *From Courtesy to Civility*, 143.

64 Crosse, *Vertues common-wealth*, Lv.

65 Vaughan, *The Golden-Grove*, book 2, chapter 26, P6.

66 Boose discusses the word 'shrew,' which – like the words 'harlot,' 'hoyden,' 'scold,' 'baggage,' 'brothel,' 'bordello,' and 'bawd' – became transposed from its original sense as a contemptuous expression for a lower-class man into a term used to denigrate a rebellious woman ('Good Husbandry,' 222).

67 David Underdown, 'The Taming of the Scold: The Enforcement of Patriarchal Authority in Early Modern England,' in Fletcher and Stevenson, eds., *Order and Disorder*, 119–20.
68 Ibid., 132, 127.

4. The Italian Vice and Bad Taste in *Edward II*

1 Bourdieu, *Distinction*, 244.
2 John Summerson, *History of Architecture in Britain, 1530–1830*, as in Greenwood, *Shifting Perspectives*, 35.
3 Greene, *The Life and Complete Works*, 11:226.
4 Joseph Hall, *Quo Vadis? A Just Censure of Travel as it is commonly undertaken by the Gentlemen of our Nation* (London, 1617), as in Michael J. Redmond, '"I have read them all": Jonson's *Volpone* and the Discourse of the Italianate Englishman,' in Marrapodi and Hoenselaars, *The Italian World of English Renaissance Drama*, 133.
5 Cynthia in George Chapman, *The Widow's Tears* (London, 1612), as in Floyd-Wilson, *English Ethnicity*, 138. Michael J. Redmond also emphasizes the perceived 'susceptibility of travelers to Italian influences' as a theme in early modern English travel writing, in his '"I have read them all,"' 122.
6 MacCaffery, 'Place and Patronage,' 101. On the new breed of court aspirant, see also Bryson, *From Courtesy to Civility*, 119, and Starkey, 'The Age of the Household.'
7 MacCaffery, 'Place and Patronage,' 101; Greene, *The Life and Complete Works*, 11:221.
8 Ascham, *The Schoolmaster*, 60. *The Schoolmaster* was published in 1568 and reprinted in 1570, 1579, and 1589. On the popularity of Ascham's cautionary travel narrative, see Redmond, '"I have read them all."' Greene describes himself as 'ruffeled out in my silks, in the habit of a *malcontent*,' after having returned from a tour of Italy, in *The Repentance of Robert Greene*, as in Hentschell, 'A Question of Nation: Foreign Clothes on the English Subject,' in Richardson, *Clothing Culture*, 62.
9 Thomas Nashe, *The Unfortunate Traveller* in *Works*, 2:301.
10 Sharon Tyler, 'Bedfellows Make Strange Politics: Christopher Marlowe's *Edward II*,' in 'Drama, Sex, and Politics,' ed. James Redmond, *Themes in Drama* 7, special issue (1985): 56.
11 Dympna Callaghan describes Gaveston as staging 'a spectacle of power' befitting his illicit rise in status, in 'The Terms of Gender: "Gay" and

"Feminist" in *Edward II,*' in Valerie Traub, M. Lindsay Kaplan, and Dympna Callaghan, eds., *Feminist Readings of Early Modern Culture* (Cambridge: Cambridge University Press, 1996), 285.

12 Dollimore, *Sexual Dissidence*, 8. See, for example, Claude J. Summers's discussion of Gaveston's penchant for extravagant apparel, in 'Sex, Politics, and Self-Realization in *Edward II,*' in Friedenreich et al., '*A Poet and a Filthy Play-maker,*' 221–40; and Gregory Woods, 'Body, Costume, and Desire in Christopher Marlowe,' in Summers, *Homosexuality in Renaissance and Enlightenment England*, 69–84.

13 Marlowe, *Edward the Second*, scene 1.6 and scene 1.2. Hereafter cited within the text by scene and line number.

14 *Oxford English Dictionary*, s.v. 'pert,' s.v. 'dapper,' and s.v. 'brisk.'

15 Ibid.

16 On Henri III as a possible historical referent for Marlowe's Edward II, see Curtis Perry, 'The Politics of Access and Representations of the Sodomite King in Early Modern England,' *Renaissance Quarterly* 53 (2000): 1054–83; DiGangi, *The Homoerotics of Early Modern Drama*, 108; and Julia Briggs, 'Marlowe's *Massacre at Paris*: A Reconsideration,' *Review of English Studies* 34.135 (August 1983): 257–78.

17 *Holinshed's Chronicles*, 2:550. The argument can be made that Marlowe manipulates his historical source in much the same way that the filmmaker Derek Jarman manipulates Marlowe's play. Importantly, for my argument, Jarman honours Marlowe's emphasis on sartorial extravagance, and in his film version of *Edward II* he costumes the barons in the standard uniform of the Thatcherite bourgeoisie. They wear drab, grey flannel suits, accessorized with cheap ties and sensible shoes.

18 Ascham, *The Schoolmaster*, 66.

19 On Edward's court as a negative exemplum of Elizabeth's, see Dennis Kay, 'Marlowe, Edward II, and the Cult of Elizabeth,' and on *Edward II* as a commentary on Elizabeth's court, see John Michael Archer, *Sovereignty and Intelligence: Spying and Court Culture in the English Renaissance* (Palo Alto, CA: Stanford University Press, 1993), 77.

20 Stow, *Survey of London*, 2:212.

21 Ascham, *The Schoolmaster*, 44, 46.

22 Bryson, *From Courtesy to Civility*, 119.

23 Ibid., emphasis mine.

24 For the politics of stylistic affinity, see Bourdieu, *Distinction*, 173. On the significance of proper comportment at the English court in the late sixteenth century, see Norbert Elias, *The Civilizing Process: The History of*

Manners and State Formation and Civilization, trans. Edmund Jephcott (Oxford: Blackwell, 1994); Whigham, *Ambition and Privilege*; Anna Bryson, 'Gesture, Demeanor, and the Image of the Gentleman,' in Lucy Gent and Nigel Llewellyn, eds., *Renaissance Bodies: The Human Figure in English Culture, 1540–1660* (London: Reaktion Books, 1990), 136–53; Bryson, *From Courtesy to Civility*; Correll, *The End of Conduct*; and Harry Berger Jr, *The Absence of Grace* (Stanford: Stanford University Press, 2002).

25 Roze Hentschell, 'A Question of Nation: Foreign Clothes on the English Subject,' 53. On the link between nationalization and naturalization, see Keir Elam, '"The continent of what part a gentleman would see": English Bodies in European Habits,' in Marrapodi, *Shakespeare and Intertextuality*, 49.

26 Overbury, *Characters*, 102.

27 Ibid., emphasis mine.

28 *Holinshed's Chronicles*, 2:539.

29 Du Refuge, *Treatise of the Court* (London, 1622), trans. Reynold, as in Bryson, *From Courtesy to Civility*, 121.

30 *Oxford English Dictionary*, s.v. 'draw.'

31 Daniel Javitch, '*Il Cortegiano* and the Constraints of Despotism,' in *Castiglione: The Ideal and the Real in Renaissance Culture*, ed. Robert Hanning and David Rosand (New Haven: Yale University Press, 1983), 23.

32 As in Russell West, *Spatial Representations and the Jacobean Stage: From Shakespeare to Webster* (New York: Palgrave, 2002), 69.

33 Javitch, 'The Constraints of Despotism,' 23.

34 John Shearman writes, 'The concept *maneria* was borrowed from the literature of manners, and had originally been a quality – a desirable quality – of human deportment.' The meaning of the word survives, he notes, 'not only through its transference in Italy to the visual arts but also in its modern equivalent, style. *Maneria*, then, is a term of long standing in the literature of a way of life so stylized and cultured that it was, in effect, a work of art itself; hence the easy translation to the visual arts' (*Mannerism*, 17–19).

35 Hauser, *Mannerism*, 3.

36 Ibid., 12, 13.

37 Greenwood, *Shifting Perspectives*, 23. In describing Italian artistic production as 'mannerist,' Giorgio Vasari looks to the stylized work of Parmigianino, which he contrasted to the spare aesthetic of *istoria* associated with Alberti (as in Greenwood, *Shifting Perspectives*, 38).

38 Inigo Jones, 20 January 1615, as in Lubbock, *The Tyranny of Taste*, 163–4.

39 Ibid., 164.

40 Shearman, *Mannerism*, 104.

41 Greenwood, *Shifting Perspectives*, 29. For a comparison between the respective philosophies of Ben Jonson and his rival Samuel Daniel, see John Peacock, 'Ben Jonson's Masques and Italian Culture,' in J.R. Mulryne and Margaret Shewring, eds., *Theatre of the English and Italian Renaissance* (London: Macmillan, 1991), 73–95. On the Jonsonian masque, see Roy Strong, *Splendor at Court: Renaissance Spectacle and the Theater of Power* (New York: Houghton Mifflin, 1973); and Barish, *The Antitheatrical Prejudice*, 140–4. See also Stephen Orgel, *The Jonsonian Masque* (Cambridge, MA: Harvard University Press, 1965); and Orgel, *The Illusion of Power: Political Theater in the English Renaissance* (Berkeley: University of California Press, 1975).

42 See Thomas A. King for a discussion of the ways that the homoerotic elements of this masque were tamed, in *The Gendering of Men*, 51.

43 Thomas Wilson, *Arte of Rhetorique*, as in Kay, 'Marlowe, Edward II, and the Cult of Elizabeth,' 5. http://www.oclc.org/emls.

44 See Hauser's chapter, 'Alienation of the Key to Mannerism,' in *Mannerism*, 94–115; and Hoy, 'Jacobean Tragedy and the Mannerist Style,' 59. The main proponents of a mannerist aesthetic in early modern English drama were playwrights John Marston and Christopher Marlowe, both of whom, like the Inns of Court students for whom they wrote, attempted to secure positions at court. See Manley, *Literature and Culture*, 390–2, 428; and Finkelpearl, *John Marston of the Middle Temple*.

45 Jonson, *Every Man Out of His Humour*, ed. Ostovich, 3.3.15–17.

46 Overbury, *Characters*, 128–9.

47 Earle, *Microcosmography*, 60.

48 Ben Jonson, *Cynthia's Revels* (London, 1600) as in Overbury, *Characters*, 336.

49 *Holinshed's Chronicles*, 2:547.

50 Antonio de Guevara, *The Diall of Princes* (London, 1568), 2nd rev. ed. trans. Thomas North, as in Bryson, *From Courtesy to Civility*, 120.

51 See Marlowe, *Edward the Second*, 39n33.

52 On Italianate fencing terms as code for same-sex eroticism on the English stage, see Keir Elam, '"The continent of what part a gentleman would see": English Bodies in European Habits,' in Marrapodi, ed., *Shakespeare and Intertextuality*, 55; and Joan Ozark Holmer, '"Draw if you be men:" Saviolo's Significance for *Romeo and Juliet*,' *SQ* 45 (1994): 163–89.

53 Mark Thornton Burnett, '*Edward II* and Elizabethan Politics,' in White, *Marlowe, History, and Sexuality*, 96. Frank Whigham describes unpedigreed aspirants as shifting between attitudes of alienation and ambition in the face of being among a surplus of qualified men for few available

elite jobs (*Ambition and Privilege*, 17). Richard Mulcaster, Spenser's teacher and the headmaster of the Merchant Taylors School, was well aware by 1581 of 'the dangers of ... overproduction,' such that too many educated young men remained at court to 'loiter without living' (as in ibid., 15).

54 Burnett, '*Edward II* and Elizabethan Politics,' 96–7.

55 For a discussion of the rhetorical implications of the 'or worse' construction as code for sodomitical activity, see Goldberg, *Sodometries*, 121–3.

56 Harvey, *The Works of Gabriel Harvey*, 1:84–5.

57 Ibid., 84, 85.

58 Thomas Nashe as in *Gabriel Harvey's Marginalia*, ed. G.C. Moore Smith, 19, emphasis mine. For a slightly altered version of the same anecdote, see *The Works of Thomas Nashe*, 3:73–4.

59 Nashe, as in *Gabriel Harvey's Marginalia*, 19. In his attempt to get back at Nashe, Harvey frequently publicly identified him as the English Aretino, which apparently Nashe accepted as a compliment; see Ian Frederick Moulton, *Before Pornography: Erotic Writing in Early Modern England* (Oxford: Oxford University Press, 2000), 161.

60 Letter from Hubert Languet to Sidney, as in Montrose, 'Spenser and the Elizabethan Political Imaginary,' 932.

61 Ibid.

62 Jardine, *Still Harping on Daughters*, 54–6.

63 Javitch, *Poetry and Courtliness*, 127. See also Stone, *The Crisis of the Aristocracy*; and J.E. Neale, 'The Elizabethan Political Scene,' in *Essays in Elizabethan History* (London, 1958). On the 'new men' infiltrating Elizabeth's court, see Whigham, *Ambition and Privilege*, 10.

64 Greene, *The Life and Complete Works*, 11:236.

65 Ibid.

66 Bryson, *From Courtesy to Civility*, 147. See also Curtis, *Oxford and Cambridge in Transition*; and Wilfred R. Prest, *The Inns of Court under Elizabeth I and the Early Stuarts, 1590–1640* (London: Longman, 1972).

67 M.H. Curtis points out that 'in the difficult years of the mid-sixteenth century, when university enrollments were down and prices were rising, the temptation to admit paying students, pensioners, and fellow commoners became overpowering' (*Oxford and Cambridge in Transition*, 77). On the social *cachet* associated with attending the Inns of Court, such that gentlemen of 'somewhat lesser breed and those who wished to pass as gentlemen naturally followed suit,' see Whigham, *Ambition and Privilege*, 16–17. On the effects of a 'transitional economy' and its production of a

class of discontented young men whose ambitions at court were frustrated, see L.C. Knights, 'Seventeenth-Century Melancholy,' in *Drama and Society*, 331.

68 As in Moulton, *Before Pornography*, 163. On Aretino, see Giulio Romano et al., *I Modi, The Sixteen Postures: An Erotic Album of the Italian Renaissance*, ed. and trans. Lynne Lawner (Evanston: Northwestern University Press, 1988). Aretino's sodomitical erotica lay the ground for associations like those advanced by Henri Estienne in his 1566 *Apology for Herodotus*, in which he presumes that sodomy is the 'trade and occupation' of Italy. See Henri Estienne, *A World of Wonders*, trans. R.C. (London, 1607), as in Borris, *Same-Sex Desire in the English Renaissance*, 61.

69 Curtis, *Oxford and Cambridge in Transition*, 54. See also Cooper, *Annals of Cambridge*, 2:360–1, 2:616.

70 Cooper, *Annals of Cambridge*, 2:360, 2:616.

71 Stephen Orgel, 'Tobacco and Boys: How Queer was Marlowe,' *Gay and Lesbian Quarterly* 6.4 (2000): 558.

72 Ibid., 573.

73 Dennis Kay writes: 'When Edward falls in love with Gaveston, the king becomes a subject in and to love' ('Marlowe, *Edward II*, and the Cult of Elizabeth,' 4). See also Claude Summers, 'Sex, Politics, and Self-Realization in *Edward II*,' in Friedenreich et al., *'A Poet and a Filthy Play-maker,'* 221–40; and Bruce R. Smith, *Homosexual Desire in Shakespeare's England*, 221.

74 On the transition from the Roman definition of vice as *luxuria* to the sin of *lechery*, which was specifically associated with non-procreative sexual practices, see Mark D. Jordan, *The Invention of Sodomy in Christian Theology* (Chicago: University of Chicago Press, 1997). On the early modern conflation of luxury and lechery, see Margreta de Grazia, 'The Ideology of Superfluous Things: *King Lear* as Period Piece,' in Stallybrass et al., *Subject and Object in Renaissance Culture*, 17–43; and John Sekora, *Luxury: The Concept in Western Thought, Eden to Smollett* (Baltimore: Johns Hopkins University Press, 1977).

75 In his film, *Edward II*, Derek Jarman charts the trajectory of Isabella's increasing haughtiness and progressive political boldness by costuming her in successively outrageous ensembles, which she flaunts with overweening confidence.

76 DiGangi argues that even though 'the play may represent the *homoerotic* relations between the king and his favorites as disorderly, scandalous, improvident, or parasitical, it locates the political crime of sodomy in a

rebellious peer's transgressive access to the royal body'; see DiGangi, 'Marlowe, Queer Studies, and Renaissance Homoeroticism,' in White, *Marlowe, History, and Sexuality*, 209.

77 Correll, *The End of Conduct*, 40.

78 Judith Haber sees Marlowe's play as effectively submitting Edward to history, which is expressed by the triumph of the dominant ideology associated with Mortimer and the barons. Her paradigmatic example is the manner of Edward's death. His execution, she avers, expresses the 'logical punishment-fitting-the-crime aspect,' and thus serves as a 'figure for the literal truth, the intelligible, the determinate, the (patri)lineal, the causal, and the historical'; see 'Submitting to History: Marlowe's *Edward II*,' in Richard Burt and John Michael Archer, eds., *Enclosure Acts: Sexuality, Property, and Culture in Early Modern England* (Ithaca: Cornell University Press, 1994), 180. Albeit with a different emphasis, Purvis Boyette also argues that this particular mode of murder is fitting since 'Edward's execution "purifies" the king in the brutally violated image of his sexual pleasure,' in 'Wanton Humor and Wanton Poets: Homosexuality in Marlowe's *Edward II*,' *Tulane Studies in English* 12 (1977): 48. In keeping with my argument, Wiggins and Lindsey discuss the trend in production to have the same actor play Gaveston and Lightborne; Introduction, *Edward the Second*, 34. On this doubling trend in performance, see also Alan Stewart, '*Edward II* and Male Same-Sex Desire,' in Garret A. Sullivan Jr et al., eds., *Early Modern English Drama: A Critical Companion* (Oxford: Oxford University Press, 2006), 85.

79 *Holinshed's Chronicles*, 2:587.

80 *Oxford English Dictionary*, s.v. 'gear.'

81 Ascham, *The Schoolmaster*, 66.

82 *Oxford English Dictionary*, s.v. 'bravery.'

83 Gosson, *The School of Abuse*, C4.

84 Bruce R. Smith, *Homosexual Desire*, 223. Along similar lines, Emily Bartels notes that 'in the representations of both Gaveston and Edward, Marlowe begins to open up the stage, state, and status quo to the possibility of homosexuality'; see Bartels, *Spectacles of Strangeness: Imperialism, Alienation, and Marlowe* (Philadelphia: University of Pennsylvania Press, 1993), 167. Claude J. Summers emphasizes that 'Marlowe's presentation of homosexual love as casual, occasionally elevated, frequently moving, and always in human terms is unique in sixteenth-century English drama'; see 'Sex, Politics, and Self-Realization in *Edward II*,' in Friedenreich et al., *'A Poet and a Filthy Play-maker,'* 222.

85 Bruce R. Smith, *Homosexual Desire*, 223.
86 My exploration of *Edward II* has been guided by David M. Halperin's approach to the history of sexuality; in asking *how* people were 'gay,' Halperin investigates those objects that the queer-identified enjoyed and with which they surrounded themselves. By exploring how certain objects may have served as vehicles of collective identification, Halperin develops 'a modified constructionist approach' that enables him to tease out transhistorical continuities and to integrate them into his analyses of (homo)sexuality. See his *How to Do the History of Homosexuality*, 106.
87 Nashe, *The Unfortunate Traveller*, in *Works*, 2:301.
88 Thomas Hoby, trans. *The Courtier* (London, 1561), as in Floyd-Wilson, *English Ethnicity*, 61.

5. Plotting Style in Ben Jonson's London

1 Guilpin, *Skialetheia*, Satire 5, 84.
2 *Ben Jonson: The Complete Works*, 2:21; hereafter referred to as Herford and Simpson. On the difficulties with this play in production, see Hereford and Simpson, 9:185–8; David Riggs, *Ben Jonson: A Life* (Cambridge, MA: Harvard University Press, 1989), 64–5; Joel Shapiro, *Rival Playwrights: Marlowe, Jonson, Shakespeare* (New York: Columbia University Press, 1991), 56; and Anne Barton, *Ben Jonson, Dramatist* (Cambridge: Cambridge University Press, 1984), 63–5. For an overview of the negative critical reception of this play, see *Every Man Out of His Humour*, ed. Helen Ostovich, Introduction, 38–41.
3 Herford and Simpson, 1:379; Robert N. Watson, *Ben Jonson's Parodic Strategy: Literary Imperialism in the Comedies* (Cambridge, MA: Harvard University Press, 1987), 9. David Kay makes a strong case for the importance of this play for studies of early modern dramaturgical innovations, in 'The Shaping of Ben Jonson's Career: A Re-examination of Facts and Problems,' *Modern Philology* 67 (1970): 228–30.
4 Henry S. Turner discusses the derivation of the term 'plot' and cites Dryden's *Essay* of 1668 as 'the canonical point of articulation' for the use of the word in reference to the total mimetic action of a literary work in, 'Plotting Early Modernity,' in Turner, *The Culture of Capital*, 87.
5 In Jonson's character descriptions, a member of the chorus, Cordatus, identifies himself as 'the author's friend; a man inly acquainted with the scope and drift of his plot' ('Character Descriptions,' *Every Man Out*, ed. Ostovich, 105–6).

6 According to Lawrence Manley, 'between the death of Thomas More and the death of Milton, the population of London increased from 50,000 souls to half a million, transforming a late medieval commune into a metropolis that would soon become the largest capital and *entrepôt* in Europe' (*Literature and Culture*, 125). London's population reached its zenith in the 1590s, when England's political and economic life became centred in London and a series of crises in provincial economies led to widespread migration into the city. See E.A. Wrigley, 'A Simple Model of London's Importance in Changing English Society and Economy, 1650–1750,' *Past and Present* 37 (July 1967); and A.L. Beier and Roger Finlay, 'The Significance of the Metropolis,' in Beier and Finlay, *London 1500–1700*, 1–35.

7 Manley, *Literature and Culture*, 14. On behavioural urbanization, see also Agnew, *Worlds Apart*; and Bruster, *Drama and the Market*. Fran C. Chalfant estimates that there are on average twenty-nine references to different London locales in each of Jonson's comedies; see her *Ben Jonson's London: A Jacobean Placename Dictionary* (Athens: University of Georgia Press, 1978). Jonathan Haynes identifies William Haughton's *Englishmen for my Money* (1598) as the first London comedy, followed by *Every Man Out* (1599), in *The Social Relations of Jonson's Theatre* (Cambridge: Cambridge University Press, 1992), 7. On city comedy, see Knights, *Drama and Society in the Age of Jonson*; Leggatt, *Citizen Comedy in the Age of Shakespeare*; and Brian Gibbons, *Jacobean City Comedy*, 2nd ed. (London: Methuen, 1980).

8 Bryson, *From Courtesy to Civility*, 133.

9 *Wentworth Papers*, as in Greaves, *Society and Religion*, 513. On the pressures placed on young men to appear credit worthy in urban contexts, see Shepard, *Meanings of Manhood*, 188–95.

10 Lemnius, *The Touchstone of Complexions*, Iv.

11 Ibid.

12 Sarah Thornton defines 'subcultural capital' as capital that may be either objectified or embodied, which confers status on its owner in the eyes of the relevant beholders. She notes that subcultural capital may not be converted into economic capital with the same ease or financial reward as cultural capital; see 'The Social Logic of Subcultural Capital,' in Gelder and Thornton, *The Subcultures Reader*, 202–3.

13 Guazzo, *Civil Conversation*, 1:56.

14 Brathwait, *The English Gentleman*, B3v.

15 Earle, *Microcosmography*, 16.

16 Ibid., 16–17.

17 Dekker, *The Guls Horne-booke*, 35, 37.

18 *Every Man Out* is the first play Jonson published under his name, and critics have speculated that Jonson regarded the genre of 'comical satire' as first and foremost a form for printed text rather than for performance. Lending some credence to this claim, *Every Man Out* went through three editions in the first year of its publication and was the most popular published play of the period; Herford and Simpson, 3:374, 3:408–9.

19 See Helen Ostovich, '"To Behold the Scene Full": Seeing and Judging in *Every Man Out of His Humour*,' in Martin Butler, ed., *Re-Presenting Ben Jonson: Text, History, and Performance* (New York: St Martin's Press, 1999), 76.

20 Ostovich, Introduction to *Every Man Out*, ed. Ostovich, 46.

21 Robert Greene, *The Second Part of Cony-Catching* (London, 1592), in Harrison, *Elizabethan and Jacobean Quartos*, 31.

22 For instance, during royal pageants official representatives of the twelve city companies dressed in full regalia and lined the processional route in orderly ranks, forming a boundary between the crowd and the monarch, thus serving as a symbolic reminder of the city's role as mediator in the task of governance; see Manley, *Literature and Culture*, 220. Steven Mullaney discusses communal rituals like Rogationtide, as well as ceremonies such as the monarch's progress, in *The Place of the Stage: License, Play, and Power* (Chicago: University of Chicago Press, 1988), as do A.L. Beier and Roger Finlay in 'The Significance of the Metropolis,' in Finlay and Beier, *London 1500–1700*, 1–35; and Glynne Wickham, *The Medieval Theatre* (1974; repr., Cambridge: Cambridge University Press, 1987), 76.

23 John Stow, as in Manley, *Literature and Culture*, 240.

24 Stow, *A Survey of London*, 1:95.

25 See Finkelpearl, *John Marston of the Middle Temple*, 61.

26 Gurr, *Playgoing in Shakespeare's London*, 155. Gurr speculates that with its absence of physical comedy and emphasis on verbal wit, *Every Man Out* would have been performed by Paul's boys if the company had been operational (161).

27 Ibid., 155.

28 For a discussion of evolving forms of satire after 1599 Bishop's Ban, see Manley, *Literature and Culture*, 372–409.

29 Dedication to the Holmes Folio, lines 8–10, emphasis mine, in *Every Man Out*, ed. Ostovich, Appendix C, 383–4. On the relationship of *Every Man Out* to the Inns of Court revels, see Ostovich, Introduction, 28–41.

30 Thomas Middleton and Thomas Dekker, *The Roaring Girl*, Dedicatory Epistle, 1–2, in Bevington et al., *English Renaissance Drama*.

31 See John Marston, *The Malcontent*, Ind. 16, in Bevington et al., *English Renaissance Drama*.
32 In the revised version of *Every Man in His Humour*, which is set in London, Jonson describes one of the characters as a 'Paul's man': 'a fashionable man-about-town, specifically, a frequenter of the middle aisle of St Paul's, then both a centre of business and a place ... in which "to be seen."' See The New Mermaids edition, ed. Martin Seymour-Smith (London: Ernest Benn, 1966), 'The Persons of the Play,' l.16.
33 Manley, *Literature and Culture*, 239.
34 Simpson, *Chapters in the History of Old St. Paul's*, 152.
35 Harding, *The Dead and the Living*, 87. See also Millar MacLure, *Register of Sermons Preached at Paul's Cross, 1534–1642*, ed. Jackson Campbell Boswell and Peter Pauls (Ottawa: Dovehouse, 1989).
36 Thomas Dekker, *The Dead Tearme*, in *The Non-Dramatic Works*, 4:51.
37 Middleton, *The Black Book*, in *The Works of Thomas Middleton*, 8:32.
38 Earle, *Microcosmography*, 93.
39 Paul L. Hughes and James F. Larkin, eds., *Tudor Royal Proclamations*, vol. 1, *The Early Tudors (1485–1553)* (New Haven: Yale University Press, 1964), 1:489.
40 Hughes and Larkin, *Tudor Royal Proclamations*, 2:92.
41 Ibid., 2:232–3.
42 Henry Hart Milman, *Annals of St Paul's Cathedral* (London, n.d.), as in *Every Man Out*, ed. Ostovich, 3.1, note 3.
43 *Oxford English Dictionary*, s.v., 'loiter.'
44 Ibid.
45 Thomas Harman, 'A Caveat for Common Cursitors' (London, 1566), in Kinney, *Rogues, Vagabonds, and Sturdy Beggars*, 153.
46 Andrew McRae, 'The Peripatetic Muse: Internal Travel and the Cultural Production of Space in Pre-revolutionary England,' in MacLean et al., *The Country and the City Revisited*, 46.
47 Peter Burke, 'The Language of Gesture in Early Modern Italy,' in Jan Bremmer and Herman Roodenburg, eds., *A Cultural History of Gesture* (Ithaca: Cornell University Press, 1991), 80. Burke discusses the English disdain for the bodily excesses putatively displayed by Italian and French men (80–1).
48 Thomas Wilson, *The Arte of Rhetorique*, as in Bryson, *From Courtesy to Civility*, 179.
49 Guazzo, *Civil Conversation*, 130.
50 William Whately, *A Bride Bush* (London, 1623) as in Shepard, *Meanings of Manhood*, 85.
51 Wright, *The Passions of the Mind in General*, 184.
52 Ibid., 185.

53 Ibid.
54 Cleland, *Hero-Paideia*, 170.
55 *Every Man Out*, ed. Ostovich, 'Characters,' 104, line 34.
56 Stephen Gosson, *Plays Confuted in Five Actions* (London, 1582), ed. Peter Davison, (New York: Johnson Reprint, 1972), FIv.
57 *Oxford English Dictionary*, s.v. 'flux.' Primarily a term of physiology, in the early modern period flux was understood to be 'an abnormally copious flowing of blood, excrement, etc., from the bowels or other organs; a morbid or excessive discharge' and 'an early name for dysentery.'
58 Dekker, *Guls Horne-booke*, 38.
59 The conflation between Fastidious's body and his clothes is later established by Fastidious himself when he describes the 'injuries' he sustains in a duel solely in terms of the damage done to his and his opponent's apparel (4.3.390–433).
60 George Puttenham, *Arte of English Poesie* (1589), as in Henry S. Turner 'Plotting Early Modernity,' in Turner, *The Culture of Capital*, 103.
61 Bray, *Homosexuality in Renaissance England*, 54–5; Stephen Orgel, 'Nobody's Perfect: or Why Did the English Stage Take Boys for Women?' *South Atlantic Quarterly* 88.1 (winter 1989): 19; and Jackson I. Cope, 'Marlowe's *Dido* and the Titillating Children,' *ELR* 4.3 (1974): 318.
62 J.N. Adams, *The Latin Sexual Vocabulary* (Baltimore: Johns Hopkins University Press, 1982).
63 Crosse, *Vertues common-wealth*, I3.
64 Tobacco provided an especially rich dramatic symbol for Jonson because it was an imported commodity that was perceived alternately as a curative herb and as a corrosive elixir that transgressed geographical boundaries and dangerously altered the smoker's physiological integrity. For an overview of the contested discourse around tobacco in early modern English culture, see Craig Rustici, 'The Smoking Girl: Tobacco and the Representation of Mary Firth,' *Studies in Philology* 92.2 (spring 1999): 159–80.
65 *Oxford English Dictionary*, s.v. 'shift.'
66 McRae, 'The Peripatetic Muse,' 49. For early modern satiric accounts of shifters, see Harman, 'A Caveat for Common Cursitors'; and Dekker's *Lanthorne and Candle-Light* (London, 1609), in *Non-Dramatic Works*, 3:171–303.
67 Richard Johnson, *Look On Me, London* (1613), as in Twyning, *London Dispossessed*, 63.
68 *Oxford English Dictionary*, s.v. 'shift.'
69 *Every Man Out*, ed. Ostovich, 'Characters,' 108 lines 80–3. On Pict Hatch, Ostovich writes, 'a rendezvous of thieves and prostitutes located behind

a turning called Rotten Row [a red light district] on the east side of Goswell Road; the name derives from the half-door surmounted by spikes which was often used in brothels' (ibid., 108n82).

70 Burton, *The Anatomy of Melancholy*, part 1, section 1, 158.

71 Cooper, *Annals of Cambridge*, 3:27. On the perceptions of tobacco and the activity of smoking more generally in early modern England, see Jeffrey Knapp, *An Empire Nowhere* (Berkeley and Los Angeles: University of California Press, 1992), 134–74.

72 Crosse, *Vertues common-wealth*, C3.

73 Agnew, *Worlds Apart*, 50.

74 Three quarters of adult men in London belonged to livery companies and identified themselves as citizens. 'Freemen' of the city distinguished themselves as regular participants in London's administrative and commercial affairs; see Boulton, *Neighbourhood and Society*; and Rappaport, *Worlds within Worlds*.

75 On 'biting' usury, see William Shakespeare, *The Merchant of Venice: Texts and Contexts*, ed. M. Lindsay Kaplan (London: Bedford/St Martin's, 2002), Introduction, 1–21.

76 On the fees charged to debtors incarcerated in London's Counters, see William Fennor, *The Compter's Commonwealth* (London, 1617); and Muldrew, *The Economy of Obligation*, 257.

77 Burton, *The Anatomy of Melancholy*, part 3, section 2, 98.

78 Cleland, *Hero-Paideia*, 215.

79 Crosse, *Vertues common-wealth*, K3v.

80 Hall, *Characters of Virtues and Vices*, 85.

81 Jean Baudrillard, *For a Critique of the Political Economy of the Sign*, trans. Charles Levin (St Louis: Telos, 1981), 87.

Epilogue: The Twilight of Sumptuousness, the Dawn of Style

1 Vincent, *The Young Gallant's Academy*, 8. Vincent does not provide an updated version of Dekker's chapter addressing gallant conduct at St Paul's Cathedral.

2 Evelyn, *Tyrannus*, 12.

3 Thomas Dyche, *A New General English Dictionary* (1735), and Samuel Johnson, *Dictionary; The Dictionary of Love* (London, 1795), s.v. 'fop,' as in Carter, *Men and the Emergence of Polite Society*, 141.

4 In particular, Kuchta, *The Three-Piece Suit*, 17–51; and Whigham, *Ambition and Privilege*, 148.

5 Evelyn, *Tyrannus*, 14, 15.
6 Ibid., 29.
7 Flugel, *The Psychology of Clothes*, 113.
8 Evelyn writes, 'The Mode is a Tyrant' (*Tyrannus*, 29).
9 Kuchta, *The Three-Piece Suit*, 90.
10 Fashion historians have attributed the rise of sartorial modesty to the cultivation of bourgeois virtues of industry and thrift, described as the 'bourgeoisification' of the aristocracy. Yet, as Kuchta points out, neither the ideology nor the practice of masculine modesty was initially a middle-class ideal, but rather a strategy of a court under siege whose members were compelled to dispel the charges of extravagance levelled against them (*The Three-Piece Suit*, 162–72).
11 Thomas Hall, *The Loathsomeness of Long Hair* (London, 1653), as in Twyning, *London Dispossessed*, 113.
12 For instance, Katherine Eisaman Maus, 'Playhouse Flesh and Blood: Sexual Ideology and the Restoration Actress, ' *ELH* 46.11 (winter 1979): 595–617; and Stephen Greenblatt, *Shakespearean Negotiations: The Circulation of Social Energy in Renaissance England* (Berkeley and Los Angeles: University of California Press, 1988), 66–93.
13 Thomas Laqueur, *Making Sex: Body and Gender from the Greeks to Freud* (Cambridge, MA: Harvard University Press, 1990), 5–6.
14 Susan C. Shapiro provides a list of effeminate male stage characters, in '"Yon Plumed Dandeprat,"' 409.
15 For a complete list of eighteenth-century fops, see Staves, 'A Few Kind Words for the Fop,' 415.
16 George Etherege, *The Man of Mode; or, Sir Fopling Fop* (1676), in *Three Restoration Comedies*, ed. Gamini Salgado (Baltimore: Penguin, 1968), 1.1.59; 3.2.89; Staves, 'A Few Kind Words,' 414.
17 Clement Ellis, *Gentile Sinner*, as in Carter, *Men and the Emergence of Polite Society*, 140; Butler, *Characters*, 291.
18 See Samuel Butler, *Characters* 292; and Carter, *Men and the Emergence of Polite Society*, 156.
19 Staves, 'A Few Kind Words,' 419.
20 Michael Kimmel, 'From Lord to Master to Cuckold and Fop: Masculinity in Seventeenth Century England,' *University of Dayton Review* 18 (1986–7): 94–6.
21 Carter, *Men and the Emergence of Polite Society*, 149. According to Carter, the fop pushed 'men towards more manly forms of refinement' (ibid., 140). Susan Staves sees the fop in a more positive light, as an early

example of the refined masculinity that would come to be associated with the values of sentiment and civility in the early nineteenth century (Staves, 'A Few Kind Words,' 428).

22 Randolph Trumbach has argued that there was a shift in the representation of the effeminate man, away from the bisexual, rake libertine of the early seventeenth century, to the homosexual molly of the early eighteenth century, in 'The Birth of the Queen: Sodomy and the Emergence of Gender Equality in Modern Culture, 1660–1750,' in Martin Duberman et al., eds., *Hidden from History: Reclaiming the Gay and Lesbian Past* (New York: Meriden Books, 1989), 129–40. See also Trumbach's 'Sex, Gender, and Sexual Identity in Modern Culture: Male Sodomy and Female Prostitution in Enlightenment London,' *Journal of the History of Sexuality* 2 (October 1991): 186–203; and 'Sodomitical Subcultures, Sodomitical Roles, and the Gender Revolution of the Eighteenth Century.' In keeping with Trumbach's trajectory, Stephen Orgel identifies Vanbrugh's character Coupler in his 1697 *The Relapse* as 'the first character ... who would be recognizable as gay in the modern sense' (*Impersonations*, 61). Susan Shapiro demonstrates that the 1691 pamphlet *Mundus Foppensis, or, The Fop Displayed* connects foppery with sodomitical practice by equating the wearing of long-toed shoes with the practice of buggery ('Yon Plumed Dandeprat,' 401).

23 Faramerz Dabhoiwala, 'Sex, Social Relations, and the Law in Seventeenth- and Eighteenth-Century London,' in Braddick and Walter, eds., *Negotiating Power in Early Modern Society*, 91.

24 Edward Ward, *The History of London Clubs* (London, 1709), as in Bray, *Homosexuality in Renaissance England*, 86.

25 Bray, *Homosexuality in Renaissance England*, 92.

26 Vanessa Harding, 'The Population of London, 1550–1700: A Review of the Published Evidence,' *London Journal* 15 (1990): 111–28.

27 See Reay, *Popular Culture in Seventeenth-Century England*.

28 The 1703 *London Spy* describes a 'gaudy crowd of fellows' composing a 'fluttering assembly of snuffing peripatetics' at Man's coffee-house, and the 1774 *Universal Magazine* depicts Frank Fopling as 'flutter[ing] up and down' St James Park, as he is seen 'adjusting his hair ... contemplat[ing] his legs, and the symmetry of his breeches'; as in Carter, *Man and the Emergence of Polite Society*, 149.

29 Susan Sontag, 'Notes on "Camp,"' in Cleto, *Camp*, 63.

Select Bibliography

Agnew, Jean-Christophe. *Worlds Apart: The Market and the Theater in Anglo-American Thought, 1550–1750*. Cambridge: Cambridge University Press, 1986.

Amussen, Susan Dwyer. *An Ordered Society: Gender and Class in Early Modern England*. London: Blackwell, 1988.

Archer, Ian. *The Pursuit of Stability: Social Relations in Elizabethan London*. Cambridge: Cambridge University Press, 1991.

Armstrong, Nancy, and Leonard Tennenhouse, eds. *The Ideology of Conduct: Essays on Literature and the History of Sexuality*. New York: Methuen, 1987.

Ascham, Roger. *The Schoolmaster*. 1570. Ed. Lawrence V. Ryan. Ithaca, NY: Cornell University Press, 1967.

Baldwin, Frances Elizabeth. *Sumptuary Legislation and Personal Regulation in England*. Baltimore, MD: Johns Hopkins Press, 1926.

Barish, Jonas. *The Antitheatrical Prejudice*. Berkeley and Los Angeles: University of California Press, 1981.

Barry, Jonathan, and Christopher Brooks, eds. *The Middling Sort of People: Culture, Society, and Politics in England, 1550–1800*. London: Macmillan, 1994.

Beier, A.L. *Masterless Men: The Vagrancy Problem in England, 1560–1640*. London: Methuen, 1985.

– and Roger Finlay, eds. *London 1500–1700: The Making of the Metropolis*. New York: Longman, 1986.

Ben-Amos, Ilana Krausman. *Adolescence and Youth in Early Modern England*. New Haven, CT: Yale University Press, 1994.

Bevington, David, et al., eds. *English Renaissance Drama*. New York: Norton, 2002.

Boose, Lynda E. 'Scolding Brides and Bridling Scolds: Taming the Woman's Unruly Member.' *SQ* 42.2 (1991): 179–213.

– '*The Taming of the Shrew*, Good Husbandry, and Enclosure.' In *Shakespeare Reread: The Texts and in New Contexts*, ed. Russ McDonald, 193–225. Ithaca, NY: Cornell University Press, 1994.

Borris, Kenneth, ed. *Same-Sex Desire in the English Renaissance: A Sourcebook of Texts, 1470–1650*. New York: Routledge, 2004.

Boulton, Jeremy. *Neighbourhood and Society: A London Suburb in the Seventeenth Century*. Cambridge: Cambridge University Press, 1987.

Bourdieu, Pierre. *Distinction: A Social Critique of the Judgment of Taste*. Trans. Richard Nice. Cambridge, MA: Harvard University Press, 1984.

Braddick, Michael J., and John Walter, eds. *Negotiating Power in Early Modern Society: Order, Hierarchy, and Subordination in Britain and Ireland*. Cambridge: Cambridge University Press, 2001.

Brathwait, Richard. *The English Gentleman: Containing Sundry Excellent Rules how to Accommodate Himselfe in the Manage of Publike or Private Affaires*. London, 1630.

Bray, Alan. *The Friend*. Chicago: University of Chicago Press, 2003.

– *Homosexuality in Renaissance England*. 2nd ed. New York: Columbia University Press, 1995.

Bristol, Michael, *Big-time Shakespeare*. New York: Routledge, 1996.

Bruster, Douglas. *Drama and the Market in the Age of Shakespeare*. Cambridge: Cambridge University Press, 1992.

Bryson, Anna. *From Courtesy to Civility: Changing Codes of Conduct in Early Modern England*. Oxford: Clarendon, 1998.

Burnett, Mark Thornton. *Masters and Servants in English Renaissance Drama and Culture: Authority and Obedience*. New York: St Martin's, 1997.

Burton, Robert. *The Anatomy of Melancholy*. Ed. Holbrook Jackson. New York: New York Review of Books, 2001.

Butler, Samuel. *Characters*. Ed. Charles W. Daves. Cleveland, OH: Press of Case Western Reserve University, 1970.

Carson, Neil. *A Companion to Henslowe's Diary*. Cambridge: Cambridge University Press, 1988.

Carter, Philip. *Men and the Emergence of Polite Society, Britain 1660–1800*. Harlow, England and New York: Pearson Education, 2001.

Chambers, E.K. *The Elizabethan Stage*. 4 vols. Oxford: Clarendon, 1923.

Chapman, George, Ben Jonson, and John Marston. *Eastward Ho*. Ed. R.W. Van Fossen. Manchester: Manchester University Press, 1999.

Cleaver, Robert, and John Dod. *A Godly Form of Household Government: For the Ordering of Private Families According to the Direction of God's Word*. London, 1621.

Cleland, James. *Hero-Paideia, or, the Institution of a Young Nobleman*. London, 1607: repr. New York: Scholars Facsimiles and Reprints, 1948.

Cleto, Fabio, ed. *Camp: Queer Aesthetics and the Performing Subject*. Ann Arbor: University of Michigan Press, 2002.

Colman, E.A.M. *The Dramatic Use of Bawdy in Shakespeare*. London: Longman, 1974.

Cooper, Charles Henry. *Annals of Cambridge*. 5 vols. Cambridge: Cambridge University Press, 1842–53.

Correll, Barbara. *The End of Conduct: Grobianus and the Renaissance Text of the Subject*. Ithaca, NY: Cornell University Press, 1996.

Crosse, Henry. *Vertues common-wealth, or, the Highway to Honour*. London, 1603.

Curtis, M.H. *Oxford and Cambridge in Transition, 1558–1642*. Oxford: Clarendon, 1959.

de Certeau, Michel. *The Practice of Everyday Life*. Trans. Steven Rendall. Berkeley and Los Angeles: University of California Press, 1988.

de Grazia, Margreta, Maureen Quilligan, and Peter Stallybrass, eds. *Subject and Object in Renaissance Culture*. Cambridge: Cambridge University Press, 1996.

Dekker, Thomas. *The Guls Horne-booke*. 1609. Ed. R.B. McKerrow. London: De La More, 1904.

– *The Non-Dramatic Works of Thomas Dekker*. Ed. Alexander B. Grosart. 5 vols. New York: Russell & Russell, 1963.

DiGangi, Mario. *The Homoerotics of Early Modern Drama*. Cambridge: Cambridge University Press, 1998.

Dollimore, Jonathan. *Sexual Dissidence: Augustine to Wilde, Freud to Foucault*. Oxford: Clarendon, 1991.

Earle, John. *Microcosmography*. 1628. Ed. Alfred West. Cambridge: Cambridge University Press, 1920.

The English Courtier and the Country Gentleman, or, Civil and Uncivil Life. London, 1586. In *Inedited Tracts: Illustrating the Manners, Opinions, and Occupations of Englishmen during the Sixteenth and Seventeenth Centuries*, ed. W.C. Hazlitt. London: The Roxburghe Collection, 1868.

Evelyn, John. *Tyrannus, or, the Mode: In a Discourse of Sumptuary Laws*. London: G. Bedel and T. Collins, 1661.

Finkelpearl, Philip J. *John Marston of the Middle Temple: An Elizabethan Dramatist in His Social Setting*. Cambridge, MA: Harvard University Press, 1969.

Fitzgeffrey, Henry. *Satyres and Satyrical Epigrams*. London, 1617.

Fletcher, Anthony. *Sex, Gender, and Subordination in England, 1500–1800*. New Haven, CT: Yale University Press, 1995.

– and John Stevenson, eds. *Order and Disorder in Early Modern England*. Cambridge: Cambridge University Press, 1985.
Floyd-Wilson, Mary. *English Ethnicity and Race in Early Modern Drama*. Cambridge: Cambridge University Press, 2003.
Flugel, J.C. *The Psychology of Clothes*. London: Hogarth, 1930.
Foakes, R.A., ed. *Henslowe's Diary*. 2nd ed. Cambridge, MA: Harvard University Press, 2002.
Friedenreich, Kenneth, Roma Gill, and Constance B. Kuriyama, eds. *'A Poet and a Filthy Play-maker': New Essays on Christopher Marlowe*. New York: AMS, 1988.
Gates, Henry Louis. *The Signifying Monkey: A Theory of African-American Literary Criticism*. Oxford: Oxford University Press, 1988.
Gelder, Ken, and Sarah Thornton, eds. *The Subcultures Reader*. New York: Routledge, 1997.
Gillis, John. *Youth and History: Tradition and Change in European Age-Relations, 1770 to the Present*. New York: Academic Press, 1981.
Goldberg, Jonathan. *Sodometries: Renaissance Texts, Modern Sexualities*. Stanford: Stanford University Press, 1992.
– ed. *Queering the Renaissance*. Durham, NC: Duke University Press, 1994.
Gosson, Stephen. *Plays Confuted in Five Actions*. London, 1582. In *The English Drama and Stage under the Tudor and Stuart Princes, 1543–1664*, ed. W.C. Hazlitt. New York: Burt Franklin, 1869.
– *The School of Abuse*. London, 1579.
Gouge, William. *Of Domestical Duties*. 2nd ed. London, 1626.
Greaves, Richard L. *Society and Religion in Elizabethan England*. Minneapolis: University of Minnesota Press, 1981.
Greene, Robert. *The Life and Complete Works in Prose and Verse of Robert Greene*. Ed. Alexander B. Grosart. New York: Russell and Russell, 1964.
– *A Notable Discovery of Coosnage, 1591; The Second Part of Conny-Catching, 1592*. Ed. G.B. Harrison. Edinburgh: Edinburgh University Press, 1966.
Greenwood, John. *Shifting Perspectives and the Stylish Style: Mannerism in Shakespeare and his Jacobean Contemporaries*. Toronto: University of Toronto Press, 1988.
Griffiths, Paul. *Youth and Authority: Formative Experiences in England, 1560–1640*. Oxford: Clarendon, 1996.
– Adam Fox, and Steve Hindle. *The Experience of Authority in Early Modern England*. New York: St Martin's, 1996.
Guazzo, Steven. *The Civil Conversation of M. Steven Guazzo: The First Three Books Translated by George Pettie*. 1581. Ed. Charles Whibley. New York: Knopf, 1925.

Guild, William. *A Yong Mans Inquisition, or Triall.* London, 1608.
Guilpin, Everard. *Skialetheia, or, A Shadow of Truth in Certain Epigrams and Satyres.* 1598. Ed. A. Allen Carroll. Chapel Hill: University of North Carolina Press, 1974.
Gurr, Andrew. *Playgoing in Shakespeare's London.* Cambridge: Cambridge University Press, 1987.
– *The Shakespearean Stage, 1574–1642.* 3rd ed. Cambridge: Cambridge University Press, 1997.
Hall, Joseph. *Characters of Virtues and Vices.* 1608. In *A Book of Characters*, ed. Richard Aldington. London: Routledge, 1924.
Hall, Stuart, and Tony Jefferson, eds. *Resistance Through Rituals: Youth Subculture in Post-War Britain.* London: Hutchinson, 1976.
Halperin, David M. *How to Do the History of Homosexuality.* Chicago: University of Chicago Press, 2002.
Halpern, Richard. *The Poetics of Primitive Accumulation: English Renaissance Culture and the Genealogy of Capital.* Ithaca, NY: Cornell University Press, 1991.
Harte, N.B. 'State Control of Dress and Social Change in Pre-Industrial England.' In *Trade, Government and Economy in Pre-Industrial England: Essays Presented to F.J. Fisher*, ed. D.C. Coleman and A.H. John, 132–65. London: Weidenfeld and Nicolson, 1976.
Harvey, Gabriel. *The Works of Gabriel Harvey.* Ed. Alexander B. Grosart. London: Printed for Private Circulation, 1884–5.
Hauser, Arnold. *Mannerism: The Crisis of the Renaissance and the Origin of Modern Art.* Vol. 1. Trans. Eric Mosbacher. New York: Knopf, 1965.
Hazlitt, W.C., ed. *Inedited Tracts: Illustrating the Manners, Opinions, and Occupations of Englishmen during the Sixteenth and Seventeenth Centuries.* London: The Roxburghe Collection, 1868.
Heal, Felicity. *Hospitality in Early Modern England.* Oxford: Clarendon, 1990.
Hebdige, Dick. *Subculture and the Meaning of Style.* New York: Methuen, 1979.
Hitchcock, Tim, and Michèle Cohen, eds. *English Masculinities, 1660–1800.* London: Longman, 1999.
Holinshed's Chronicles of England, Scotland, and Ireland in Six Volumes. A compilation of 1577 and 1587. London, 1807.
Hooper, Wilfred. 'The Tudor Sumptuary Laws.' *English Historical Review* 30 (1915): 433–49.
Hoy, Cyrus. 'Jacobean Tragedy and the Mannerist Style.' *Shakespeare Survey* 26 (1973): 49–67.
Hughes, Paul L., and James F. Larkin, eds. *Tudor Royal Proclamations.* Vols. 2

and 3, *The Later Tudors (1553–1603)*. New Haven: Yale University Press, 1964–9.
Hunt, Alan. *Governance of the Consuming Passions: A History of Sumptuary Law*. New York: St Martin's, 1996.
Jardine, Lisa. *Still Harping on Daughters: Women and Drama in the Age of Shakespeare*. 2nd ed. New York: Columbia University Press, 1989.
Javitch, Daniel. '*Il Cortegiano* and the Constraints of Despotism.' In *Castiglione: The Ideal and the Real in Renaissance Culture*, ed. Robert Hanning and David Rosand, 17–28. New Haven: Yale University Press, 1983.
– *Poetry and Courtliness in Renaissance England*. Princeton, NJ: Princeton University Press, 1978.
Jones, Ann Rosalind, and Peter Stallybrass, eds. *Renaissance Clothing and the Materials of Memory*. Cambridge: Cambridge University Press, 2000.
Jonson, Ben. *Ben Jonson: The Complete Works*. 11 vols. Ed. C.H. Herford and Percy Simpson. Oxford: Clarendon, 1925–63.
– *Every Man Out of His Humour*. Ed. Helen Ostovich. Manchester: Manchester University Press, 2001.
Kay, Dennis. 'Marlowe, *Edward II*, and the Cult of Elizabeth.' *Early Modern Literary Studies* 3.2 (1997), http://www.oclc.org/emls: 1–30.
King, Thomas A. *The Gendering of Men, 1600–1750*. Vol. 1, *The English Phallus*. Madison: University of Wisconsin Press, 2004.
Kinney, Arthur F., ed. *Rogues, Vagabonds, and Sturdy Beggars: A New Gallery of Tudor and Stuart Rogue Literature*. Amherst: University of Massachusetts Press, 1990.
Knights, L.C. *Drama and Society in the Age of Jonson*. London: Chatto and Windus, 1937.
Korda, Natasha. *Shakespeare's Domestic Economies: Gender and Property in Early Modern England*. Philadelphia: University of Pennsylvania Press, 2002.
Kuchta, David. *The Three-Piece Suit and Modern Masculinity, England 1550–1850*. Berkeley and Los Angeles: University of California Press, 2002.
Kussmaul, Ann. *Servants in Husbandry in Early Modern England*. Cambridge: Cambridge University Press, 1981.
Lane, Joan. *Apprenticeship in England, 1600–1914*. London: University College of London Press, 1996.
Larkin, James F., ed. *Stuart Royal Proclamations: Royal Proclamations of King James I, 1603–1625*, Vol. 1. Oxford: Clarendon, 1973.
Leggatt, Alexander. *Citizen Comedy in the Age of Shakespeare*. Toronto: University of Toronto Press, 1973.
Leinwand, Theodore. *The City Staged: Jacobean Comedy, 1603–1613*. Madison: University of Wisconsin Press, 1986.

Lemnius, Levinus. *The Touchstone of Complexions*. Trans. Thomas Newton. 3rd ed. London, 1633.

Lenton, Francis. *The Young Gallants Whirligigg; or, Youth Reakes*. London, 1629.

Lubbock, Jules. *The Tyranny of Taste: The Politics of Architecture and Design in Britain, 1550–1960*. New Haven: Yale University Press, 1995.

M., I. *A Health to the Gentlemanly Profession of Servingmen: or, The Servingmans Comfort*. 1598. In *Inedited Tracts: Illustrating the Manners, Opinions, and Occupations of Englishmen during the Sixteenth and Seventeenth Centuries*, ed. W.C. Hazlitt. London: The Roxburghe Collection, 1868.

MacCaffery, W.T. 'Place and Patronage in Elizabethan Politics.' In *Elizabethan Government and Society: Essays Presented to Sir John Neale*, ed. S.T. Bindoff, J. Hurtsfield, and C.H. Williams. London: University of London Press, 1961.

MacLean, Gerald, Donna Landry, and Joseph P. Ward, eds. *The Country and the City Revisited: England and the Politics of Culture, 1550–1850*. Cambridge: Cambridge University Press, 1999.

Manley, Lawrence. *Literature and Culture in Early Modern London*. Cambridge: Cambridge University Press, 1995.

Marlowe, Christopher. *Edward the Second*. The New Mermaids Edition. Ed. Martin Wiggins and Robert Lindsey. New York: Norton, 1997.

Marrapodi, Michele, ed. *Shakespeare and Intertextuality: The Transition of Cultures Between Italy and England in the Early Modern Period*. Rome: Bulzoni, 2000.

– and A.J. Hoenselaars, eds. *The Italian World of English Renaissance Drama: Cultural Exchange and Intertextuality*. Newark: University of Delaware Press, 1998.

Marston, John. *The Plays of John Marston in Three Volumes*. Ed. H. Harvey Wood. London: Oliver and Boyd, 1939.

– *The Poems of John Marston*. Ed. Arnold Davenport. Liverpool: Liverpool University Press, 1961.

McIntosh, Marjorie Keniston. *Controlling Misbehavior in England 1370–1600*. Cambridge: Cambridge University Press, 1998.

Mertes, Kate. *The English Noble Household, 1250–1600: Good Governance and Politic Rule*. Oxford: Blackwell, 1988.

Middleton, Thomas. *The Works of Thomas Middleton*. 8 vols. Ed. A.H. Bullen. London: John C. Nimmo, 1886.

Moisan, Thomas. '"Knock me here soundly": Comic Misprision and Class Consciousness in Shakespeare.' *SQ* 42.3 (fall 1991): 276–90.

Montrose, Louis Adrian. 'Spenser and the Elizabethan Political Imaginary.' *ELH* 69.4 (2002): 907–56.

Muldrew, Craig. *The Economy of Obligation: The Culture of Credit and Social Relations in Early Modern England*. London: St Martin's, 1998.
Mun, Thomas. *A Discourse of Trade, From England Unto the East-Indies*. London, 1621.
Nashe, Thomas. *The Anatomy of Absurdity*. London, 1589.
– *Pierce Penniless his Supplication to the Devil*. London, 1592. In *Thomas Nashe Selected Writings*, ed. Stanley Wells. Cambridge, MA: Harvard University Press, 1965.
– *Works*. 5 vols. Ed. R.B. McKerrow. Oxford: Blackwell, 1958–66.
Neill, Michael. *Putting History to the Question: Power, Politics, and Society in English Renaissance Drama*. New York: Columbia University Press, 2000.
Newman, Karen. *Fashioning Femininity and English Renaissance Drama*. Chicago: University of Chicago Press, 1991.
Orgel, Stephen. *Impersonations: The Performance of Gender in Shakespeare's England*. Cambridge: Cambridge University Press, 1996.
Overbury, Thomas. *Characters, or, Witty Descriptions of the Properties of Sundry Persons*. In *A Book of Characters*. London, 1614. Comp. and ed. Richard Aldington. New York: Routledge, 1924.
R[ankins], W[illiam]. *The English Ape, the Italian Imitation, or, The Foot-Steps of France*. London, 1588.
Rappaport, Steve. *Worlds within Worlds: Structures of Life in Sixteenth-Century London*. Cambridge: Cambridge University Press, 1989.
Reay, Barry, ed. *Popular Culture in Seventeenth-Century England*. New York: St Martin's, 1985.
Richardson, Catherine, ed. *Clothing Culture, 1350–1650*. Aldershot: Ashgate, 2004.
Seaver, Paul S. 'Declining Status in an Aspiring Age: The Problem of the Gentle Apprentice in Seventeenth-Century London.' In *Court, Country, and Culture: Essays on Early Modern British History in Honor of Perez Zagorin*, ed. Bonnelyn Young Kunze and Dwight D. Brautigam, 129–47. Rochester, NY: University of Rochester Press, 1992.
Sermons or Homilies Appointed to be Read in Churches in the Time of Queen Elizabeth of Famous Memory. London: The Church of England, The Prayer Book, and Homily Society, 1824.
Shakespeare, William. *The Complete Works of Shakespeare*. Ed. David Bevington. 5th ed. New York: Longman, 2004.
– *The Taming of the Shrew: Texts and Contexts*. Ed. Frances E. Dolan. New York: St Martin's, 1996.
Shapiro, Susan C. '"Yon Plumed Dandeprat": Male Effeminacy in English Satire and Criticism.' *Review of English Studies: A Quarterly Journal of English Literature and the English Language* 39.155 (August 1988): 400–12.

Shearman, John K.G. *Mannerism: Style and Civilization*. Harmondsworth: Penguin, 1967.
Shepard, Alexandra. *Meanings of Manhood in Early Modern England*. Oxford: Oxford University Press, 2003.
Simpson, W. Sparrow. *Chapters in the History of Old St. Paul's*. London: Elliot Stock, 1881.
Sinfield, Alan. *Faultlines: Cultural Materialism and the Politics of Dissident Reading*. Berkeley and Los Angeles: University of California Press, 1992.
Slack, Paul, ed. *Rebellion, Popular Protest, and The Social Order in Early Modern England*. Cambridge: Cambridge University Press, 1984.
Smith, Bruce R. *Homosexual Desire in Shakespeare's England: A Cultural Poetics*. Chicago: University of Chicago Press, 1991.
Smith, G.C. Moore, ed. *Gabriel Harvey's Marginalia*. Stratford-Upon-Avon: Shakespeare Head Press, 1913.
Starkey, David. 'The Age of the Household: Politics, Society, and the Arts c.1350-c.1550.' In *The Context of English Literature: The Later Middle Ages*, ed. S. Medcalf, 225–90. New York: Holmes and Meier, 1981.
Staves, Susan. 'A Few Kind Words for the Fop.' *Studies in English Literature, 1500–1700* 22.3 (summer 1982): 413–28.
Stephens, John. *Satirical Essays, Characters, and Others*. London, 1615.
Stone, Lawrence. *The Crisis of the Aristocracy, 1558–1641*. Oxford: Oxford University Press, 1965.
– 'Social Mobility in England, 1500–1700.' *Past and Present* 33 (April 1966): 16–55.
Stow, John. *A Survey of London*. Ed. C. Lethbridge Kingsford. 2 vols. Oxford: Clarendon, 1908.
Stubbes, Phillip. *Phillip Stubbes' Anatomy of the Abuses in England in Shakespeare's Youth, A.D. 1583*. Ed. Frederick J. Furnivall. London: The New Shakespeare Society, 1877–9.
Summers, Claude J., ed. *Homosexuality in Renaissance and Enlightenment England: Literary Interpretations in Historical Context*. New York: Haworth, 1992.
Trumbach, Randolph. 'Sodomitical Subcultures, Sodomitical Roles, and the Gender Revolution of the Eighteenth Century: The Recent Historiography.' *Eighteenth Century Life* 9.3 (May 1985): 109–21.
Turner, Henry S., ed. *The Culture of Capital: Property, Cities, and Knowledge in Early Modern England*. New York: Routledge, 2002.
Twyning, John. *London Dispossessed: Literature and Social Space in the Early Modern City*. New York: St Martin's, 1998.
Vaughan, William. *The Golden-Grove, Moralized in Three Parts*. London, 1600.

Vincent, Samuel. *The Young Gallant's Academy, or, Directions How He Should Behave Himself in All Places and Company*. London, 1674.

Wall, Wendy. *Staging Domesticity: Household Work and English Identity in Early Modern Drama*. Cambridge: Cambridge University Press, 2002.

Ward, Joseph P. *Metropolitan Communities: Trade Guilds, Identity, and Change in Early Modern England*. Stanford: Stanford University Press, 1997.

Whigham, Frank. *Ambition and Privilege: The Social Tropes of Elizabethan Courtesy Theory*. Berkeley and Los Angeles: University of California Press, 1984.

White, Paul Whitfield, ed. *Marlowe, History, and Sexuality: New Essays on the Life and Writing of Christopher Marlowe*. New York: AMS, 1998.

Whitney, Charles. '"Usually in the werking Daies": Playgoing, Journeymen, Apprentices and Servants in Guild Records, 1582–1592.' *SQ* 50.4 (winter 1999): 433–58.

Wright, Thomas. *The Passions of the Mind in General*. Ed. William Webster Newbold. New York: Garland, 1986.

Wrightson, Keith. *English Society, 1580–1680*. Oxford: Oxford University Press, 1982.

Index

Lightning Source UK Ltd.
Milton Keynes UK
UKHW040627230223
417513UK00001B/36